Fathers and Mothers

Robert Bly

James Hillman

Augusto Vitale

Marion Woodman

Patricia Berry

Mary Watkins

Jackie Schectman

Ursula K. Le Guin

Erich Neumann

C. G. Jung

FATHERS AND MOTHERS

Second Edition, Revised and Enlarged

Edited by

PATRICIA BERRY

Spring Publications, Inc.
Dallas, Texas

First printing of *Fathers and Mothers*, second edition, 1990. Published by Spring Publications, Inc., P.O. Box 222069, Dallas, Texas 75222. Text printed on acidfree paper. Printed in the United States of America

Interior art by Mary Vernon. Cover design and production by Margot McLean

International distributors:
Spring; Postfach; 8803 Rüschlikon; Switzerland.
Japan Spring Sha, Inc.; 12–10, 2-Chome, Nigawa Takamaru;
    Takarazuka 665, Japan.
Element Books Ltd; Longmead Shaftesbury;
    Dorset SP7 8PL; England.
Astam Books Pty. Ltd.; 162–168 Parramatta Road;
    Stanmore N.S.W. 2048; Australia.
Libros é Imagenes; Apdo. Post 40–085;
    México D.F. 06140; México.
Zipak Livraria Editoria Ltda; Alameda Lorena 871;
    01424 São Paulo SP; Brazil.

Library of Congress Cataloging-in-Publication Data

Fathers and mothers / edited by Patricia Berry. — 2nd ed., rev. and enl.
        p.   cm.
    Includes bibliographical references.
    ISBN 0-88214-344-1 (pbk. : alk. paper)
    1. Mothers—Psychology.   2. Fathers—Psychology.   3. Archetype (Psychology) 4. Jung, C. G. (Carl Gustav), 1875–1961.   I. Berry, Patricia.
HQ759.F28   1990
306.874—dc20   90–39373
                                                                    CIP

Contents

Editor's Preface

MUCH OF THE literature nowadays regarding parenting involves descriptions of, and ways to overcome, abuse—sexual abuse, emotional abuse, the abuse caused by dysfunctional families. Generally, approaches to these topics locate the child as victim of a malaise caused by the wounded adults of unhealthy familial and societal systems.

The collection here offered is of a different sort. Here the reader encounters approaches grounded less in the child as singular and secular and more in the child as archetypally based and of the imagination. Seen in this way, the child becomes one of the players in a drama of primordial actions and interactions. Mothers and fathers become many-sided figures, images, based in the continual flux of creation and re-creation.

Rather than schemata for solving 'issues' by working through grids listing traits and areas of malfunction, you will find in these essays insights emerging directly from deeper levels of parents and parenting.

An advantage of viewing figures and events archetypally is that the archetype—this primordial form, as Jung delineates it in his essay on the mother archetype—is inherently ambivalent. It shows many faces. In Neumann's treatment this ambivalence becomes a creative flux of lunar inspiration. Le Guin births ambiguity poetically as a Persephonic moment of awareness. With Watkins the ambivalent becomes an interplay of childlike desire, alike in parent as in child.

Ambivalence also requires an ability to see darkness. Several of these essays directly confront this unavoidable and irreducible phenomenon. Bly, Hillman, and Vitale wrestle through the son's agonies with the dark father. Schectman explores the step-mother as she appears in fairytales; Woodman traces the killing mother through a series of dreams; Hillman treats the feelings of the 'bad' mother in childrearing; and I look to the negativity and emptiness of mother's matter.

The archetypal view that the essays in this book demonstrate is at once mythic and personal, cultural and clinical. The book as a whole offers an encompassing imagination to inescapable complexes of human life.

Scholars might also note that this version of Jung's essay "The Psychological Aspects of the Mother Archetype" is that given at the Eranos Conference, 1938, published first in *Spring 1943,* translated by Cary F. Baynes and Ximena de Angulo and later retranslated and edited for *The Collected Works.*

Patricia Berry
Cambridge 1990

Acknowledgments and a Note to the Reader

The first edition of *Fathers and Mothers*, edited by Patricia Berry (Zürich: Spring Publications, 1973), was composed of five chapters, of which three are reprinted here. References to *The Collected Works of C. G. Jung* are cited throughout the present volume in a consistent style by volume and paragraph numbers.

"The Hunger for the King in a Time with No Father" appears here for the first time in print. In changed form it will be part of the author's *Iron John: A Book about Men* (Reading, MA.: Addison-Wesley Publishing Co., Inc., forthcoming).

"On Senex Consciousness" appeared first in *Spring 1970*: 146–65 and is composed of excerpts from the draft of an extended revision of "Senex and Puer: An Aspect of the Historical and Psychological Present," in *Eranos Jahrbuch* 36 (Zürich: Rhein Verlag, 1968). Notes and references have been omitted here. Further elaboration of senex psychology with complete notes and references can be found in the author's "The 'Negative' Senex and a Renaissance Solution," *Spring 1975*: 77–109.

"The Archetype of Saturn or the Transformation of the Father" was presented in a series of lectures at the C. G. Jung Institute, Zürich, Summer Semester 1970, and was published first in the first edition of *Fathers and Mothers*, pp. 5–39.

The material in "Mother as Patriarch" appears in different form in the author's *The Ravaged Bridegroom: Masculinity in Women*,

no. 41 in the series Studies in Jungian Psychology by Jungian Analysts (Toronto: Inner City Books, 1990).

"What's the Matter with Mother" was first presented as a lecture
sponsored by the Guild of Pastoral Psychology, Oxford University,
Oxford, England, 1976, and was published first as a chapter in the
author's *Echo's Subtle Body: Contributions to an Archetypal Psychology* (Dallas: Spring Publications, Inc., 1982), pp. 1–16.

"The Bad Mother" was written for the 1982 Nippon Life Insurance Foundation Symposium, "The Parents–Child Bonding," and
delivered in Osaka, November 1982. The revision published here
appeared first in *Spring 1983*, pp. 165–81, and includes a coda and
other adaptations made for a seminar on "Education of the Imagination" held in January 1983 at The Dallas Institute of Humani-
ties and Culture.

"Mother and Child" is comprised of excerpts from the author's
work in progress *Heart's Desire: Habits of Being*.

"The Step-Mother in Fairytales" will appear in the author's *The
Step-mother in Fairy Tales* (Boston: Sigo Press, forthcoming).

"A Child Bride" first appeared in *Terry's Universe* (1987) under
the title "Kore 87" and is reprinted here by permission of the author and the author's agent Virginia Kidd.

"The Great Mother, Her Son, Her Hero, and the Puer" is a chapter of a work in progress on the archetypal psychology of the puer
aeternus and was published for the first time in the first edition of
Fathers and Mothers, pp. 75–127. See A Note to the Reader at the
conclusion of these acknowledgments.

"On the Moon and Matriarchal Consciousness" appeared originally in German in the *Eranos Jahrbuch* 18 (Zürich: Rhein Verlag,
1950) and later in the author's *Zur Psychologie des Weiblichen*
(Zürich: Rascher, 1953). The English translation by Hildegard Na-
gel, which is an abbreviated adaptation made at the suggestion of
Dr. Neumann, was published first in *Spring 1954* with the kind

permission of the Rascher Verlag. It was reprinted in the Spring Publications booklet *Dynamics of the Psyche* and was republished in the first edition of *Fathers and Mothers,* pp. 40–63, with the kind permission of Mrs. Julia Neumann. It is reprinted here by permission of the heirs of the Neumann estate.

"The Psychological Aspects of the Mother Archetype" is reprinted here by permission of Princeton University Press, which publishes a revised version of the essay in *The Collected Works of C. G. Jung,* trans. R. F. C. Hull, Bollingen Series XX, Vol. 9, I: *The Archetypes and the Collective Unconscious,* Copyright © 1959, 1969. For this edition of *Fathers and Mothers,* Spring Publications has edited out Jung's references to the Eranos Conference—where the paper was first read in German—and updated the endnotes to refer to volumes in *The Collected Works.*

A Note to the Reader

The following article ["The Great Mother, Her Son, Her Hero, and the Puer"] forms one chapter of a long and still unfinished book about the archetype of the puer aeternus, and so this article was originally not intended to stand on its own. Some of its themes refer to other chapters of that work where they are developed more adequately, and both the method and the style of expression belong to a larger whole. However, I felt there was an urgent reason for printing this piece even if dissociated from its context: the idea of "the mother-complex" still dominates in the analysis of young men. It is still considered to be the background of the "puer problem" and of "ego development." I believe this is a dreadful mistake having individual and collective consequences. To see only mother-complex neurosis in puer phenomena means making the spirit ill and missing the opportunities for movement that the spirit urges onto the collective psyche through its incarnation in puer-dominated men and women. For I believe puer characteristics may best be understood in terms of a phenomenology and psychopathology of the spirit which is the main approach of the book. Some chapters of the planned book have appeared in *Loose Ends* (Spring Publications, 1975) and mainly in *Puer Papers* (Dallas: Spring Publications, 1979), including the essay (my Eranos Lecture for 1967)

"Senex and Puer: An Aspect of the Historical and Psychological Present," from which sprung the larger plan. Also, in what follows, I am assuming some familiarity with the classic views of analytical psychology toward puer phenomenology.

JH
1973

The Hunger for the King in a Time with No Father
Robert Bly

I. New Terrors and New Flights

WE'LL BEGIN THIS essay with the thought I have heard in so many phrasings from so many men: "There is not enough father." They speak as if father were a substance like salt, which in earlier times was sometimes in short supply, or like ground water, which in some areas now has simply disappeared.

Geoffrey Gorer remarked in 1940 in his book *The Americans* that for a boy to become a man in the United States only one thing is required, namely, that he reject his father.[1] American fathers, he noted, expect to be rejected. Young men in Europe often have seen the father as a demonic being to be wrestled with (and the son in Franz Kafka's "The Judgment" does wrestle his father to the death and loses), but sons in the United States accept the father as an object of ridicule to be made fun of in comic strips and television commercials. One young man summed it up: "A father is someone who rustles newspapers in the living room."

When the father-table, the ground water, drops (so to speak) and there is too little father, instead of too much father, the sons find themselves in a new situation. What do they do: hoard father, drill for new father, distill mother-ocean water into father-water, change crops? We are not going to speculate here on what can be done but instead talk about the phenomenon of too little father and what it feels like.

Some cultures have had an abundance of father. Uncles in

traditional cultures discipline, warriors instruct; and if we are to take Bruno Bettelheim's word for it, fathers and sons in many societies live in an amused tolerance of each other and spend hours walking together, whittling, or repairing a spear or a wheel.[2] It still happens sometimes. When it does, a vitamin-like food passes from the father's body to the son's body.

Our contemporary mind might want to describe this transmission as a likening of attitude, a *mimesis*, but I think it was physical. Some substance was and is still passed directly to the cells. The son's body—not his mind—receives food on a sort of cellular level, and the father gives it at a level far below consciousness. The son does not receive a hands-on healing but a body-on healing; and beyond that, his cells receive some knowledge of what an adult masculine body is. Learning at what frequency the masculine body vibrates, the younger body begins to grasp the song that adult male cells sing and how the charming, elegant, lonely, courageous, half-shamed male molecules dance.

During the long months the son spent in the mother's body, his body got well-tuned to female frequencies: it learned how a woman's cells broadcast, who bows to whom in that resonant field, what animals run across the grassy clearing, what the body listens for at night, what the upper and lower fears are. How swiftly the son's body became, before birth and after, a good receiver for the upper and lower frequencies of the mother's voice! The son either tunes to that frequency or he dies.

Now, standing next to the father, as the two repair arrowheads, or repair ploughs, or wash pistons in gasoline, or care for birthing animals, the son's body has the chance to retune. Slowly, over months or years, that son's body strings begin to resonate to the harsh, sometimes demanding, testily humorous, irreverent, forward-driving, silence-loving older masculine body. Both male and female cells carry marvelous music, but the son needs to resonate to the second as well as to the first.

Sons who have not received this tuning or retuning will have father-hunger all their lives. I think calling the longing "hunger" is accurate: the son's body needs salt, or water, or a protein, just as a starving person's stomach and digestive tract need protein. If it finds none, the stomach will eventually eat up the muscles themselves. Such men hang around older men as the homeless around a soup kitchen. Like the homeless they feel shame over their condition, and it is a nameless, bitter, unexpungeable shame.

Women cannot, no matter how much they sympathize with their starving sons, replace that missing substance. Many contemporary sons recognize this father-hunger that no one knows how to satisfy.

In agricultural societies as far back as we can see, and in the craft cultures and hunter-gatherer societies that preceded them, fathers and sons worked, if not closely together, at least together. As late as 1900 in the United States, about ninety percent of fathers were engaged in agriculture. The son characteristically saw his father working at all times of the day and all seasons of the year. Only one hundred and forty years have passed since factory work began in earnest in the West, and we see in each succeeding generation less bonding between father and son, with catastrophic results. A close study of the Enclosure Acts of England shows that, toward the end of that long legislative process, the English government denied the landless father access to free pasture and common land with the precise aim of forcing him—and sometimes his family as well—to travel to the factory.

By 1950, a massive change had taken place: the father works, but the son cannot see how he works, with whom he works, or what he produces. Does the son fantasize that his father is a lord, does he fill in positive details of the father's work place and the father's actions there, idealizing his father as a hero, a fighter for good, a saint or grand person? The answer is sad: a hole appears in the son's psyche, a hole that fills with demons.

This metaphor of the hole that fills with demons was contributed by the German psychoanalyst Alexander Mitscherlich, following on his forty years of research with young German men. He reports on that investigation in his masterful book *Society Without the Father.*[3]

Suspicion of older men is the demons' theme. The demons admire *Lawrence of Arabia* and *The Dead Poets' Society* because they remind us how absolutely the corrupt old men betray the young male idealist. One's father may be an ex-Nazi living in Brazil: we remember Dustin Hoffman in *The Marathon Man* marching the Nazi up Fifth Avenue to the water purification plant. The sixties' men said, "Never trust anyone over thirty."

Each of us furnishes an apartment in his mind for his father, but when we do not know for sure what he does at work, we cannot keep it furnished. The demons move in, take down photographs of the father, substitute paintings of Stalin or themselves, throw the sofas out the window, tie little black dogs to the radiators, plant letters signed by the head of the CIA. Mentorship becomes difficult to sustain; initiation is rejected; we believe that elders in primitive cultures perform sadistic and humiliating acts on young men under cover of initiatory ritual. A young architect ridden by these demons secretly rejoices when a Louis Sullivan building gets knocked down, and the young rock musician plays with a touch of malice music that his grandfather could never understand.

Because the son has used up much of his critical, cynical energy on old men, he will compensate by being naive toward young people. He may assume a young woman knows more about a relationship than he does, allow her moods to run the house, assume she is attacking him "for his own good." Such a young man might take on the feminist agenda without questioning it and agree that the penis is the same as the rocket, etc. He may allow a male partner in business to steal all his money, or allow himself to be manipulated by a man his own age whom he imagines to be his friend, or accept betrayal and humiliation under cover of teaching. Having all the suspicion in one place—toward older men—often leads to disaster in relationships and great isolation in spirit and soul.

The demons will certainly insist that he reject the Father God and be suspicious of all disciplines associated with any religion, art, or mythology to which men of the past have contributed images or concepts. The fatherless son then—without "intending to"—becomes a person who disparages all masculine achievement in past centuries, ruling out of his life all influence from it. He seems independent, but he is actually, unconsciously, being ridden by the demons that have invaded the soul.

We can expect to see in the next decade these demons of suspicion cause more and more damage to the masculine vision of what a man is. Over fifty percent of American households now live with no father present, and the demons there have full permission to rage. One has to expect that daughters will suffer more and more from these demons as well.

So much for the demons. A new situation for the father is that, when he returns home at night to the father-holding households, he has nothing to teach. The children have some genetic expectation of teaching. If the father is working for a corporation, what is there to teach? He is reluctant to tell his son what is really going on. The fragmentation of decision-making in corporate life, the massive effort to produce shoddy products, the corporate willingness to destroy animals and land for the sake of profit, the prudence, even cowardice, that one learns in bureaucracy—who wants to teach that?

We know of rare cases in which the father brings sons or daughters into the factory, judge's chambers, used-car lot, or insurance building, and those efforts do reap some of the rewards of teaching in craft cultures. But in most families today, the sons and daughters receive, when the father returns home at six, an irritable mood and that is all.

The successful father brings home a manic mood, the unsuccessful father depression. What does the son receive? A bad disposition, springing from powerlessness and despair mingled with long-standing shame and the numbness peculiar to those who hate their jobs. Fathers in earlier times could often break through their own defective dispositions by teaching rope making, fishing, post-hole digging, grain cutting, drumming, harness making, animal care, even singing and storytelling.

The king who is able to bless and encourage remains alive inside the father, but fossilized; and the son receives instead the nonblesser, the threatened, jealous "Nobodaddy" as Blake calls him—no one's father—the male principle that lives in the Kingdom of Jealousy. Daughters take in poisonous moods and suffer damage as well. The father's domineering remoteness may severely damage their ability to participate good-heartedly in later relationships with men. Much of the rage that some women direct to the patriarchy amounts to a vast disappointment experienced over this lack of teaching from their own fathers. Both the son and daughter may soon begin to experience a second disappointment around the mother's inability to bless as the mother works more and more hours away from the home.

We have said that "the father" as a living energy in the home disappeared when those forces demanding industry sent him on various railroads out of his various villages. No historical models prepare us for the contemporary son's psychic condition; we have to imagine new furniture, new psychic interiors, new demon possessions, new terrors, new incapacities, new hungers, new rages, new generosities, new flights.

The group father—which is another name for the King in the political world and for the patriarchy—died, for the most part, in the nineteenth century. The Western cultural attacks on the patriarchy, so massive in recent decades, oddly have arrived when there is no longer a patriarchy. Each patriarchy is complicated anyway, being matriarchal on the inside; and each matriarchy we know of is complicated as well, being patriarchal on the inside. The genuine patriarchy brings down the sun through the Sacred King into every man and woman in the culture. The death of the Group Father means that we now live in a system of industrial domination, which is not patriarchy, and honor is given neither to the male mode of feeling nor to the female. The industrial mode of domination determines how things go with us in the world of resources, values, and allegiances; and in the mode of industrial domination there is neither King nor Queen. What concerns us here is the effect the death of the Group Father has had on sons and daughters. This effect is surprising: everyone becomes a sibling.[4]

Since we don't have the space here to go into this development with the attention and detail it deserves, we will make only a few observations—and these primarily about men. When a culture retains a living Group Father, sons know where the authority is. Gold carriages, bowing men, stately processions, Forbidden Cities, titles, epaulets, uniforms, large moustaches, crowns of gold, thrones, stairs let everyone know who the authority is. If a young man wants this authority, he kills the King and takes it; that is how Mao got the Forbidden City, how Lenin did, and Cromwell. But in a sibling society, the young ones look sideways for their orientation and don't particularly want the authority or the responsibility that goes with it. Sons in a sibling society don't feel as much murderous jealousy of the father as they did in Vienna. They often win the mother soon after birth and then don't know what to do with her. Such siblings are not violent revolutionaries; authority, being relatively impalpable, does not evoke as much anger as it did in the old father societies.

But we know that among family siblings envy is a primary emotion. Siblings want a higher standard of living, because they compare themselves with other "siblings" living everywhere else on the planet. Shopping malls then are a sibling phenomenon. Even though the sibling society is just in its beginning phase, we notice that men and women have become highly envious of each other. We are accustomed to anger between men and women, defense of territory, contempt, alienation, rage, incomprehension, but not envy. Ivan Illich remarks that he knows of no other time in history in which envy between men and women has played such a large part.[5] Some ground beneath each gender having been taken away, men and women are envious of each other, Illich says, for the meager rewards that the capitalist society offers: promotions, high salaries, prestige. Blue collar men envy women for being able to stay at home; women envy men for their being able to go out, etc.

Violent revolution, then, does not belong to the sibling way. If friends of Mao in Beijing hold power achieved by the old father-killing mode and a hundred thousand siblings occupy a nearby square, the stage is set for a vast misunderstanding. The old men did not grasp that what the students really wanted was a higher standard of living; they did not in fact want the old men's deaths. That incomprehension led to the hideous massacre of the student camp, simmering with the new post-father emotions. I emphasize this drama in order to remind us how far-reaching the changes are. We have to look hard at the culture of siblings we now have all over the industrialized world. The conservative agenda—buttressing present authority, resurrecting the father discipline and police power, centering national energy on hating the father authority in some other nation—will not work. Gorbachev is one of the first leaders to understand the sibling aspirations.

Enormous changes have appeared at the last minute, and I suspect that the masculine psyche, particularly, is not prepared for them. I have mentioned so far the lack of "cellular tuning" that young men remain hungry for; the arrival of the demons that want nothing to do with older men; the disappearance of the father's teaching in practical matters; the death of the Group Father and the subsequent appearance of the sibling society which is taking shape everywhere on the planet. All of these events work to hedge the father around with his own paltriness. D. H. Lawrence says: "Men have been depressed now for many years in their male and splendid selves, depressed into dejection and almost abjection. Is that not evil?"

The final change I want to look at here is the increasing caretaking of the "endarkened" father by the son and that son's attempt to redeem the father by becoming "enlightened." James Hillman's essay elsewhere in this volume has brought this longing for redemption into the light, offering a new view of what is called the "puer aeternus" or flying boy.

He sees the mythical model for the flight of so many contemporary young men in the flights of the Egyptian God Horus, about whom one hieroglyphic script declares: "Horus soars up into the sky beyond the flight of the original god's soul, and beyond the divinities of former times. . . . I have gone beyond the bounds of Seth. I am unique in my flight."

Horus's father, Osiris, was imprisoned by his brother Seth in a coffin that drifted down the Nile, across the Mediterranean to Byblos, where it became incorporated into a tree trunk, then shaped in turn into a pillar, where it remained for years. Horus's father then was truly in "darkness."

This comparison of the flying boy with Horus helps us to understand the possibility that a young man in these times may be ascending because he sees that his father is immersed in demonic darkness, the sort of darkness suggested by the words workaholism, weakness, submission, isolation, alcoholism, addiction, abusiveness, evasion, cowardice. Or—to simplify the perception—the son sees the darkness in his father's lack of purpose.

I don't mean to imply that meditation and spiritual labor in young men are a mistake or something that should not be or have been. But timing is important; the spirituality may come too soon in a life. When some of us look back on our own acts of ascension during our twenties, they seem more a sacrifice than a growth; and we ask: for whom was this sacrifice being made?

All over our culture we see sons who do not fight to defeat their own fathers or the Group Father's authority, but instead ascend above them, beyond them. We have Transcendental Psychology, which is at once Sibling Psychology and a psychology of people determined to have a higher consciousness than their fathers.

The young man's flight toward light and enlightenment has usually been understood in psychological literature as a revolt against the chthonic, conservative, possessive, commitment-mad maternal part of the feminine, as Marie-Louise von Franz has laid it out so brilliantly in her book *Puer Aeternus*.[6] I prefer James Hillman's view of this flight; it seems truer to my own experience. And so this ascension of sibling males all over our culture I add to our list of imbalances brought about by the exile and belittling of the personal father.

The demons who have set up a propaganda shop in the son's psyche convince him that his father's darkness is deeper than he ever imagined. He senses that his mother cannot redeem his father and that she doesn't want to. So the only one who can do it is the son. There is a social quality in this flight: it is the family name that is redeemed more than the father himself. The son cannot rescue the father, for he is flying away from the father and not toward him. But I, like many other sons, have accepted years of anguish, foolishness, abuse from others, inappropriate aspirations, thin air, and the loneliness of the long-distance flyer in order to ascend like Horus, "farther than any of the other gods."

Society without the father produces these bird-like men, so intense, so charming, so open to addiction, so sincere, as those great bays of the Hellespont produced the cranes Homer noticed that flew in millions toward the sun.

II. A Digression on the King

"King and Queen" have a long and honorable history in fairy stories where the words do not imply human beings—let alone persons of gender—and in the history of monarchy where they do. Without attempting to be exhaustive, we'll distinguish three levels on which human beings experience the King: upper, middle, and lower.

The middle ground refers to the political earth where the flesh and blood King lives. Kings as leaders of huge cities and empires, holding broad powers, are first noticed during the second millennium B.C., in the city states of Mesopotamia. A Sacred King united heavenly sun power and earthly authority. The Chinese elaborated this double Kingship in fantastic detail. The King held societies together until the eighteenth and nineteenth centuries, and then the powers failed. Under the names of Kaiser, Czar, Emperor, Maharajah, Sultan, Bey—one after another, the Kings fell throughout Europe and its colonies.

Our nation's rejection of the flesh and blood King George (1776) preceded the beheading of Louis XVI by a few years, and we celebrate the moment with Fourth of July fireworks. We repeat that rejection of the King with less and less joy each July, perhaps because the brilliant and ascending explosion of victory, followed by the descending failure, casts its shadow down on our fathers.

In the Middle Ages the King would sometimes take a tour of his realm. Waiting in village lanes to see him go by, hundreds of people would feel some blessing from the King at the moment he passed. When the flesh and blood King, for good reasons or bad, disappears through exile or death, each of us finds it more difficult to visualize the King on the other two levels. I am not declaring that the King-killing was a historical error, or that we should resurrect the King and send him out along the lanes again, but I do urge the contemporary person not to blame himself if he finds it difficult to grasp vividly the Kings on the other two levels.

When the outward or flesh-and-blood King falls, his plunge downward entangles the frail Kings in the other two layers, increasing the speed of their descent. It accelerates their fall by sympathetic magic.

John Weir Perry calls the sacred King who unites sun power with political authority the "Lord of the Four Quarters," and in the book of that same name he has written brilliantly about this force.[7]

The surviving flesh-and-blood Kings now live out their lives in *The National Enquirer*, along with Duke Ellington, Count Basie, "Elvis, the King," and Prince. When the patriarchy collapses, the sun energy cannot get down to the earth. Celtic legends give the image: eagles sit on the tops of trees with dead animals underneath their claws, and rotting bits of flesh fall through the branches to the ground beneath, where the meat is eaten by swine. We are the swine. When all that comes down from the eagles is rotten flesh, the sons and daughters do not receive the true meat, and the scavengers get what there is. Naturally, everyone is dissatisfied.

The upper King, the King in his eternal space—who sits with the Queen and does not undermine her power—lives in a mythological, eternal, and luminous realm. We could call the space where he and the Queen live the "mythological layer." Joseph Campbell remarked often that the mythological layer in the West collapsed around 1000 A.D., when imaginative energy and prayer held it up no longer. It was felt as an overarching inner heaven where the Virgin Mary lives, where Dionysus lives, where Zeus and Athena live, where Freya, Odin, Thor, and Jehovah live.

There is room also for witches, giants, and dwarfs, all three well-remembered in fairytales even after the collapse. Mythological thinking means the ability to imagine these Gods and what they do boisterously, vigorously, and well, keeping the layers well-distinguished. Catholic priests (one could say) stopped doing that, mingled the layers and, around 1300, began confusing witches with living women and burning the women. Partly because so much imaginative energy went into science, European men and women after the Renaissance stopped feeding beings in the mythological layer with the intensity of their imagination. The inner heaven collapsed, and we see all around our feet broken glass. We know that the Gods are somehow "at our feet."

The Protestant path did not amount to a reversal or turn for the Catholic imagination—it was more of the same. Calvinists, Quakers, and Lutherans gave evidence through the pure, white inner walls of their churches that the Protestant imagination could not celebrate, nurture, honor, laugh with, interpenetrate with these old God images any longer.

The Sacred King of the upper world, to follow John Weir Perry, is the principle of order in whose presence the Cosmos takes shape. He does not create order; where he is, there is order. He blesses and by that means encourages the creativity in others. Because he and the Queen are in the right space together, the fig tree blossoms, the apple trees bear fruit abundantly, ditches run with milk and honey. Robert Moore, the Jungian analyst and theologian, reminds us that the Sacred King's brother—the Shadow King, or Poisoned King, or Twisted King, or Herod King—exists in that eternal and mythological space as well, as some traditions hold the Devil to be the brother of Christ.[8]

It remains then to discuss the "Third King," whom we'll call the Inner King. He lives in the roots in the sense that he inhabits the human soul-world, the lower world, which we sometimes call "the unconscious," though wrongly, for it may be more conscious than we. "Lower" does not imply lesser. It means a place we find when we break contact even briefly with our womb-like world of obsessive social light. We go down to it, guided by Dionysus or Persephone. The Inner King is one of a company of root people that includes the Trickster, whom the native Americans have always loved, and the Wild Man, who is discovered lying at the bottom of a pond.

When we were born, our Inner King was perfectly alive and willing to fight for what we want. Those people who spent their childhoods in alcoholic families or in families messed up in some other way sense that their Kings were killed early on. The child's realm, which we will call his mood, counts for nothing in the messed-up family. The mood of the dominant parent is the only mood in the house, and the spouse and children all adapt to that mood, tiptoe around it, serve it, sacrifice their mood to that "greater" mood. The Inner King then dies, over and over, in the son or daughter.

The Inner King is able to set the course for the rest of one's life—set it for the next hour, the next day, the next month, the next year, the next ten years—without being contaminated in that decision by the opinions of others. Recovering the Inner King means overcoming the victimhood that has become habitual to us since childhood, then feeding and honoring with our adult energy the Inner King until he stands up once more.

I have often spoken of the disappearance of the Wild Man. Many men of the seventies and eighties find themselves out of touch with him, and they long for him out of sight below the waters of their lives. But contemporary men long just as deeply to be in touch with the Inner King. The diminishment of the father, as well as the collapse of the other two Kings, makes the longing for the Inner King intense, almost unbearable.

I would say that the growth period that men want at midlife starts off not so much with camping trips and resolutions as with long grieving over the dead Inner King, the dismembered Warrior, and the buried Wild Man inside ourselves and our fathers.

III. Widening the Father's Apartment

Sons today see their fathers as dejected and abject, and that vision is a new phenomenon. We see the fathers diminished, reduced to stick-figure cartoons, "unable to fare forward or retreat," no match for feisty, furious women. We see the father as misguided or purposeless, a thing any self-respecting wife or son could get along without.

It is through the radiance of the Virgin Mary shining down into a woman that the Christians see a woman's purity and sweetness,

and through the radiance of great witches—Baba Yaga, Kali, and
Durga—that the Russians and the Hindus see a woman's violence,
her strength, her openness to death, her longing to conquer death.
We who are sons hope that through the radiance of the Sacred
King, the radiant Arthur, shining down into the father, we will be
able to see his bravery and his generosity; and we know that
through the great poisoned Fathers and Kings—Herod, Cronos,
Stalin, the Thornbush Cock Giant—we see his devouring hunger,
his fear of death, his insistence that everyone live in disorder.

Let me mention three ways we have of thinking about our personal father. We'll call them the concrete way, the psychological
way, and the mythological way. All three are good. When we
remember our father concretely, we say he did this and did that,
and that's over, so why talk about it? Concrete thinking feeds itself
on anger, and a lot of blaming gets done. Sons remember each
blow, each time the father did not take them fishing. Adolescent
sons have very little to say about their fathers beyond the facts.

When we think psychologically, we discover that some acts of
our father that we disliked carried other implications: a father's
drinking may reveal a longing for "spirits"; the father's "dropping"
the son may be a teaching about the world; his flashes of anger
may suggest an honesty heroically preserved against his own parent's wishes. Then we may soften, give up blaming so much, and
feel the heart begin to melt. Psychological thinking, which our culture has taught with such persistence the last four decades, is in-
finitely valuable: it tends to bring in forgiveness, complication,
humor, symbolic subtlety, and compassion. Eventually, however,
it leads us to think of the father as a victim. We understand that his
own father did not love or support him; we take childhood trauma
into account; we say he got no help. Psychological thought rarely
enlarges a father. He falls into a place we reserve for wounded
animals and defeated generals, and rather than see what he did,
good or evil, we see what he could not help but do. Psychological
thinking leaves him the same size, perhaps smaller—simultane-
ously more acceptable and less original.

If we take the next step, toward mythology, we go to stories,
and then the dark side of the father becomes vivid. We recall that
in Kafka's *Metamorphosis* the father changed his son into a shelled
insect who lived under the bed in the son's room.[9] The son-insect
exercised occasionally by crawling around on the living room walls

while the father was absent. The father returned unexpectedly one day and, on seeing the son-insect up on the wall, threw an apple that dented the shell and damaged the son's soft interior body. As the apple from the Garden of Eden hits the son, the father in our eyes grows larger: he carries something of a maligned Jehovah or perhaps a shamer on a cosmic scale. We can take one more example from Kafka: the aged and apparently senile father in "The Judgment" changes size several times.[10] While the son is carrying the old man to his new room, he appears to be a small baby who plays with the son's watch chain; but once in bed, he leaps up, touching the ceiling with his fingers, and then condemns his son to death by drowning. The authority is so great that the son carries out the sentence within five minutes.

We'll call this method of enlarging the father apartment "contemplating his dark side." Each father carries on his dark side qualities of the Destructive King, as well as the corrupt Shaman, the brutalized Warrior, the Shadow Wild Man, the bitter Trickster, and the deformed Grief Man. That father side curses the son, pushes him into a world of disorder, refuses to share power with the Queen, undermines the son's self-respect. We need consciously to build another room on our father apartment to house this Destructive King and his relatives.

We are so used to the witch image that we too soon give her credit for hideous transformations. The witch's daughter in the Grimm Brothers' story "The Six Swans" does change the King's six sons into swans. But we find out that earlier the father, or the fear-ridden, cowardly part of the father, arranged for all that. Lost in the forest of the world, fearing for his life, he bought his way out by agreeing to marry the witch's daughter. Our own father, through his fear, may have arranged our disasters before we were born. Buddha blessed all his sons by standing fast when the Demons of Death threatened him, but most of us do not have a Buddha father. The Buddha, sitting under the Bo tree, drew down the energy of the steadfast Divine King; our father, who had no tree, who sold out to save his life, draws energy too, but from the Shadowy King. For the six swans, it was the father who let the forces of evil into the house.

Each father inherits thousands of years of cunning and elaborate fatherhood. The apparently weak father can control the entire family from beneath with his silences. Should the father be an alcoholic, his alcoholism may be a massive operation, carried out with Napoleonic thoroughness, so that he rules his house by the most economical means. He withdraws energy from his community; energy pours into his dynamos, rather than out of them, in a way familiar to us from the lives of great tyrants.

To widen the father apartment we need, like Kafka, to increase our capacity for horror, life-hatred, tyranny, jealousy, murderousness. Blake imagined a being named Urizen who curses, condemns, and blasts "the fairest joys," while he weeps from blind eyes. Blake's fantasy amounts to an extra room he added on to his father's space.

By remembering the mythologies of the Destructive, Twisted, Urizenic, Poisoned Father, we enlarge our father's space, and we are good at this activity. Why not then enlarge the space still more by dwelling on mythological stories of the Good Father? We are not so good at that, and looking for stories we may come up short. Good fathering of the kind we want is rare in fairytales or in mythology. Who are the good and kind fathers? There are none in Greek mythology—a shocking fact—and very few in the Old Testament. Ouranos, Kronos, and Zeus exhibit three styles of horrendous fatherhood. Abraham, a famous Old Testament father, was perfectly willing to sacrifice Isaac; and his grandson Jacob was good to Joseph, but apparently not to his other eleven sons, and he certainly didn't protect Joseph from them. In Celtic legend, we don't think of Cuchulain primarily as a father (and in the end he killed his son in battle), nor do we think of any other great Celtic heroes that way. We love the lively and bizarre Kings in fairytales for qualities other than their fathering.

We also notice few examples of close or chummy father–son relationships in mythology. King Arthur radiates generosity, but he does not do so as father, but as uncle, as initiator and guide of young men. We know that in some ancient cultures the father did little besides conceive the son. Warriors taught the child, uncles disciplined him, old men initiators guided him. It was only in our time, after all the helping older men had disappeared, that those sacred responsibilities fell on the father, and one reason he seems small is that he cannot possibly carry them all.

We cannot have the closeness we want from our fathers. "Male," John Layard says, "symbolizes that which is 'set apart', as masculinity is set apart or separated from the matrix of femaleness biologically, and as monoliths are set up and separated from the places where they are found."[11] The father is set apart not only from his wife but from his son. Sitting on the western cliff of the main Aran Island, I wrote of my father:

> Aren't you farther out
> from the mainland
> even than these granite cliffs?
>
> Perhaps I want you
> to be still farther from land
> than these Aran Islands,
> to be at the edge
> of all human feeling.

We want our father to be close, and at the same time we want him to be "at the edge of all human feeling," where he already is.

As sons we are drawn to light, and we resist learning what the dark side of our father is. His positive qualities and his horrendous qualities may both belong to the monolith in him that is "set apart."

As I close this essay, I have two brief points. We have to be satisfied with a relationship to our father that is not close. He's not the type. If we want blessing, order, sympathy, and encouragement of our creativity, we are confusing him with the Sacred King. We can develop an Inner King, and he will do that blessing and evoke the order.

Secondly, in a time when the Group Father has fallen, we approach the Sacred King and the Inner King with tremendous longing. We want them to approach us. But how can we invite them to be guests in our psyche when the rooms we keep for our own father are so small? The apartment we keep for our father is where the mentor, the Inner King, and the Sacred King will eventually live. We begin our invitation to the King then by enlarging those rooms, and we do that by renewed attention to our personal father and particularly to his dark side. To regard our father with respect for his size is more difficult for us than it was for the men for whom these myths and stories were composed thousands of years ago. If we are to believe anthropologists, they had mentor fathers, warrior fathers, initiate fathers. We have only one, and so we say, "He is not enough." He'll have to be.

We think for a long time that we want a Sacred King as father; we want to be up above with him and to forget how dark he is. We want closeness, but that's not the way it is. The myths on the whole testify to that distance. The father gives us a dam, and our water gets piled up behind it. He gives us the intensity of dammed water and its agony. A man said to me: "My father gave me a red-hot poker in the gut. He gave me a nail that will not loosen. This house will fall before this nail will come out."

His gift then is not closeness. The father gives with his sperm a black overcoat around the soul, invisible in our black nights. He gave, and gives, a sheathing, or envelope, or coating around the soul made entirely of intensity, shrewdness, desire to penetrate, liveliness, impulse, daring. The father's birth gift cannot be quantified. It has something to do with a love of knowledge, love of the mind, and a way to honor the world of things.

1. G. Gorer, *The Americans* (New York, 1940).

2. B. Bettelheim, *Symbolic Wounds* (New York, 1954).

3. A. Mitscherlich, *Society Without the Father* (London, 1969).

4. Ibid.

5. I. Illich, *Gender* (New York, 1982).

6. M.-L. von Franz, *Puer Aeternus* (Santa Monica, 1981).

7. J. W. Perry, *Lord of the Four Quarters: Myths of the Royal Father* (New York, 1966).

8. R. Moore, *Rediscovering Masculine Potentials* (four tapes) (Wilmette, IL, 1988).

9. F. Kafka, *Metamorphosis* (New York, 1968).

10. F. Kafka, *The Complete Stories* (New York, 1983).

11. J. Layard, *The Virgin Archetype* (Zürich, 1972).

On Senex Consciousness
James Hillman

SENEX IS THE Latin word for old man. We find it still contained within our words *senescence, senile* and *senator.* In Rome the time of the senex was "from the latter half of the fortieth year onward." It could apply to old woman too. But as we shall inquire into this idea, senex will come to mean more than old person or old age. The imaginal notions condensed into this short term extend far beyond whatever personal ideas we might have of oldness, beyond our concerns with old age, old people and the processes of time in personal life. Perhaps, however, at this first level, where the senex affects our lives and aging we can grasp its import most easily.

The discussion that follows makes two assumptions: first, the senex is an archetype; second, this archetype is the one most relevant for the puer, as if its 'father.' By this we mean that the senex is a *complicatio* of the puer, infolded into puer structure, so that puer events are complicated by a senex background. A phenomenological review of this archetype becomes necessary for our study of the puer. Although these two archetypal structures are intertwined, we shall draw the portrait of the senex away from the puer, in sharpest relief and contradistinction, in order to reflect the psychological tension between them. Nevertheless, the senex archetype is more than something 'psychological,' a derivative of experience, an aspect of man and his behavior, an icon foisted upon life by man's idolatrous imagination. Rather, the senex is one of the crystallizations of God, one of his *numen multiplex,* or, the senex is itself a God, a universal reality whose ontological power is expressed in nature and culture and the psyche of man.

As natural, cultural and psychic processes mature, gain order, consolidate and wither, we witness the specific formative effects of the senex. Personifications of this principle appear in the holy or old wise man, the powerful father or grandfather, the great king, ruler, judge, ogre, counselor, elder, priest, hermit, outcast and cripple. Some emblems are the rock, the old tree, particularly oak, the scythe or sickle, the time-piece and the skull. Longings for superior knowledge, imperturbability, magnanimity express senex feelings as does intolerance for that which crosses one's systems and habits. The senex also shows strongly in ideas and feelings about time, the past and death. Melancholy, anxiety, sadism, paranoia, anality and obsessive memory ruminations reflect this archetype. Moreover, the main image of God in our culture: omniscient, omnipotent, eternal, seated and bearded, a ruler through abstract principles of justice, morality and order, a faith in words yet not given to self-explanation in speech, benevolent but enraged when his will is crossed, removed from the feminine (wifeless) and the sexual aspect of creation, up high with a geometric world of stars and planets in the cold and distant night of numbers—this image depicts a senex God, a God imaged through the senex archetype. *The high God of our culture is a senex God; we are created after this image with a consciousness reflecting this structure.* One face of our consciousness is inescapably senex.

Because this archetype expresses all that is old, ordered and established, it has particular bearing upon our culture and its supposedly dead or dying God. The breakdown of structure is the death of this particular structure, who is the principle of Structure; if this central fixation of our religious consciousness has aged into remote transcendence, there to wither and die, then the image in which we have been cast, reflecting this main God, is also passing away. A kind of consciousness departs. The 'de-struction' of culture and the breakdowns in individual lives result from this transition of the senex dominant which has also been a senex dominance: *the usurpation of one God over many,* of one archetypal form over others, of one kind of consciousness pressing others into unconsciousness. Although the theology of our culture gives witness to the death of the senex God by proclaiming reform and loosening principles, an archetypal power does not 'die' in the

sense of emptied out, inoperant and still. It continues in the imaginal realm through which it influences our fantasy and emotion
and continues to receive its due worship through the psyche in
ways we shall discover as this part proceeds. Although fading as
an icon, an image 'out there' with a name and an observance,
it catches us from within, through its immanence in the fantasy
levels of the psyche. What the Greeks called Kronos, the Romans
Saturn, our tradition has worshiped as "Our Father who art in
Heaven." But gone from Heaven—and Heaven gone too—the
senex now can be best encountered indirectly, through a psychological phenomenology.

I. Senex Characteristics in Saturn

From astrology, from the medicine of the humors, from lore and
iconography, from the collections of the mythographers, we can
piece together the major characteristics of Kronos–Saturn as archetypal image of the senex. One basic text on which we rely and
from which are condensed many of the formulations in this part is
the Warburg Institute's study *Saturn and Melancholy,* by Klibansky, Saxl and Panofsky.

The double nature of the senex we have already mentioned.
This duplicity must be kept in mind as we read through his qualities; one characteristic is never safe from inversion into its opposite. We shall never encounter the good wise old man without
recognizing him as an ogre at the same time, nor come upon one
destructive trait that cannot be saved into virtue by turning it upside down.

The temperament of the senex is cold, which can also be expressed as distance. Senex-consciousness is outside of things, lonely,
wandering, a consciousness set apart and outcast. Coldness is also
cold reality, things just as they are, dry data, unchangeable cold
hard facts. And coldness is cruel, without the warmth of heart and
heat of rage, but with slow revenge, torture, exacting tribute,
bondage. As lord of the nethermost, Saturn views the world from
the outside, from such depths of distance that he sees it all 'upside
down,' and to this view the structure of things is revealed. He sees
the irony of truth within the words, and the city from the cem-

etery, the bones below the games of skin. Thus the senex view gives the abstract architecture and anatomy of events, plots and graphs, presenting principles of form rather than connections, inter-relations or the flow of feeling.

The senex emblem of the skull signifies that every complex can be envisioned from its death aspect, its ultimate psychic core where all flesh of dynamics and appearances is stripped away and there is nothing left of those hopeful thoughts of what it might yet become, the 'final' interpretation of the complex at its end. The end gives the pessimistic and cynical reflection as counterpart to puer beginnings. As complexes can cloud themselves with puer-illusions, senex-consciousness penetrates these illusions with its fantasy of 'bitter truth' and 'cold reality,' of seeing through all exteriors. The fantasy of 'laying bare' is a favorite one of the philosopher, like Jeremiah the prophet or Diogenes the Cynic, exposures of truth to the bone, 'where it hurts.' The fantasy of this consciousness is that a complex can be dissolved by concentration upon itself, penetrating to a self-knowledge, a truth which can be known and is unpleasant. Ultimately, this fantasy turns into a lifestyle of permanent cynicism for all complexes, the seeing through of everything: vanity, all is vanity.

The skull also refers to the concern of senex-consciousness with structure and intellectual abstraction. In Medieval and Renaissance imagery, Saturn was often depicted together with instruments of geometry and astronomy. Structure and abstraction point yet deeper: to the principle of order itself. Kronos–Saturn as original governor of the universe is the *nous*—an idea that can be traced back to Plato (*Laws,* 4, 713b–14a). Hesiod's Kronos ruled at the beginning of things. The senex provides the original order, or *nous*, its ideal form, the foundations, principles and axioms upon which a state is built. He promulgates its law and its order. The state and its government are also the state of the complex and that ruling fantasy by which it is governed. The structure of the complex, the rules by which it abides, making it repetitive in responses and so difficult to dismantle or even argue against except in the terms of its official, habitual logic—this is the senex aspect of the complex.

Senex fantasies such as the longing for law and order, for return to a golden age where there might be contentment in agrarian simplicity under patriarchal solidity can be found in Greece and in Rome in connection with the festivals of the senex, the Cronia and the Saturnalia. Then, the senex power was honored with anarchy and propitiated from hardening into its despotic tendency. The rigid structure of the complex cured itself, so to speak, by providing for its own de-struction. Its order included anarchy; the festivals of Kronos and Saturn provided for a fantasy of leisure, peace and bounty, food and drink without toil, an end of slavery and property. We no longer use these homeopathic cures. Instead, we attempt to break down the senex power from without, introducing violence to topple the structure. These attacks upon it merely reinforce the ruling complex by increasing the rigor of its law and the vigor of its order. When the senex forgets its form of renewal through its own asocial and anarchic fantasy, it loses one side of its structure, becoming onesided. By its banning breakdown, breakdown is ensured.

Within the individual psyche, we find the same senex fascination with order. We want to get the complexes into order in accordance with the first principles of what complexes are, their rules of behavior, their analysis through association experiment plotted by means of time on graphs, so as to discover their laws and to master them through these laws. Whenever we make order we ask the senex to enter. And he enters through every fantasy of structural analysis and therefore has his place in this study and its fantasy.

Saturn and his attributes show many ways in which order can be brought about: through time, through hierarchy, through scientific system of measurements. Order may be brought also by setting limits and exclusions, by the logical thought of negation and contradiction, through establishing and extending power, by conserving what exists and fulfilling duty. Saturn's order may also be made by relating events to the fixity of the earth and the definition of shape that earth gives. Order may also refer to a spiritual order and a spiritual discipline which requires inwardness, isolation and reflection, which virtues too belong to Saturn. To grasp the senex at work in our lives is to watch the way in which we order our lives. Habit is the movement of Saturn through our days; so too is counting; so too is remembering. Our relation to the clock, the calendar, and the passing years show Saturn. The principles by which we live, the limits we set ourselves and the world around us, the scale of values (less the values than their hierarchy), and—

above all—the order brought through control, self-control and control over others express this senex nature.

The senex makes order particularly through boundaries. Senex-consciousness draws division lines: your kingdom and mine; conscious and unconscious; body and mind. Also, as Norman O. Brown exhibits with his characteristic brilliance, our idea of the ego and its notion of order require a boundary between real and fantasy, between inner and outer. Boundary is necessary for properties and possessions, for territory and ownership. One's own is within one's boundaries. The idea of a self, an enclosed and individual proprium, requires boundary, and boundary is made by the senex.

But boundaries are set—to carry on from Brown—for religious reasons, too. *Fanum* and *temenos* mark off the sacred. The boundary differentiates districts of being; it permits ontological distinctions and the possibility of symbols. Senex-consciousness, by maintaining the wall and law against something which does not like a wall and a law, makes possible the psychological region of the borderline and a host of symbols whose existence requires boundaries. Without boundaries there would be no container and no preserves; without boundaries, what sense in gates, doors, openings, barricades, exits and entries, secrets, initiations, election, esotericism. Saturn draws the lines and therefore rules both sides: the exaltation of holiness and the degradation of the profane, the city and the outcast, the king and the slave, the ego and its repression.

Slow, heavy, chronic, leaden—these analogous qualities referred to Saturn. Lead was especially important for the alchemical work of redemption. The work could not be begun nor completed without lead, and Saturn in some alchemical systems was the beginning and the end. A senex quality was required to give realization through time and dense corporality. The alchemist's accomplishment came through his own leadenness, his chronic patient labor and the accompanying depressed states of mind. Lead was not merely a metal; it was a quality of consciousness which the alchemist had to have inherently present in order to do his work with the metal. He and the substances had to correspond. The lead remained to the end as a necessary ingredient of the Stone, so the depressed state of mind survived to the end, reflecting a consciousness that survives through and by means of depression. It was not all done away with, all transmuted into shining gold. The poisonous lead, its evil and its dullness were the curse of the work, yet necessary to it.

From early Greek to late Roman times, superstitious curses were inscribed on leaden tablets (*defixiones*). These curses (*katadesmoi, katadeseis*) literally mean "bindings." They were left in tombs or buried for the spirits of the underworld. Evidently in popular imagination Saturn had a special relation with the spirits beyond the grave and the black art of manipulating these spirits. The same charge in another language is brought against senex-consciousness today for its affinity with what is dead and buried and its binding curse upon present life through manipulation of past history. For some critics of senex-consciousness, institutions such as the medical profession, university instruction and parliamentary government are 'black arts' that bind the soul. The laws and prescriptions written by these institutions are, for some, tablets of lead, *defixiones*, curses of the senex. The mixture of knowledge with power and the magical use of it for evil seem one propensity of senex-consciousness. This archetype bridges to lower powers, as Saturn–Dis at the *imum coeli*, as Hypete the gravest note and longest chord, as lead the heaviest of the classical metals. Below is the place of the dead and the uncanny; it is also in our tradition the locus of evil.

For this reason, extreme inwardness (involution) and downwardness (dejection of melancholia, from the Greek word for black bile, Saturn's humor)—of all psychic disorders—have been met with especial suspicion. The melancholic has long been regarded not only as seriously ill but as particularly sinful. The black color associated with Saturn—besides standing for winter, night, death, distance—also in many different cultures evokes decay and evil. Hildegard of Bingen combines the theological and medical condemnation of this aspect of senex-consciousness in her *Of Causes and Cures*. The *humour melancholicus* originates in Adam's sin and the Fall of Man; it is a direct poisoning from the bite of the apple at the suggestion of the devil, and as such an incurable hereditary taint. Our resistance to depression, including the radical methods of shock and pep, continues to exhibit the fear of those black extremes to which senex-consciousness can penetrate through its melancholy.

From another regard, the lead of Saturn is the downward and

inward pull of gravity into subjectivity. The plumb-line drops ever deeper, straight to the grave, and below, to time past and the underworld spirits. The inward and downward pull into oneself and one's death implies that the senex is the chief force at work in some descriptions of individuation. The end-goal is often presented in senex imagery: isolation, unity, stones, cosmic systems and geometric diagrams, and especially the structured mandala and the Wise Old Man. Even 'wholeness through integration' can reflect Father Saturn who ate all the other Gods, swallowing his children.

Furthermore, the method of arrival at these goals is also determined by senex fantasies: depression (not inflation), suffering (not laughter), and introversion and imagination require turning away from the world. At the same time the ego is to be stable, ordered and strong. There is a distinct stress on numbers as archetypal root-structures, a belief in compensation as a psychic law (karma, retribution, revenge and the balance of opposites belong to Kronos–Saturn), and a profound occupation with archeology, history, religion, prophecy and outcast or occult phenomena. Part of the discipline, in this description of the way, is the intellectual study of abstract subjects, a scrutiny of dreams and oracular procedures (*I Ching*), prolonged and constant loyalty to the analysis of the unconscious. Natural man, as peasant, woodchopper or stonecutter, is idealized. Here we find a parallel in Marsilio Ficino who believed that one became a child of Saturn by turning to those occupations and habits that belonged to Saturn: ". . . hence, by withdrawal from earthly things, by leisure, solitude, constancy, esoteric theology and philosophy, by superstition, magic, agriculture, and grief, we come under the influence of Saturn." The senex archetype profoundly affects Jungian collective consciousness and, as we shall come to later, equally affects the Jungian judgments against the puer.

Slow, heavy, chronic, leaden: these qualities produce weight. Senex-consciousness ponders; it weighs things, as did the scales in the Roman temples to Saturn and the long history of the balance image associated with melancholy and Saturn. The voice of this consciousness carries weight, sometimes felt as lead-weight, too pessimistic and dry and altogether untimely, as if from a perspective that is both outmoded and prophetic. The weight represents congealing and coagulation, for Saturn is the personification of the *coagulatio* as it was called in alchemy. Coagulation makes things stick and hold together, becoming solid, trustworthy and time-worthy, but also dense and immobile.

The experience of coagulation is classic to depression, the inhibition and congealing of all psychic reactions to the degree of static inertia, a dry hunk of wood, a block of stone. This condition was once called the sin of *acedia*—only partially rendered by our *sloth* (cf. S. Wenzel, *The Sin of Sloth*, 1967). The main affliction was less of the body and its members than of the spirit and its expression. Although the heaviness shows particularly in the head—the melancholic is usually depicted with his head held up by a hand or dejectedly thrown forward onto a table—it is the voice that is "rendered mute, like a spiritual aphonia, a true 'extinction of the voice' of the soul. . . . Interior being closes in on itself in its mutism and refuses to communicate with the outside. (Kierkegaard will speak of *hermetism*)."

When Ficino refers to "leisure" and the "withdrawal from earthly things," or the Jungians speak of introversion as dominating behavior, or the alchemists of the hermetic vessel, or the clinician of depressive inhibition, we find the background to these manifestations of *acedia* to be senex-consciousness. As long ago as the Medieval period, a treatment for involutional withdrawal was work, since work (and prayer) were precisely what *acedia* was preventing. Treatments for depression through work and occupational therapy are prefigured in these older cures for the sin and disease of sloth. Work is the enemy of the devil; and again the senex provides a cure within its own archetype in accord with its own kind of consciousness, which includes toil and prayer as well as sloth and spiritual inertia. The recipe of work for 'curing the puer,' of course, will not have the same success because work is not rooted in the puer's own structure.

The pattern of two-sidedness continues through the collection of traits, thereby affecting especially the moral attributes of this consciousness. They become two-sided, dubious. Saturn presides over honest speech—and deceit; over secrets, silence—and loquacious slander; over loyalty, friendship—and selfishness, cruelty, cunning, thievery and murder. He is the just executioner and the criminal executed, the prisoner and the prison. He is retentive but forgetful, slothful and apathetic but rules the vigil of sleeplessness. His eyes droop with depression, apathetic to all events, and they stare inconsolably open, the super-ego eye of God, the Father, taking account of everything. He makes both honest reckoning and fraud. He is God of manure, privies, dirty linen, bad wind—and he is cleanser of souls.

Senex duality presents moral values inextricably meshed with shadow; good and bad become hard to distinguish. Because of the inherent antitheses, a morality based on senex-consciousness will always be dubious. No matter what strict code of ethical purity it asserts, there will be a balancing loathsome horror not far away, sometimes quite close—in the execution of its lofty principles. Torture and persecution are done in the best of circles for the best of reasons: this is the senex.

II. Saturn's Sexuality and Fertility

The relation of Saturn to sexuality is also dual: on the one hand, he is patron of eunuchs and celibates, being dry, cold and impotent; on the other hand, he is represented by the dog and the lecherous goat. Certain kinds of sexual disorder could be controlled by means of lead, according to Albertus Magnus: "The effect of lead is cold and constricting, and it has a special power over sexual lust and nocturnal emissions. . . ." Here, the senex constricts; yet it also imagines with the inordinate goatish desire of the 'dirty old man.' In either case, sexuality is at its extremes, transcending the normal and expected, so that these characteristics no longer refer to actual sexuality but to a fantasy of it. The dog and goat describe the impersonality of the desire, its commonplace and uninhibited earthiness, all eros-sentimentality shed. Impotence, on the other hand, prevents even the dog and goat level of connection, isolating the person and the drive itself to purely imaginal happenings. Impotence, like castration, is a pathological disturbance only when one expects sexuality to perform in the normative sense of generation and intercourse, sexuality in the service of life and love. But these are only two of its possible fantasies; sexuality may also be impotent for life and yet have potency in other aspects.

We must ask what is implied when sexuality is powerless to move externally, when it is contained altogether within; what is a man who is not a male, a force without an issue, a lifelessness of that which is generally considered the creative. Impotence as a death in the midst of life opens another avenue of sexual

exploration so that senex consciousness offers the complex
another kind of sexual possibility, another way of coming to terms
with the meaning of its sexuality and of creativity. Without the
senex and his inhibiting impotence, sexuality would exhaust itself
in exteriority, the copulative delights, the ceaseless generations.

That senex consciousness is associated with extremes of irrational and thus ungovernable sexuality is an idea that can be traced
back to the *Problemata* attributed to Aristotle. This idea has been
summed up in *Saturn and Melancholy* (p. 34):

> Melancholics followed their fancy entirely, were uncontrolled
> in every respect and were driven by ungovernable lust. . . .
> They were greedy, and had no command over their memory,
> which refused to recall things when wanted, only to bring
> them to mind later and unseasonably. All these weaknesses . . .
> came from the immoderate irritability of their physical con-
> stitution, so that neither could love give them lasting satisfac-
> tion nor gluttony alter their congenital leanness. In both cases
> they sought enjoyment not for its own sake but simply as a
> necessary protection against an organic failing; for just as their
> sexual craving came from excessive tension, so did their greed
> spring from metabolic deficiency. . . .

"Especially to visual images" were they susceptible, so that in sum
one could say they were characterized by an "exaggerated irritability of the 'vis imaginativa'" (p. 35).

The "excessive tension" as well as the excess of libido has its
source—according to the Aristotle of the *Problemata*—in an "excess of pneuma." The sexuality of the senex is given a pneumatic
source. Its disorders, whether in the form of lechery or of impotence, become ultimately accountable through the *heightened
power of imagination*. Senex consciousness presents a sexuality of
the *vis imaginativa,* an appreciation of sexual behavior itself as one
more form of fantasy. Impotence and lechery are aspects of the imagination first of all; they find their expression in sexuality, but in
other areas too. So we can look again at the castration of Uranos
by his youngest son Kronos, not merely as an emblem of sexual
impotence where the father is dethroned when his fertility is replaced by the usurping heir. The tale tells as well that the reign

of the old sky God as a myth maker and creator of imaginal possibilities is over when the sexual aspect of the *vis imaginativa* no longer functions.

If lechery and impotence both originate in the heightened imagination, we may detect in these apparently dissimilar phenomena a latent identity. Commonly, because old men are impotent, they, of course, have dirty thoughts. Dirty thoughts are, commonly, inferior substitutes for the 'real thing.' But turned the other way around, 'real' sexuality dwindles in order to stimulate dirty thoughts. These fantasies are the sexualization of consciousness, the needed erotic stimulation to fertilize the imagination. The transition to a lecherous spirit and an impotent body is the transition from the normal to the *noetic*, where impotence may become the precondition for a potent imagination. A similar transition can occur through senile memory-loss which opens the way from the normal to the noetic memory, to the remembrance via early childhood of the archetypal as described in Plato's *Meno* and *Phaedo*.

To be filled therefore with lecherous fantasies means Saturn is near, and depression too; these fantasies offer access to this archetypal perspective and to all the complications that come with this senex structure. So, too, with impotence: Aphrodite may not want it, nor Zeus, nor Pan, but its appearance demands that sexuality be re-imagined now through the senex. As senex pertains not only to old people but to a structure of consciousness, so senex sexuality refers not only to the sexual behavior of old people but to a kind of sexual consciousness, which provides the imaginal background for both impotence and lechery.

Despite the impotence, Saturn retains the attributes of Kronos; he is a fertility God. Saturn invented agriculture; this God of the earth and the peasant, the harvest and the Saturnalia, is ruler of fruit and seed. Even his castrating sickle is a harvesting tool. It would have to be Saturn who invents agriculture: only the senex has the patience equaling that of the soil and can understand the soil's conservation and the conservatism of those who till it; only the senex has the sense of time needed for the seasons and their chronic repetition; the ability to abstract so as to master the geometry of ploughing, the essence of seeds, the profitable counting, the dung, the loneliness and the affectionless, objectivized sexuality.

III. The Senex and the Feminine

According to Hesiod, in the Golden Age when Kronos ruled there were no women. The lore of Saturn in the astrological-magical texts continues the tradition of an estrangement between the senex and the feminine. Those born under Saturn "do not like to walk with women and pass the time." "They are never in favour with woman or wife."

Even if constant in feeling, Saturn is associated with widowhood, childlessness, orphanhood, child-exposure, and he attends childbirth so as to be able to eat the newborn. The original Saturn figure of Rome was not married (even if his Greek parallel, Kronos, had his sister-wife, Rhea). His feminine counterpart in Republican Rome was principally Lua (Goddess of the spoils of war, the plundered fields, the booty), who had the power of working evil (lues) on women, crops and harvest. Crops were spoiled or became the spoils of war. In later imagery, of which Dürer's *Melancolia* is the paradigm, Saturn's feminine aspect is Dame Melancholy. The mood of depression, with Saturn's usual attributes including the signs of wisdom, is now carried by the *anima tristis*. In a sense, Dame Melancholy is the senex vision of Sophia: senex wisdom may be depressing; senex depression may be wise.

Despite the disregard for women, senex-consciousness may keep the feminine imprisoned in secret, a secret soft-spot or a secret mistress. Like the Old King with the Princess in the keep, he does not let out his feminine side, warding off with cruelty and wiles anyone trying to rescue it. Or, the femininity of the senex may be an enactment of Dame Melancholy. Then the feminine side of the negative senex is a moody consort with whom no one can get along. It is not merely the anima-complex turned sour, bitter, resentful, complaining; the moody consort emanates like an atmosphere from any moribund complex, giving it the stench of Saturn.

For complexes, when they lose their life, putrefy. Putrefaction belongs to Saturn as God of agriculture, dung and dying. Putrefaction in alchemy was natural disintegration necessary for change. Such putrefaction is ferment, decomposition into elements through the release of sulphuric aggressive fumes which assault and insult

one's sensibilities. Its purpose is a re-ordering of 'matters.' But
when the senex has lost its child, then the rot is stagnation, nothing flowing in, nothing flowing out. One turns around and around
in one's own mess. Matters do not change. A dying complex in-
fects all one's psychic life. It can be recognized by grief and helped
with mourning; therewith we acknowledge the fact of decay. But
when ignored it spreads to the life of others. We become old
witches, old devils, old monsters that the world would put away
because of the death spread by the old dying complexes. In our
delusions of strength and power, we refuse to bear witness to our
decay.

Saturn's female partner, Lua, shows growth gone wrong
through Saturn's aggrandizement, the materialism and the greed.
Without awareness of the *anima tristis* component of Saturn, Lua's
reign may extend. Thus though senex-consciousness intends be-
nevolence, wisdom and order, senex-unconsciousness in the control of the feminine counterpart spreads like lues (the plague) and
looks for the battle to gain spoils. We may also read Lua as a Goddess of decay and pollution, for Saturn is the Lord of Decrease.
Senex growth is inward and downward, or backward; its force can
come through shrinkage, his power manifest in the last stage of
processes, in their decay. He rules over the spoiled, the filth and
the refuse of society not only owing to sordid anality and repression, but because senex consciousness finds its awareness in the
underside of the complex and as it decays. So accustomed are we
to growth, and to what Eliot calls "superficial notions of evolution / Which becomes, in the popular mind, a means of disowning
the past," and to the Positive Great Mother doctrines of milky-way
philosophy, onward and upward with Teilhard de Chardin, that
we miss Lua, the spoiler, the consciousness that is possible through
the natural process of decomposition. For "decay is inherent in all
composite things," so that what we work at, according to this last
dictum of the Buddha, is not our growth, but the modes of our rot.

Dame Melancholy may also appear as the embodiment and vision of depression, where she brings wisdom, as she did to
Boethius, who was betrayed and thrown into prison when not yet
forty. There his suicidal melancholy conjured the feminine figure
of Wisdom, who dictated to him his *Consolation of Philosophy.*
Depression and the awakening of one's genius are inseparable, say

the texts. Yet for most of us there is much depression and little genius, little consolation of philosophy, only the melancholic stare —what to do, what to do.

Psychological clichés claim that senex-consciousness is 'cut off' from the feminine. But Kronos has mother and wife and daughters (Demeter, Hera, Hestia). Rather than dissociated femininity, this archetype shows a female counterpart—Lua, Dame Melancholy— which mirrors and is thus indistinguishable from Saturn himself. His mother Gé (Mother Earth) repeats in his sister-wife Rhea, so that Saturn's agricultural, fertility and material functions are reflected by these feminine mirrors. The urge to "build cities" and "mint money," the deep-seated concretization of the senex impulse, may very well be taken as an attribute of this mother-sister-wife complex. The *complicatio* of these earth Goddesses in Kronos involve the senex in earthiness. Thus senex preoccupation with property, with the things and matters of the established order, its hoarding and its greed, derives not from the "excess of pneuma" and the "exaggerated irritability of the 'vis imaginativa'"—that is, Saturn's own native spirit—but rather from the feminine side of this structure, the earth and its materialism to which its ties are reinforced in triplicate.

By showing saturnine traits, senex femininity presents unpleasant, even maleficent, aspects of the anima. Here we meet her mad moodiness, her peculiar fascinations with the occult, or with power and possessions, or with the 'way out' things of prisons, sewerage and magic. A state of mind occurs that seems obsessive, not anima and not feminine as we prettily conceive these notions. Senex femininity seems rather the witch side of the mother archetype. As if as we grow older, not only do we whine and need helping, but use our infirmity for power. The old man has cut off not his mother, but his father; his mother he has married; they have become one. The senex anima can be so objectionable to ruling consciousness that a life may be, so to speak, dragged into the senex state. One turns against the moody consort and her materializations, attempting indeed to 'cut off' the feminine, negating her effects by clinging to the relics of male authority, worn-out fathering postures, refusing the natural decomposition of the complexes, refusing that decay emanating through the earth-witch and depression, the senex bride and sister.

Or, to re-awaken the puer aspect, the feminine may re-appear as an object for complex-compelled falling-in-love. Enter: the girl of our dreams; out: old woman, decay and depression. Falling-in-love is a phenomenon not only of old age, but of an old attitude. It may occur at any time of life and be occasioned by the loss of any puer aspect. Then one is 'ripe for it.' It is less a *coniunctio* fantasy, nor even the renewal of the feminine, as much as it is prompted by the lost child and re-connecting to the puer in oneself. So, the woman becomes Pandora—the first female brought into the all-male Kingdom of Kronos—a magical, beautiful box of fantasies and hope for the complex to be rejuvenated, *senilis* to *juvenilis*. The fantasies bring forth Venus from the sea of unconscious emotions, suddenly ebbing and flooding again. Her birth is closely tied with the senex; she is his progeny, his sole creation. Without Kronos and the senex-despair of the complex, Aphrodite and her illusions might never float in off the foam. Venus rose from the sea after being conceived there from the fathering genitals of Uranos which Kronos–Saturn, his son, cut off with his left hand and flung away. A senex act creates her of the seminal stuff of the father.

But these genitals are of the sky-god. They are the 'upper' aspect of sexuality, sexuality's *fantasy power*. So Venus is born from imaginal froth, the sea-foam of unconscious fantasy. When one attacks sexuality with senex-repression, severing the fathering fantasies of one's own loins, throwing it away left-handedly, unconsciously, it does not cease creating. Sexual fantasies inseminate below the waves, returning in the shape of Venus. Cut-off sexuality goes on living. The images return as the father's daughter: sweet, alluring, aphrodisiacal fantasies bred of the union of sexuality's 'upper' genitals and the emotional depths.

Kronos's act fathered other daughters besides Aphrodite; her sisters were dark indeed: the Moira and the Erinyes. The latter —even called "daughters of Kronos"—were death-dealing deities; the former, Goddesses of death and chthonic powers of the fate portioned to all men. These mythical sisters of Aphrodite (like the mythical servants of Aphrodite: Custom, Grief, Anxiety) reflect their parentage in senex-consciousness and its underworldly, otherworldly associations. Even the feminine delights that might be promised the old man through a young love come to him sternly and take him to his grave. Oedipus's daughters at the end bring not refreshment and renewal but ease his parting. The complex in its senex phase is inescapably doomed to its fate and the revelation of its psychic essence through the anima of death, which however does have, as its sister in inseparable *complicatio*, the joy and beauty of Aphrodite. Only when we would have Aphrodite alone, her sisters ignored, do they come pursuing like the Erinyes, snarling with endless complications the portions of inheritance, the retributions and recriminations of a mess left behind and passed like a fateful karma to next generations.

IV. Senex Consciousness in Childhood and Midlife

If the senex as archetype is there a priori, 'from the beginning,' we must expect it in a person's life from the beginning. We must expect a show of the archetype already in childhood, the old man in the little boy. And there we do find it when the small child says "I know" and "mine" with the full intensity of its being. There is senex, too, in the child's loneliness: a sense of utter abandonment, isolation and helplessness that may not come again until old age. The senex gives that ontological loneliness, a removal from human existence, in the special world set apart for the old, the mad and small children. The child's loneliness is part of that misery we call "ego-development." We conceive the ego as having boundaries, separated and able to withstand isolation. It must be able to go it alone. Part of the heroic initiation is exposure and loneliness. Loneliness gives the ego a vision of the world from the exile of childhood where one is outside like the senex, in another state of being. The ego is a superstition born of solitude, a magical way of entering the world of full human being. Call it an enacted omnipotence fantasy.

The small child shows its senex when it is the last to pity and the first to tyrannize, when it enjoys destroying what it has built, spurs its will with envy, keeps its secret, relishes detail, performs its esoteric superstitions, carries its grief, and in its weakness produces oral omnipotence and anal sadistic fantasies, or defends its borders and tests the limits set by others. The child can be solemn and ceremonious like old men. The child is obsessed with the limitations imposed by the body, tiny sores, afflictions and complaints. Its compulsion is like that of the aged: once obsessed, it cannot let go until it suddenly forgets. The senex traits are there; we need but see them for what they are. Childhood is governed not only by the archetype of the child and by the mother. The senex is there too, just as Saturn is in the birthchart, having its effects from the beginning. Seneca put it like this: "Ere the Child has seen the light, the principle of beard and grey hairs is innate. Albeit small and hidden, all the functions of the whole body and of every succeeding period of life are there."

Although the senex is there in the child, the senex spirit nevertheless appears most evidently when any function we use, attitude we have, or complex of the psyche begins to coagulate past its prime. It is the Saturn within the complex that makes it hard to shed, dense and slow and maddeningly depressing—the madness of lead-poison—that feeling of the everlasting indestructibility of the complex. It cuts off the complex from life and the feminine, inhibiting it and introverting it into an isolation. Thus it stands behind the fastness of our habits and the ability we have of making a virtue of any vice by merely keeping it in order or attributing it to fate.

The senex of the complex appears long before a person has himself put on his *toga senilis*. Michelangelo and Voltaire complained of old age around forty though they lived long into their eighties. Dante's four ages of man (adolescence, youth, *senectus* and *senio* [senility]) placed at least two of them directly under the influence of the senex. Shakespeare considered a man of forty old. Erasmus wrote "On the Discomforts of Old Age" while still thirty-nine. Tasso, who died at fifty, wrote his autobiographical essay on his infirmity and old age when he was forty-one. Another representative of the Renaissance, Thomas Eliot, in his *Castle of Health* (1534) declared that *senectus* begins at age forty. The awareness of the senex archetype through depression, complaint and limitation, the sense of time and death, of decay and the *anima tristis* has been fundamental in the kind of awareness we attribute to the creative person. Rembrandt, yet in his twenties, painted old people; Plato, we conjecture, devoted his early dialogues to the dying of a wise old man. There is, according to Jaques, a "mid-life crisis" in regard to death which determines the course of artistic work in later life. From what we know of the senex archetype, a crisis is brought on by its demand for entry. It brings a re-orientation of consciousness—in this case, in terms of senex structures.

The need for a 'second beginning' is often put in creation myths. The first start is wiped out, and the world begins again, after the

flood. Gods and heroes have a second birth (Osiris, Dionysos), or
two tales are told of their origin, and mystical man is twice-born.
Psychology has taken this ontological image about two levels of
being and two structures of consciousness and laid it out in terms
of progressive time: first-half and second-half of life. But these
'halves' are less biological or psychological fact than they are a
mythical description of the two levels on which we live. Some men
live from a 'twice-born' state early in their youth; others go
through a midlife crisis moving from one to another; others may
repeatedly live now one, now the other in alternations. First-half
and second-half pertain to kinds of consciousness, not to periods.

So the senex may appear in dreams while we are still very young.
It manifests as the dream father, mentor, old wise man, to which
the dreamer's consciousness is pupil. When accentuated it seems to
have drawn all power to itself, paralyzing elsewhere, and a person
is unable to make a decision without first taking counsel with the
unconscious to await an advising voice from an oracle or vision.
Though this counsel may come from the unconscious, it may be as
collective as that which comes from the standard canons of the
culture. For statements of sagacity and meaning, even spiritual
truths, can be bad advice. These representations—elders, men-
tors, analysts, and old wise men—provide an authority and
wisdom that is beyond the experience of the dreamer, 'helping' to
keep him helplessly dependent. Therefore it tends to have him
rather than he it, so that he is driven by an unconscious certainty,
making him 'wise beyond his years,' ambitious for recognition by
his seniors and intolerant of his own youthfulness. According to
some research, the senex figure comes more frequently in dreams
of women than those of young men, further indicating the distance
between puer and senex in our present culture. Crucial in this discussion is that senex consciousness may be constellated at any age
and in regard to any complex.

The Archetype of Saturn or the Transformation of the Father
Augusto Vitale

IT IS OFTEN not an easy task to begin to describe a region of the collective unconscious, as I am going to do, because the subject is not a rational one that can be systematically ordered in a logical manner. It is the recollection of many empirical facts that may bring the intuition of an archetypal motif and so lead to a region of our psyche where each point can be used as the starting point for the description of the region. We can get sufficient understanding of it only when we have completed our tour.

I. Some Aspects of Melancholy

Where can we find the experience of melancholy? I will point out only in short outlines melancholy as found in psychiatry and in some peculiar conditions of so-called normal life, as in mourning, nostalgia, adolescence—also as expressed in special fields of human activity, the arts, philosophical Weltanschauung, and religion.

After that, we will look for a common motif. This common motif could introduce us, by amplification, into the psychological inquiry of archetypes. We have chosen the archetype of Saturn, of the negative father. Other motifs and archetypal images might prove equally valid, but this question will appear more clearly at the end of our inquiry.

The psychical states that we call melancholy all have some

characteristics in common. From an objective point of view, there is a lowering of energy level in most of the psychical conscious functions, relationship life and all its expressions are reduced, mental processes and activities are slowed down. Melancholy goes from total inhibition, as in some psychotic depressions, to the lightest gradations of mood, but in all cases there is a subjective consciousness of sorrow bound to a feeling of powerlessness or impotence to will or to use one's own faculties.

Let us consider some aspects of melancholy that can be easily observed. At one extreme we encounter the depression of manic-depressive psychosis, which is often simply called "melancholy" or "melancholia." Here is what Karl Jaspers, the philosopher and psychopathologist, says about the characteristics of melancholic depression:

> Its core consists of a deep and unmotivated sadness, in addition to an inhibition of all psychical activities. Besides being felt very painfully by the subject, it is also observable in his objective behaviour. All instinctive drives are inhibited; the patient does not desire anything. It ranges from a lessening of the desire for movement and activity to a complete immobility. No decision, no activity can be undertaken by the patient. He lacks psychological associations. Nothing comes to mind; he complains about his deranged memory; he feels his lack of productive capacity and laments his insufficiency, insensibility and emptiness. He experiences this deep affliction as a peculiar sensation in the breast and abdomen, almost as if it could be grasped there. In his deep sadness the world seems to him grey within grey, indifferent and disconsolate. He looks only for the unfavourable and unhappy side of everything. He feels he has had many guilts in the past; the present offers only misfortune and the future looks terrifying with visions of ruin and impoverishment. At this stage of melancholy—anxiety, boredom and despair show a way out in suicide.[1]

If we take melancholy in its everyday or literary usage, it has the meaning of a gloomy and slack state of mind, a condition of sorrow, of being sunk in meditation and irritability—or, more romantically, a state of vague and resigned dejection, a meditative and intimate pain.

If in the extreme stages inhibition prevails, in all others there are besides the apparent inactivity and apathy an innermost longing, a constant work and torment, a searching without rest, thoughts and fancies which know neither their goals nor their needs. If a desirable goal is glimpsed, the subject runs up against a painful inhibition, an unaccountable impotence or an indecisive and inconclusive turning round.

Homesickness without hope, loss of an irreplaceable good, as may be experienced in exile or in the sorrow of mourning—such feelings are contained, so to say, in the state of melancholy and permit the amplification of its meaning.

As in homesickness and mourning, happiness that was known living in that land, or near that precious being, is in the memory boundless. By now everything is dull since such happiness was once known; all existence is conditioned; everyday experiences are continuously measured with this memory, stubbornly compared with it, as if to gain confirmation that what the subject experiences today isn't worth the shadow of that which he has lost.

It is as if there existed some power opposed to the reunion with that which has been lost, an overwhelming, adverse, and inflexible power which seems to paralyze the will and provoke that painful feeling of impotence.

All this is quite well illustrated in the melancholy which frequently affects adolescents. The adult world may be perceived by the adolescent as the hard reality—arduous, unpoetic as well as inescapable—in opposition to a sentimentally colored and cherished world of dreams and poetry generally connected with fabulous memories and the nostalgia of childhood. The melancholy adolescent experiences the irresolution, perplexity, and depression of being between two opposite sides of his existence: for him, to grow older is unavoidable, but it means to be deprived of the shining, nostalgic world of childhood. He sees the grown-up world as represented by persons who cannot understand those values and, moreover, who mock them. Contrary to the adolescent, they have power, will, and self-assurance, and by their mere existence they emphasize the insufficiency and incompleteness of the young man; they affirm a reality that looks to the adolescent grey and hard.

The melancholy adolescent experiences feelings of inferiority, impotence, guilt, because he doesn't accept the values of the grown-up world, and at the same time he experiences bitterness and contempt for a world toward which he nevertheless feels drawn by an invincible underground current. He flees toward what he feels to be a more acceptable atmosphere, the mystic, artistic, or philosophical. In his practical life he experiences waste, inconclusiveness, indecisiveness, confusion, as a consequence of contradiction and perplexity, because the attempt to settle the two aspects of life has failed. The melancholy adolescent often indulges in the idea of death as the "desired wreck" that could relieve him from a ruthless reality.

In our experience we encounter other forms of melancholy which help our task of unfolding and amplifying this psychological state and trying to find its unconscious components.

Philosophical pessimism may be considered a systematic display of a temperamental melancholy that is reflected in the thinking and becomes Weltanschauung. It may seem a mere aspect of character, an obsessive tendency to see in life only what is wrong. Every aspect of life brings with it ideas of decadence, disorder, waste, danger, and improvidence, even death and oblivion. In those who experience this pessimism there is the impression that *someone* must be responsible; as Leopardi, the poet of pessimism, said: ". . . the ugly hidden power which rules for general damage,"[2] or as Hamlet says in his monologue: ". . . the whips and scorns of time. . ." (3.1.70).

In these forms of melancholy the world and reality are seen as being endowed with insurmountable power and, on the other hand, an unshakable negativity; man is seen as a toy in the hands of a mocking destiny. Every living thing in which might appear beauty and goodness gives rise at once to the contrary images of death, destruction, corruption. The fragile brings to mind destruction and the ephemeral, illusion and pain.

Until now we have spoken about the negative aspects of melancholy, but there are other manifestations that bring to light the positive side of it, those in which the subject experiences in his memory, imagination, or intuition the aspect of existence most longed-for but denied. I refer to that melancholy which may be associated with the experience of the beautiful as well as the melancholy, perhaps very similar to this, that seizes men in the field of mystical-religious experiences.

On the one hand, the meeting with the fragile flower of beauty provokes once more thoughts linked with the frailty of all things human. As Petrarch says: "All things beautiful and mortal pass and do not endure."[3] Or in the words of Heine: "To wither, to be stripped of leaves, even trampled under the rough feet of destiny; such is, my friend, the fate of the beautiful on the earth."[4] Thus, the state of melancholic contemplation is realized in which the most desirable good unites with inevitable condemnation.

But the connection between beauty and melancholy seems to be even deeper and more secret. It is certain that the tie between beauty and melancholy has been experienced by men, perhaps only a certain type of men, for ages. We can quote Socrates in the *Phaedrus:* "when one sees the beauty of here below, remembering the true one, he sprouts wings and burns with the desire to fly; but because he cannot, like a bird he turns his gaze towards the heavens, forgetting things of here below and is accused of being in a state of madness. . . ."[5] Or, as Baudelaire says: "Melancholy is the illustrious fellow of beauty, to the extent that I cannot conceive any beauty which could not have in itself any unhappiness."[6]

Marsilio Ficino, the fifteenth-century humanist founder of the Platonic Academy in Florence, has given special stress to the close connection between beauty and melancholy. In his *De vita triplici* he puts melancholy as a middle step in a kind of individuation process beginning with the knowing of beauty, which in turn provokes sadness because of its mortality. The members of the Academy say that this state of melancholy is under the sign of Saturn, the planet-god who was also the patron of that Academy. Melancholy and love for beauty provoke the will to generate in order to immortalize life. In other words, melancholy may disclose the way to creative life.

We may briefly mention the melancholy that may be encountered in religious life. In some persons the religious experience appears as a sudden crisis. In such cases it is often preceded by a state of melancholy extraordinarily similar to pathological "melancholia."

> There is a feeling of emptiness, of despair, of guilt. The world is perceived as inhabited by a monster of evil, horrible and terrifying, in whose maw man experiences the grief of continuous death. Everything is felt to be meaningless; the normal and common way of life seems impossible to understand; the subject feels abandoned and hopeless.[7]

The 'positive' aspect of the religious experience in such cases is in close relation to the preceding state, because the subject has the intuition that he can escape from that unbearable world, where prevails the perfect purity of God. Mystics are especially inclined to experience a state of union with the infinite and perfect being, in which all is full of meaning and love—a state which might be considered an opposite pole of melancholy.

II. Analogical Investigation (Amplification)

The repetition of certain motifs in a psychological state so frequent and rich in emotion makes us think that we find ourselves in the gravitational field of an archetype. As archetypes are unknowable in themselves, it is useful to look for some manifestations of the same gravitational field in other spheres of human expression.

Mythology generally has a peculiar possibility in research of this type because of the spontaneity, variety, and wealth of its expressions. As regards melancholy, a very old tradition, respected even today, associates the name of Saturn with that of melancholy. In Greco-Roman mythology the figures of Saturn and Cronus overlap, and therefore we will make reference to both myths. Let us try to analyze the myth of Saturn, keeping in mind the phenomenology of melancholy. Mythical and psychological elements should mutually clarify, amplify, and explain each other.

As melancholy is so undifferentiated, elementary, and common, it is fitting that it be found in a mythological amplification equally primeval and archaic. This is the case of the myth of Cronus–Saturn, which tells of the very first origins of human cosmogony; it deals neither with the stage of heroes nor with that of anthropomorphic Gods but with the Titans and the origin of the divine race itself.

According to Hesiod, the story of Cronus unfolds itself in three stages.[8] At the beginning he is "Cronus the cunning" whose power consists in astuteness and surprise attack, the youngest of the sons of Uranus and Rhea, the original couple. Uranus prevents the birth of his sons out of their mother's body. The mother gives Cronus the sickle with which the son castrates and kills his father, thus freeing himself and the other Titans from the mother's body.

In the second stage, Cronus himself becomes King of the Gods; but, forewarned by his mother's prophecy, he fears being in turn dethroned by one of his sons, and therefore to avoid this danger he swallows each son his wife Rhea generates.

In a third stage, by means of Rhea's stratagem, the sons are liberated from their father's stomach. Rhea gives her husband a stone in place of the last-born, Jove. The latter, grown up in secret on the island of Crete and protected by the Corybantes, who hide his crying with the noise of their instruments, dethrones Cronus, liberates his brothers, and becomes King of the Gods. The old God, dethroned, whose symbol remains that of the sickle, is sent to the end of the world, where he will reign over the island of the blessed, God and king of the happy Golden Age.

The story of Saturn coincides with that of Cronus.[9] He is the antique Italic god of agriculture whose symbol is the sickle. Dispossessed by Jove, he finds shelter in the region of Latium where he later becomes king, during a prosperous and ancient age of happy and peaceful life. The feast of Saturn, among the most important of the year, was celebrated in the winter solstice. It was characterized by the exchange of gifts, merry-making, and a temporary abolition of the differences between slave and master. Cronus–Saturn is therefore God of Agriculture, of the mown harvest, and also of sowing.

As we attempt to approach the myth beyond the apparent, superficial meaning, we begin to perceive the vastness of the horizon and of the forces that come into play. Let us try to grasp intuitively the meaning contained in the myth.

The destiny of Cronus develops in three stages, during which his potentiality unfolds and manifests itself. In the first stage the birth of Cronus is a violent and revolutionary crisis. Cronus succeeds in coming into the world only at the price of a violent rebellion against his father. A second stage follows in which the figure of Cronus takes on its central characteristic: placed between heaven and earth (his parents) he becomes an independent being, contradictory, dangerous, and problematic. He generates sons who are destined to deprive him of the power he has conquered. He had experienced in the first stage the severe test of a father who prevented his liberation from the fertile and enveloping womb, and against that obstacle he had turned the unmeasurable violence of his thirst for liberty. Now he himself is threatened by that same force and violence, born as inevitable consequence of his life and destiny. This stage we can call the conservative stage.

In the first and second stages the story of Cronus is essentially constituted by a father–son relationship of mutual competition, challenge, and violence. As in the first stage Cronus endures the hardness of the selfish father, so in the second stage he himself is the father who is frightened by the possibilities of his sons, and he too turns to deceit and violence in order to survive and keep his power.

In the third stage we see the breakdown of this dramatic figure: he is deprived of his reign, and while the generation of the Olympic Gods begins, Cronus turns to the other side of his destiny. We see him now as king over a land very different from the Titanic battlefield. The nature of the God is transformed: he is the wise and beneficent sovereign of happy men; the earth produces her goods in abundance; men and animals live in harmony.

According to another tradition—again referred to by Hesiod—Cronus, after being confined in the depths of the earth, sends beneficent spirits to men, making them capable of wise resolutions. This third stage we can call the "transformation."

We can now try to gain a better understanding of the archetype of Cronus–Saturn, amplifying its contents by the elements we find in other contexts. In the hermetic tradition, one speaks explicitly about Saturn, also in astrology, alchemy and in folklore. In the hermetic tradition Saturn, the planet whose orbit is the largest, corresponds to reason—or better, to the intellect in the non-rationalistic sense of the Greek *nous,* which is a faculty of knowing by giving unity and shape to the object, the *principium individuationis* in the scholastic sense. (For the Neoplatonic Academy of Florence, the etymology of Saturn was *sacer nous,* holy mind.)

Among the metals Saturn is lead, the dark and heavy beginning in the scale of values toward gold. In the most ancient representation of the zodiac, every planet has two houses situated at the same level on both sides of a double course, first descending and then ascending. Saturn occupies the house at the lowest point, where descent ends and ascent begins. Here Saturn corresponds to the night sun; it is the winter solstice, the place of darkness and death. His symbol represents the sickle of the moon in the lowest position with respect to the cross. In terms of consciousness this corresponds to a state of chaotic submersion in the body. On the other hand, the transformation, the changing from descent to ascent, occurs really in the house of Saturn. The life of sun and gold is hidden in the deep and obscure chaos of lead, where light and warmth seem to extinguish.

In the alchemical myth the King Gold must be killed and buried in order to be able to rise again in his full glory, and it is precisely in the house of Saturn that he is buried. The tomb of the king is therefore called Saturn. The adept must complete a journey in order to have the revelation of hermetic wisdom. The starting point of the journey is the most westward of the seven mouths of the Nile, and there lives Saturn—the coldest, heaviest, and farthest from the sun, the planet symbolizing obscurity, melancholy, abandonment, and fear, the star of bad omen, the mysterious and sinister senex. They all transform upon arrival in *dormus barbae,* the house where the "wisest of all," Hermes (Trismegistos), "three times the greatest," imparts wisdom.

In the transformation process of alchemy the first stage, which is dominated by Saturn, corresponds to the blackening and darkening, to the *putrefactio* and *mortificatio.* Grey and black are Saturn's colors, but the ashes that remain after the burning, the calcination of the base metals, the raw material are also the precious material, the sediment from which afterward gold will be obtained. It will be the *sal sapientiae* or *Sal Saturni,* the bitter salt of wisdom, which makes undrinkable, though limpid, the water of life, the *aqua permanens.* This is the tincture, the womb of the *filius philosophorum,* that longed-for heavenly substance.

T. Burckhardt, in his commentary on this first stage of magisterium, says:

> At the beginning of the spiritual realization there is death, as a dying of the world. Consciousness must be turned away from the senses and converted to the innermost. But the interior light has not yet risen; and therefore this withdrawal from the exterior world is experienced as a deep dark night, *nox profunda.*[10]

Christian mysticism compares this state with the grain of corn, which for fructifying must remain in the earth and die. Saturn is also called by alchemists "the governor of the prison," the man who has the power to keep imprisoned or to set free; he is the supreme judge.

In astrology Saturn is the master of the sign of Capricorn; he is characterized by the qualities of profundity, austerity, and renunciation, by pessimism, diffidence, and selfishness. Saturn is represented as an old man with a white beard and white hair, often with signs of bodily infirmity, brandishing the sickle and the hourglass. He corresponds to the "father" or to an important and aged person. Many of his characteristics tend toward a single point: a passionate concern, deep and continuous, in his own destiny, which may be manifested as concentration and forbearance in duty, or as exhausting doubts and introspection about the duty itself, as envy, mistrust, bad temper, or hypochondria. Saturn represents the driving power of the action which urges man to fulfill his own destiny; he is the tendency toward thorough examination of his own thoughts and feelings, continually dissecting his own actions, tormenting without rest himself and others. But Capricorn is also the sign of wisdom and spiritual perseverance, of the capacity of renunciation, austerity, and concentration.

Saturn is also the master of the sign which follows Capricorn —i.e., Aquarius, which means astrologically possible transformation toward socially positive values of humanitarianism and universal brotherhood. This fact reminds us of the last stage of the myth of Saturn: the Golden Age.

In fairytales we often encounter the figure of the old man. He is the "wise old man," or the "wizard," or the "spirit of the mountain" who lives in a castle or in a cave. He has an ambiguous nature and a surprising capacity for transformation. In some fairytales this ambiguous and transforming nature is expressed by the fact that the old man has only one side—one eye, one leg, one hand— the other side being invisible and revealing the old man's antithetical nature. He plays the role of the helper or the enemy, or a young man on his way to become a "hero," and also the role of the father or the one who holds imprisoned the princess for whom the hero is destined.[11]

As C. G. Jung says:

> The old man always appears when the hero is in a hopeless
> and desperate situation from which only profound reflection
> or a lucky idea—in other words, a spiritual function or an

endopsychic automatism of some kind—can extricate him. [This appearance is] a purposeful process whose aim is to gather the assets of the whole personality together at the critical moment, when all one's spiritual and physical forces are challenged, and with this united strength to fling open the door of the future. No one can help the boy to do this; he has to rely entirely on himself. There is no going back. This realization will give the necessary resolution to his actions. By forcing him to face the issue, the old man saves him the trouble of making up his mind. Indeed the old man is himself this purposeful reflection and concentration of moral and physical forces that comes about spontaneously in the psychic space outside consciousness when conscious thought is not yet—or is no longer—possible.[12]

But "the old man has a wicked aspect too, just as the primitive medicine-man is a healer and helper and also the dreaded concocter of poisons."[13] He is "a helper, but also the contriver of a dangerous fate which might just as easily have turned out for the bad."[14] "He is a murderer . . . he is accused of enchanting a whole city by turning it to iron, i.e., making it immovable, rigid, and locked-up."[15]

On account of his role of keeper of the princess, "the fateful archetype of the old man has taken possession of the King's anima—in other words, robbed him of the archetype of life which the anima personifies—and forced him to go in search of the lost charm, the 'treasure hard to attain,' thus making him the mythical hero, the higher personality who is an expression of the self. Meanwhile, the old man acts the part of the villain and has to be forcibly removed. . . ."[16] "So . . . we see the archetype of the old man in the guise of an evil-doer, caught up in all the twists and turns of an individuation process that ends suggestively with the *hieros gamos,*"[17] the sacred marriage.

III. Characteristics of the Cronus–Saturn Archetype

As will be said more extensively later, speaking about an archetype is not a harmless affair. We always risk losing its meaning if we try just to explain it, as if it were a rational or mechanical construction. We have to content ourselves with a description. But, to quote Jung, "The ultimate core of meaning [of an archetype] may be circumscribed, but not described. Even so, the bare circumscription denotes an essential step forward in our knowledge. . . ."[18] We should not forget to consider the peculiar characteristics of the archetype, not as definite concepts, but as images rich in emotional content and never isolated from their interrelationship. Let us try therefore to outline the common structural nucleus, the active archetype, in all these expressions and human creations that explicitly refer to the image of Cronus–Saturn.

The Greek myth refers to an elementary and primeval aspect of endopsychic development: the father–son relationship. Cronus is first the son who is prevented by the father from coming out of the mother's body; then he is the murderer of his father; then he himself is the father who swallows his own sons.

The entire story of Cronus seems guided by the leitmotif of his dogged search for and defense of his own individuality. This dramatic aspect is that which distinguishes Cronus from the other Gods—from the Olympians, for instance, whose attributes are defined right from the beginning.

The risks Cronus runs are basically those of death: in the first stage, a death in the form of non-birth, of being prevented from being born; in the second stage, a death as loss of himself. In both cases, the threat of death enters into the father–son relationship, and the murderer is always Cronus, who kills always in self-defense. There is a fundamental and absolute antagonism between these father and son aspects, for existence splits them apart. The dominant feeling is an unbearable yet unavoidable presentiment of death. Depression and anguish are recognizable in the hermetic and alchemic processes as the condition of gold hidden and imprisoned within lead, of the sun within the dark bowels of night, of burial within the earth, which means tomb and putrefaction, ignorance, obscurity, and abandonment.

The potentiality of transformation is also evident in the alchemic, as well as hermetic, tradition. Saturn is the lowest point of the parabola, the most profound seat where the descent ends and the re-ascent begins. The direction is inverted, the meaning of his being is transformed: descent becomes the possibility for re-ascent, burial becomes contact with the fertile and profound womb of the night, depth becomes possibility for wisdom, putrefaction becomes liberation from death. That which is dead breaks down and dissolves, freeing the precious element which before was bound with an impure one.

The father–son conflict of Cronus says, in the incomparable way of mythical images, what philosophers have expressed in their abstract language as the essential dynamic of being and becoming. The old generates the new. But this continuity does not happen peacefully, because the old experiences the transformation as a threat, to which he reacts by swallowing every new offspring. The new, revolutionary forces oppose this reactionary and conservative phase in a confrontation without compromise: one of the two must die, and the winner will reign. Hermetically, Cronus–Saturn is the highest tester, the trial to be overcome, the governor of the prison in whose hands is liberation or confinement.

Another important aspect of the saturnic depression is the inhibition of will. It is neither a lack nor a primitive weakness of will but a block provoked by an encounter with a contrary and more powerful will. If we look beneath the surface of psychotic melancholy, it is not a matter of an extinction of the will (as, for instance, seems to happen in catatonic schizophrenia) but rather an impossibility to get free from the snarls and obstacles that hinder, a wracking of one's brains about possible ways out, and a continuous collision with a greater and stronger obstacle. It is the condition of being swallowed and buried, just as happens to the sons of Cronus, or to gold in the stage of lead, or to the king in the tomb. Just as water becomes petrified in ice, so the cold and dry Saturn stops the movement and spontaneous flowing of the will. In the depressive phase of manic-depressive psychosis, it often seems that the incessant activity of the manic phase is reversed toward the inside; and here it is feverishly manifested as an exaggerated lucidity in perceiving the negative aspects of existence and foreseeing damage and sorrow as inevitable developments of the present.

It may be said that saturnic inhibition is the fruit of an excess of awareness, of a harmful lucidity which paralyzes every step forward by the vision of a catastrophic and terrible failure. But the anxiety which derives from it is also a consequence of the fact that the subject does not perish but witnesses with lucidity his continuous perishing. An extreme type of psychiatric melancholy shows these characteristics in their pure state. It is the Cotard syndrome, which is fairly frequent in involutive forms of melancholy.[19]

It begins with transformation ideas; the subject feels his body in a state of decomposition, noted as a petrification of his organs. Then the idea of negation, in which the patient expresses a monstrous and terrible experience: he is no longer alive, and yet he will not be able to die, and he feels destined in eternity to witness his death and dissolution.

The melancholic inactivity joins with an interior hyper-activity, blocked in its possibilities of manifestation. It is not to be considered a contradiction, therefore, if in folklore we find in the large family of the sons of Saturn[20] men who continuously strive for repairing and contrive as artisans and farm workers, carpenters and shoemakers, tailors and masons, artists and poets. This motif of continuous work (though often not visible) approaches and overlaps the already considered motifs of drive toward transformation and individuation.

The meaning of being swallowed by the father, which is a constant of the saturnic psychology, may be explained as the blocking of an urge toward transformation. It is an archetypal expression for a peculiar moment in the process of the ego toward differentiation. Here the "hardened"—that is, all that has been already done, the established powers, "history"—impedes the drive of the youth toward the chances of the future; and the fascinating but regressive "chances of the past," linked with the realm of the mother, emerge from the darkness.

This state shows an exaggeration of awareness, of mental lucidity, of perfection in accomplishment. The power for which puer is longing is already possessed; the experience which he desires has already been experienced; the truth he seeks is already known. Cronus shows his unpleasant senex face to the juvenes, and the latter feels the urgency to cast aside all that the father has done. Springing with the freshness of mourning from the maternal womb, and directed with determination toward the process and the transformation, the protagonist meets the rigid figure of Cronus, unavoidable and contrary as death.

Another side we can look at, continuing this *circumambulatio* of the figure of Cronus, is the omnipresent awareness of death. Death accompanies the various stages of the process as an inevitable counterpoint; there is no transformation without it. Among the characters participating in the tragic drama of the development of consciousness, there seems no possibility for agreement but through the death of one of the opponents. Every victory and affirmation of one must correspond to the defeat and death of the other. Father and son see reflected in each other what is in store for them—unavoidable old age and decadence for the youth, confiscation and discredit for the old.

In clinical manifestations of melancholic psychosis there is very often a delirium of guilt. A sense of guilt is hidden in the thoughts of the melancholic philosophers, in the passionate impetus of mystics. Cronus is dominated by a "bad conscience." He has earned existence at the price of his father's murder and the violent splitting of the undifferentiated unity of his parents. It is the original sin which religion and existential philosophy speak about. In the hermetic and alchemic tradition, this guilt is the impurity of the commingling of the precious element with ashes, earth, and lead. The impurity reveals itself as original guilt, to the extent that it is negation and absence of the final state toward which the whole process aims.

The revolutionary need for new values must suffer and overcome, or go through the phase of opposition to, the established values, which makes for the guilt in every process of transformation of the new toward the old. But there is also the obscure guilt of the old toward the new, because the old knows he must succumb and that his being and doing contradict this superior law of transformation. Psychologically, it seems that guilt accompanies a certain phase in every transformation process, in which one aspect of guilt will join others: the need for transformation, the inhibition of the will, the awareness of death. The necessity for transformation seems a fundamental threat to present being, for the "horizon" of the ego is bound to its present identifications and nonetheless obliged to change.

Guilt is psychologically bound to punishment, to the feeling of being in the hands of a power which can destroy. For the son this power is Cronus, the old king, the negative father. Cronus–Saturn is the archetype of the test one must pass, the person with whom you must settle the account, whose place you must take. He is bigger, wiser, more powerful, and the fear of facing him causes a stop in the transformation process and a stagnation of libido, but also an increase of endopsychic tension.

In speaking about Hermes–Mercury in alchemy and hermetics, Jung says that the ambivalent nature of this figure may be considered as a process which begins with evil and ends with good. Saturn, he says, represents the evil side which is contained in Mercury. In his work on the Spirit-Mercury, Jung says also that the *principium individuationis* may be seen as the spirit that has been confined and imprisoned. He who has imprisoned it is "the Lord of Souls," but he did so with good intentions, for only through the sense of guilt which arises from the separation of good and bad can the moral conscience be developed. He says, "Since without guilt there is no moral consciousness . . . we must concede that the strange intervention of the master of souls was absolutely necessary for the development of any kind of consciousness and in this sense was for the good."[21] In the same work, Jung reminds us that for pessimistic philosophy, as for Schopenhauer and for Buddhism, the principle of individuation is the source of every ill. So Cronus–Saturn, the star of depression, separation, moral suffering, guilt, master of the prison, represents the necessary negative moment of the individuation process.

In the *Mysterium Coniunctionis* Jung expresses the moment in which guilt reveals its positive possibility: "Only then will he realize that the conflict is *in him,* that the discord and tribulation are his riches, which should not be squandered by attacking others; and that, if fate should exact a debt from him in the form of guilt, it is a debt to himself."[22]

But Cronus–Saturn becomes the God of agriculture, who reigns over men and teaches them the arts of cultivation, only after he has been knocked down and forced to vomit his swallowed sons. The seed which dies is that which fructifies; the sickle, symbol of death, becomes the tool which harvests fruit and nourishment.

In the ancient representations of the Zodiac, Saturn is the lowest and final point of descent. Therefore, it is the negative pole toward which we must direct ourselves in order to be able to turn toward the positive pole. In other words, it is to seek darkness, pain, death, to be able to re-ascend into light, joy, and life. The astrological symbol of Saturn has the shape of a sickle, the waning moon, at the lowest point of the cross; it is the place of death *for* transformation, which is the meaning of sacrifice.

Also in the alchemical process the king must be killed in order to arise again in glory. He is buried in the house of Saturn, which has the double significance of the tomb, where the old decays and the seed is contained which prepares the new birth. An Orphic hymn to Cronus speaks to the God: "Thou devourest, but to increase."[23]

At the end of his story, Cronus–Saturn, with his last transformation, seems to go beyond time, thereby disclosing the full meaning of his process. According to the tradition handed down by Hesiod, Cronus reigns over the men of the Golden Age, who lived without worry, effort, or complaint, as Gods. The misery of old age did not threaten them; with bodies eternally young, they enjoyed their feasts free of ill. They died as if overcome by sleep. Every good was available to them: the fields, givers of life, produced their fruits in great abundance. They lived gladly from such fruits in peace, in a community composed entirely of good people. They were rich in flocks and were friends of the blessed Gods. When this generation sank, by the will of Zeus, into the hidden depths of the earth, they became the good spirits which moved about the earth as protectors of men, defenders of justice, givers of wealth, invisibly present everywhere.

Hesiod also tells that Cronus, after his dethronement, is appointed by Zeus to govern the islands of the blessed; at the end of the world, surrounded by the ocean, these islands are inhabited by heroes after their deaths. There the fertile fields bear fruit three times a year; "honey drips from the oak trees." This is the last transformation of the Titanic devourer of his sons; now he is friend of men and guides them on paths of peace and love. In terms of the anima, all the qualities that characterize this phase of the reign of Cronus are the gifts which wisdom brings to men. Wisdom, which is creative possibility because it discloses interior wealth, is also justice, because it is the capacity of unity and harmony between contrary forces and needs.

The analysis of depression, dominated by the ambiguous symbol of the old man with the sickle, brings us therefore to a dynamic nucleus of the collective psyche. We can try to circumscribe this nucleus by bipolar images or concepts of opposites—such as death and eternal life, chaos and wisdom (for Gnostics, Saturn is the son of Chaos!), impurity and purity, petrification and transformation, confusion and lucidity, guilt and glorification, punishment and reward, torment as mere suffering and sacrifice, sterile poverty and fertile wealth, violent opposition and the harmony of justice.

IV. Correlations and Dynamics of
the Cronus–Saturn Archetypal Field

In the same manner as forces from different fields meet to create a complex field of energy, we can notice other archetypes converging upon that of the old man. Also, as one cannot try to describe the function of an organ without being compelled, at a certain point, to cross over into the function of another organ, so it is that the Cronus–Saturn figure is in part superimposed upon and joined with other archetypes. These analogies with the physical concept of "field" and with the physiological concept of "organ" perhaps help better to understand the real state of affairs in the world of the collective unconscious.

When one inquires thoroughly enough into an archetype, one reaches the moment in which the figure fades and, gradually losing its clear outlines, dissolves into other closely related figures, which seem to aid in understanding but at the same time deprive the original archetype of its singular value. Every archetype seems clarified when we discover its vital connection with other archetypes, but in so doing it is dismembered by and dissolves into the others. This is especially evident when inquiring into that totality of the self, the supra-ordinate personality. Here, we cannot affirm anything of the archetype in itself, except that which is manifested by the images of dreams, myths, fantasy, etc. We cannot help but approach these psychic elements first with our intuitive and affective faculties, and then more and more with our thinking, since we no longer naively experience the myth but want to be scientific in our attitude. Our analysis, however, does not find an end. As soon as we try to abstract the very essence of the archetypal image, it fades and evaporates. Only the image itself, presented in its usual context, is clear, perspicuous, and unequivocal.[24] The main experience we have in studying an archetype is not only its infinite possibility to be analyzed but also the loss of its singularity and individuality. We perceive the fundamental relationship with other archetypes; we discover the underground identifications between opposites and the ever-present dialectical structure between them. Therefore, we should always, when facing the difficult task of speaking about an archetype, refer first to the fundamental lines of relationship with neighboring archetypes and, second, to their transformation in the individuation process.

With this in mind, we turn again to Saturn, where we find two other archetypes related directly to him. Inasmuch as Saturn is the old man, he unites with and opposes puer. Inasmuch as he is the father, he unites with and opposes the mother. Puer and senex are the personifications of the two extremes into which the libido in a certain condition splits. In the old man the process has stopped in an excess of egocentric differentiation, which has exhausted the transformation potential; it has become petrified, and the old man, detaining the power, tends to block and petrify the process around him. By now Cronus is hardened by his thirst for power and by his fear of what is new. The youth represents the need to become the new man but can achieve this only to the extent that he collides with the petrified wall of the senex. The two archetypes are the poles of a singular dynamic aspect.

The archetype of the mother is in mutual relationship with the father (mythology, alchemy, and hermetics are full of material in this regard). But the mother is also allied with the son in his struggle against the father, as is shown in the story of Cronus and repeatedly by alchemists. The mother is bound to puer in an energy-loaded relationship, but the positive or negative value of such a relationship depends on how the father constellates. The negative father, the overwhelming test, the threatening opposition of the rival castled in his established power, the hardened parent as a judge provoke the withdrawal of puer toward the all-understanding mother and her infinite capacity for transformation as the undifferentiated Great Mother. So puer's drive toward the future is stopped and is compelled to reverse its course. This is the leitmotif of the tendency toward death, which is one aspect of puer. Certainly, it is a death essentially different from that which is threatened by the father-devourer, a death this time not feared but desired, ecstatic suicide and dissolution.

The clinical manifestations of melancholy do not lack concrete examples of this aspect of the archetype: on the one hand, the fear of guilt and punishment and, on the other, the desire for death as a way out. In adolescent depression one may see expressed an ambivalent link with the mother; she would be seen as a protective refuge against the threatening and excessive demands of the father, while the father as *principium individuationis* would be felt as a threat because he seems to represent the loss of contact with the infinite possibilities of the mother. In this case, the mother would be only a pseudo-positive figure, because she herself now represents the petrification of the process. She carries now the Saturn-characteristics and thus becomes, in an ambiguous and deadly manner, the negative, devouring mother.

But the mother contains also the elements of the anima: inexhaustible richness of sentiment and emotion, fertility, creativity. She is the source of birth and rebirth, renewal, transmutation. The anima personalizes the mother and brings her to an individual level and is, therefore, guide and connection to the unconscious.

When puer and senex collide irreducibly, the breakdown in the process may be overcome through the anima. Puer fears the old man precisely because puer feels in him the hardness and aridity that derive from the old man's lack of contact with eros, from the absence of instinct and creative emotion.

According to alchemists it is necessary that the hardened element be dissolved, dismembered, and buried in the primeval, formless matter in order to be able to rise again as a new man. Naturally, this is feared by the old man, whose meaning is contrary to the formless, the mutable, the multiform, the not-yet-constituted and not-individualized. He is the powerful drive of the libido toward definite forms—just what puer fears as death! One could say that puer and senex project their shadows upon each other. Let it be said in parentheses: this affirmation might be purely analogical and could risk a certain confusion. "Shadow" must perhaps be said in reference to a person and "projection" to a personal relationship. But every archetypal personification has a shadow sui generis which might be appropriately called syzygy, a term which Jung has taken from astrology. It means the positions of the moon in junction or in opposition to the sun; astrologically speaking, syzygy has the significance of a couple yoked together.

The mixture of the personal sphere with that of the archetypal can lead the Jungian student into dangerous confusion. It is advisable not to waste any of the precious possibility for clarification when one deals with a field so complex and difficult to grasp.

The resolution of the puer–senex conflict can be found in the mediating function of the anima. In the myth of Cronus the resolution is the transformation of Cronus–Saturn into the God of Agriculture, founder and ruler of the Golden Age, or Lord of the

Tartars and sender of good spirits. Here the relation with the feminine is fundamental, for the old man must be dissolved. In the everlasting process of transformation, every completed form must decay, every conquered power must be lost, everything born must die.

The senex can signify that the process has stopped, that the subject has not had the courage to sacrifice what has been conquered and does not trust the mysterious and antithetic regenerating power of the formless, the unconscious, whose messenger is the anima.

For puer it is not a matter of withdrawing himself from the influence of the old man nor of opposing him. This would be impossible if we reflect that puer and senex, syzygial aspects of the archetype, are born one from the other! Puer must accept his own death, and that is the meaning of his collision with the old man. The youth has just been born and still carries with him the fascinating memory of the infinite, immortal depth of the mother. He has no form, but unlimited possibilities. He fears every form like death. Such an attitude is peculiar to puer aeternus, since the "changeling" wants to remain such and not take only one form. But when the unavoidable necessity of existence compels puer to take a form, the struggle with senex, the negative father, begins. That is the *principium individuationis* as puer aeternus experiences it. The unconscious suicidal tendency is nothing but the strong drive toward transformation, which is an essential constituent of puer. Death has for puer the desperate and terrifying aspect of the old man with the sickle or, as an alternative, the fascinating realm of the mother. But the "bitter cup" which is offered by the father is also the potion which can transform the youth into hero. Death itself can therefore be transformed into "a death of what I am now in order to become what I want to be!" Transformation and redemption by sacrifice are the calling of puer. The unifying symbol and redeeming personification which can arise now for him is just that of kore or anima. She acts as mediator between the needs which the old man imposes and the values which the mother represents.

In fairytales, if the youth accepts the sacrifice that is the struggle and the risk of death (in fact the youth always dies in the struggle, but to arise transformed), then having won, he can marry the daughter of the old king—the young anima, the eternal, creative possibility contained as Sophia in the old man who dissolves. This marriage with the daughter of the old king may be compared with the agricultural or Golden Age of Cronus–Saturn, when he sends inspiring spirits from the underground.

John Pordage, the English alchemist cited by Jung in "The Psychology of the Transference," says concerning the opus: ". . . the Tincture, this tender child of life . . . must needs descend into the darkness of Saturn, wherein no light of life is to be seen; there it must be held captive, and be bound with the chains of darkness. . . ." But, he continues,

> . . . in the darkness of this black is hidden the light of lights in the quality of Saturn . . . and the tincture of life is in this putrefaction or dissolution and destruction. You must not despise this blackness or black colour, but persevere in it in patience, in suffering and in silence, until the days of its tribulations are completed, when the seed of life shall waken to life, shall rise up, sublimate or glorify itself, transform itself into whiteness, purify and sanctify itself. . . .
>
> When the work is brought thus far, it is an easy work; for the learned philosophers have said that the making of the stone is then woman's work and child's play.

And about the ultimate stage of the process he says,

> Then you will see the beginning of its resurrection from hell, death and the mortal grave, appearing first in the quality of Venus, . . . and the gentle love-fire of Venus quality will gain the upper hand, and the love-fire tincture will be preferred in the government and have supreme command. And then the gentleness and love-fire of Divine Venus will reign as lord and king in and over all qualities.[25]

In the final stage the opus has therefore gained a purified and bright space, in which the archetype of the anima appears. Meister Eckhart says:

> The first of the seven planets is Saturn; know that he is the purger. . . . In the heaven of the soul, Saturn becomes of angelic purity, bringing as a reward the vision of God; as the

Lord has said, "blessed are the pure in heart, for they shall see God."[26]

In psychological terms, one would say that the old man uses the function of anima as a link between the unconscious and the conscious ego. This connection has the power of inspiring good decisions, positive and concrete actions. It is the peculiar power of Sophia or of Athena, the daughter born from her father's head.

This final synthesis between the masculine and feminine is also seen in the Hermaphroditus, as the alchemists call the final work of the process. In regard to this, Jung quotes a German poem written in the first half of the sixteenth century, in which the nature of the Hermaphroditus is explained. In this poem the queen speaks as follows:

> Then it was that I first knew my son—and we two came together as one. There I was made pregnant by him and gave birth upon a barren stretch of earth. I became a mother and remained a maid—and in my nature was established. Therefore my son was also my father—as God ordained in accordance with nature.[27]

Also in Zosimos: "Its [the stone's] mother is a virgin, and the father lay not with her."[28] Then Petrus Bonus in *Theatrum chemicum*:

> Whose mother is a virgin and whose father knew not women. . . . God must become man, because on the last day of this art, when the completion of the work takes place, begetter and begotten became altogether one. Thus all things old are made new.[29]

This may throw some light on the destiny of old man and youth in this final stage.

As we have seen, it is not possible to describe this Cronus–Saturn aspect without mention of the essential syzygial aspects of puer and mother and without arriving at kore as correlative of the last transformation. For the sake of exposition, we can describe this journey as passing through three phases. In the first phase, consciousness is formed as that function of knowing which acts only whenever there is a separation of and tension between polarities. This is the "birth" of the ego and of knowledge. From this point on, the story of the ego will be characterized by two relationships: one with a *Mater,* from whom he must go out, unfold, grow up, express himself; another with a *Pater,* to whom he must give account and who is force and resistance to conquer, an obstacle to be overcome, a test to be accepted. These two relationships are the same as those that, in other schools of psychology, are called, perhaps in a more static and dogmatic way, pleasure principle and power principle, or Id and Super-Ego.

In the second phase of the movement of the ego toward the self, the "becoming" of consciousness is represented. Cronus is swallowed by the father. Here, too, the protagonist is shut up, inside, held in the belly—but what may be the meaning that this happens now inside the father? Is it a question of the "awareness of being swallowed" or of the state of being inside looking for the possibility of getting out?

While being swallowed into the mother is more similar to infantile unconsciousness, and perhaps to certain forms of quiet stupor in psychiatric pathology, the second type, being swallowed into the father, well describes the grief of the melancholic person. This grief can also be seen as a kind of mania reversed, introverted and inhibited, a terrible lucidity and awareness of one's own condition.

We have already mentioned the Cotard syndrome of psychotic invasion of the archetype. It might be worthwhile to quote a poem by the Italian poetess Ada Negri, which impressively expresses the same condition:

> *Anniversary*
>
> Don't call me, don't tell me anything
> Don't try to make me smile.
> Today I'm like a wild beast
> That has shut himself up to die.
>
> Turn down the light, cover the fire,
> That the room be like a tomb.
> Let me huddle in the corner
> With my head on my knees.

> Let the hours extinguish in silence
> Let the torpid waves of anxiety
> Rise up and drown me;
> I ask nothing but to lose consciousness.
>
> But it isn't granted to me.
> That face, that smile
> Are always before me
> Day and night memory is a hook
> Fixed in my living flesh.
>
> Perhaps I will never be able to die:
> Condemned in eternity
> To keep vigil of the havoc within me,
> Crying with lid-less eyes.

Consciousness of being buried, in philosophical terms, is the paradoxical experience of death which is peculiar to man. Of death itself we cannot have experience, yet it constitutes the dominating thought, the background against which we perceive life. It is just in this being buried that man seems enriched by his most original and profound values. Precisely because he realizes the meaninglessness and formlessness of life, he can find the tension which makes possible his creative life.

Cronus–Saturn, the negative father, constellates with the unconscious as the devouring father at the moment in which there is formed in the personality the drive to grow up, toward individuation. It is the moment when the subject feels swallowed by collective forms, laws, customs, systems. The swallowing by the father may present a variety of aspects, but in general it has to do with conscious depression, an *abaissement du niveau mental* together with lucid presence. Jung uses the concept of regression in a similar manner.

> The hero is the symbolical exponent of the movement of libido. Entry into the dragon is the regressive direction, and the journey to the East (the "night sea journey") . . . symbolizes the effort to adapt to the conditions of the psychic inner world. . . .

It is characteristic that the monster begins the night sea journey to the East, i.e., towards sunrise, while the hero is engulfed in its belly. This seems to me to indicate that regression is not necessarily a retrograde step in the sense of a backwards development or degeneration, but rather represents a necessary phase of development. The individual is, however, not consciously aware that he is developing; he feels himself to be in a compulsive situation that resembles an early infantile state or even an embryonic condition within the womb.[30]

This womb can as well be the father's belly—in which case the ego, being differentiated from the mother, is conscious of its confinement. The state may coincide with the phase of the hero myth that Neumann defines as "patriarchal castration," characterized by compulsory spiritual life,[31] as well as with those archetypal motifs in which a rational intellectual power acts to the rigorous exclusion of every irrational function.

At this point it might be useful to refer to a dream of a patient suffering from depressive psychosis, a recurring dream which always came some days before the beginning of the psychotic crisis. In the dream the patient relived his experience as a prisoner of war. *He found himself in a stone quarry in the concentration camp at Mauthausen. He knew that the war was over, but he could not leave the camp.* The dream, with its power of synthesis, contains many elements found in the archetypal structure of melancholy. The stone quarry is a Saturnic engulfment which, as a hostile and violent power, holds the subject prisoner. In his painful impotence, the patient recognized the awakening of an autonomous force, an archetype, compelling him to such a condition.

After about a year, during which the patient had undergone psychological treatment, he had once more a depressive crisis. This time the dream was somewhat different: *the prisoner was again in the quarry, although the war was over. A young unknown woman appeared, and the two of them weaved in and out of the quarry until the prisoner suddenly realized that in fact one could go out! But as he was about to escape, the thought came to him that they might by way of retaliation do harm to his mother. Still, he left the quarry, hoping to be able to notify her in time.* The possibility of liberation is linked with the appearance of the anima. The patient's affect, representing his deeper unconscious layer, is still bound to the mother and, therefore, still exposed to the enemy.

"Man cannot be described but as antinomies," Jung reminds us. In his "The Psychology of the Transference" and *Mysterium Coniunctionis*, Jung has described the dynamic correlations, direct and crossing, between the four persons of the "marriage quaternio." In its original alchemical aspect this quaternio was composed of king, queen, adept, and soror mystica. Such dynamic correlations risk seeming too entangled, but, as a matter of fact, they correspond to a few fundamental rules of analytical psychology: the complementary and compensatory relation between the conscious and the unconscious; the bipolarity of the archetypes; the different attitudes of the individual toward archetypes and external world—identity, identification, projection, introjection, integration; the possibility that the transference relationship occurs by means of the conscious aspect of one partner and the unconscious of the other, or by means of the unconscious of both.

When an archetype constellates, a bipolar field is formed. In this case, for example, the appearance of senex must give rise to the appearance of puer, just as in physics "every action has an equal and contrary reaction." Generally this bipolar field will be experienced by the conscious mind as an inescapable alternative. As we have seen, the opposition within the syzygy is in itself unsolvable, *tertium non datur*. In our case, there are only two alternatives for the subject. The first is the identification with senex, with his propensity for law and order and rigid form. He will then naturally project the image of puer on others—the anarchists and revolutionaries, young people who want only to destroy and flee from every duty. Or else the subject will lean toward the identification with puer and his dramatic destiny. Then appearing in his story will be senex, whom he will see, by projection, in the external world—the egoism, jealousy, repression, lack of imagination of the elder generation.

If an archetypal image appears in the objective world of interpersonal relationships, it cannot remain without effect in the opposite field of introversion, of relationship with the unconscious. We have seen that, when senex is projected into the outside world and the conscious ego identifies with puer, then the mother complex activates in the unconscious. It may be recalled that puer means the birth, from the mother or the unconscious, of a principle which is basically a need for development, change, and transformation; this will be stopped against the opposite figure which means rigor, hardness, immutability, necessity of having a definite form. Then puer has a regression toward the mother, toward the regressive aspects of the mother—that is, involution, undifferentiation, and death. This unconscious activation of the negative mother has a part in forming the shadow of puer—his melancholic aspect, unavoidable for him as a destiny.

Let us consider now the case in which the subject leans toward identification with senex and the figure of puer appears projected in the outer world.

As confirmed by mythology, hermetics, and fairytales, as well as by psychological practice, there is a peculiar connection between senex and anima: she is prisoner or in some way subject to the old man, king, wizard, or chthonic godhead. It is this imprisoned anima that activates in the unconscious of a person who has let his personality slide under the archetype of senex. In the form of wizard, he becomes malicious, cunning, transformer, hot-tempered —all signs of a certain invasion by the anima.

This schematic explanation of the dialectical relationship between archetypes—between conscious and unconscious and between the external, or extroverted, reality and the internal, or introverted, reality—may help us to understand a few interpersonal relations: for example, in the world of today, the collective collision between puer and senex, where each one identifies with one of the syzygy and projects the other one. These correlations seem to be confirmed also by the subsequent events in the story of Cronus–Saturn. In that which we called the third phase there is the solution of the drama. According to their destiny of tragic characters, the two opposing protagonists must meet death: the old man, dissolution, according to the alchemical rule of being dissolved; puer, on his part, the sacrifice. But this encounter with death, this return to the mother, is made possible by the appearance of a redeeming or demiurgic figure who achieves the transformation of Cronus–Saturn.

The new issue of Cronus is characterized by creativity, which is a positive relation with concreteness and objectivity as well as with inconstancy and wealth of possibility. There the two opposite values of senex and puer find an organic synthesis—or better, they transcend in a new form. The archetypal image which appears in this phase is, for a man, the anima. She represents the individual mediator with the world of the mother, a world that for senex and puer could only be that of death. But for the hero who *has known his own death,* who has experienced the dissolution and the *sacrifice,* who has faced the night sea journey or the underground descent, it is the encounter and marriage with the bride, a fertile joining between the opposites, individual creative activity.

The anima seems born of the unconscious and presents herself as a possibility to the ego as a result of a tension toward individuation created and maintained by the constellating of puer and senex. That is the origin of what Jung calls a symbol—the images of the anima which in each case are presented as spontaneous products of the unconscious.

The peace among animals and men on earth is a sign of a state of inner harmony, consequence of a cosmic harmony, i.e., of archetypal forces of the collective unconscious. Heaven and earth, father and mother, are no longer in conflict; the mother is now the good earth, rich in fruits; the father is the god-king, or the god-protector of good laws. Men live in harmony with each other because they are at peace within themselves. The new man, born again in *novam infantiam,* the redeemed, the arisen, owes his own existence to the end of the war between the principle of power and the principle of transformation, between him who sets the limits and him who continuously breaks them. *Creativity* is the concept which expresses the unification of the two opposites.

V. Epilogue

The final state of harmony of that individuation process manifested in the story of Cronus–Saturn seems splendidly expressed by one of the most popular, though perhaps least understood, genres of Renaissance paintings—that Renaissance in which some of the most representative men chose the figure of Saturn as "father" and as "patron god" and during which the "sacred story" was often deeply experienced in the hermetic or alchemic spirit. I speak of the innumerable representations of the Madonna with child, often accompanied by holy figures. The one I choose as an example, and one could use many others, is the "Holy Conversation," by Palma il Vecchio, which can be found in the Museum of Art History in Vienna, painted at the beginning of the sixteenth century.

Near the old tree, probably where, according to the Christian holy story, the process and the primeval splitting of the contraries in the newborn consciousness of the first couple began, the Holy Mother and child form the new couple, Man and Woman. The child is "the New Man," the *renovatum ad novam infantiam,* the "redeemer redeemed." The woman is the mother, but purified from every mortal commingling and not touched in any way by the earthly father, by all that has passed, or by any possessions. She is the Virgin; she is purity itself at its source, the inexhaustible origin.

At their side the two saints seem to be images of the two principal characters in the drama we spoke about: the old man and the youth in their irresolvable struggle. Melancholic persons doomed to death, desperate bearers of the cross, their faces express profound nostalgia or the bitter torment of search. The threefold cross of the old man is certainly related to the puzzle of unity and trinity, the eternally disappointed intellect in its search for definite truth. The lamb of the youth reminds one of innocence and sacrifice. Beside every masculine figure there is a feminine one: the two young women whom the two characters of the drama do not yet seem to notice; immersed as they are in their sorrowful "passion," promise individual mediation with the mother; they seem personifications of the anima.

One seeks in vain traces of the Great Father in these holy conversations. On the other hand, the mother and child seem to form a couple completely self-sufficient. Perhaps the squared stone at the base, a very saturnic sign, alludes to the beginning of the process. A key to understanding the relationship between the two is therefore offered by the knowledge that the Virgin is also "daughter of her son" and the "father" is in the child himself.

In effect, the old man, the father, is spread throughout the entire scene. His spirit hovers there—perhaps just because of his absence. But he is concretely present in the child as the potentiality of individuation, as *principium individuationis,* which rules without being a separate person. He is no longer in conflict with the mother because, indeed, he is continuously born from the mother, who is no more the undifferentiated *prima materia* but the inspiring Sophia or the anima—or, in the language of analytical psychology, the way to the Self, the "individuation process."

Thus seems to culminate the story of the old man, the negative father, who at the end reveals the positive possibility which is in him. Depression and melancholy can be seen as the face of the process in which the figure of the father constellates negatively. The more opposition to the archetype, the more powerful and destructive are his effects. From psychotic depressions to a neurotic restriction and fear of creativity to a depressive personality, the results of a wrong adjustment to the action of the Saturn archetype are expressed.

> We may long have known the meaning, effects, and characteristics of unconscious contents. . . . The only way to get at them in practice is to try to attain a conscious attitude which allows the unconscious to cooperate instead of being driven into opposition.[32]

These words of Jung's are the most suitable comment to the ultimate possibility of depression. When accepted, melancholy would become what Ficino called "generous melancholy." By accepting one's cosmic solitude, with its temporal and mortal destiny, and by overcoming its meaninglessness, one would discover the synthesis between two major and most compulsive and, at first glance, contrary psychic entities: the need for an everchanging state of freedom which may endlessly go beyond and the need to block the stream of life in definite, concrete, and possibly imperishable forms.

1. K. Jaspers, *Psicopatologia generale* (Rome, 1964), pp. 115 ff., translation mine.

2. G. Leopardi, "A se stesso," in *Canti,* translation mine.

3. F. Petrarca, "Sonetto in vita di madonna Laura," sonnet 205, ed. Mestica, translation mine.

4. H. Heine, "Deutschland," 23, translation mine.

5. Plato, *Phaedrus,* 30, translation mine.

6. C. Baudelaire, *Oeuvres posthumes,* translation mine.

7. W. James, *The Varieties of Religious Experience,* Italian ed. (Milan, 1904), pp. 141 ff., translation mine.

8. Cf. Hesiod, *Theogony.*

9. Cf. Virgil, *Aeneid,* 8, l. 319 ff., translation mine.

10. T. Burckhardt, *Alchemie: Sinn und Weltbild,* Italian ed. (Turin, 1961), p. 160, translation mine.

11. C. G. Jung, "The Phenomenology of the Spirit in Fairytales," in *CW* 9, i, passim.

12. Ibid., §§401–02.

13. Ibid., §414.

14. Ibid., §416.

15. Ibid., §417.

16. Ibid., §418.

17. Ibid.

18. *CW* 9, i, §265.

19. H. Ey, *Etudes Psychiatriques,* Désclée de Brouwer (Paris, 1954), translation mine.

20. R. Klibansky, E. Panofsky, and E. Saxl, *Saturn and Melancholy* (New York, 1966), pp. 204–09, 217–20.

21. Jung, *CW* 13, §244.

22. Jung, *CW* 14, §§511 ff.

23. Hesiod, *Works and Days;* cited by Kerényi, *Gli dei e gli eroi della Grecia* (Milan, 1963), 1: 188.

24. Jung, *CW* 9, i, §301.

25. John Pordage; cited by Jung in *CW* 16, §§510–13.

26. Meister Eckhart; cited by Klibansky et al.

27. Jung, *CW* 16, §528.

28. Zosimos, *Artis auriferae;* cited by Jung, *CW* 16, §529n.

29. Bonus Petrus; cited by Jung, ibid.

30. Jung, *CW* 8, §§68–69.

31. E. Neumann, *The Origins and History of Consciousness* (New York, 1954), p. 187.

32. Jung, *CW* 16, §366.

Mother as Patriarch
Redeeming the Parents as the Healing of Oneself
Marion Woodman

"DADDY'S LITTLE PRINCESS" is her father's chosen child. Blessed by his love, she may be cursed by his love. Her special place in his dynasty sets her on a throne too remote for most princes to reach. Her throne is carved in ice far from the nourishing warmth of Mother Earth.

A father's daughter whose lifeline is to her dad may try to dismiss what is not there for her in her mother. Dad has always been her cherishing mother and father. Why bother with what never was? If she decides to go into analysis, she will almost surely seek a male analyst because she respects men more than women and her energy is more vibrant with them. She may occasionally dream of her mother hidden in a mysterious room, but her own earth energy is so far from consciousness that it rarely manifests even in dreams. Moreover, her attempts to free herself from her father's castle are so demanding and so intriguing that all her energy is focused on the prince who will release her. Too often the analyst becomes the prince whose castle is no less foreboding than the king's; and, too often, if great care is not taken, the analyst may exploit his foreboding precincts for reasons he does not claim as his own. Sporadic dreams may tell her that there is real trouble in her basement, that she must go down there and clean out the swamp.

If she follows that direction, she may be obliged to go to a female analyst who will constellate the mother. Then she faces the deeper problem: the bedrock of her feminine being is not present except as an inchoate flow of lava. The loving mother who carries her unborn child in her warm, dark womb for nine months was not there to reassure her, nor was she there to welcome her into life. Instead, her months in utero were charged with Vesuvius-like fear or anger; her birth was a battle, her presence on earth a dubious gift.

A mother who cannot welcome her baby girl into the world leaves her daughter groundless. Similarly, the mother's mother and grandmother were probably without the deep roots that connect a woman's body to earth. Whatever the cause, her own instinctual life is unavailable to her, and, disempowered as a woman, she runs her household as she runs herself—with shoulds, oughts, and have tos that add up to power. Life is not fed from the waters of love but from willpower that demands perfection, *frozen* perfection. Meanwhile Dad may, in fact, not be king but prince consort, and Dad and daughter are then bonded against a tyrant queen—the mother as patriarch.

Jaffa was born into such a family. In her mid-twenties she realized she was in deep trouble. Unlike many fathers' daughters who avoid going to a male analyst because they know they will "fall in love with him," she chose a female analyst because she knew she needed a woman. She has been in analysis and body work for over five years. Together we have chosen a few dreams out of hundreds that pinpoint her path from victimization to approaching freedom, dreams that illustrate transformation that is always in process at the archetypal level.

Only at that depth does real healing take place. There the Self protects the ego, tearing away the veils of illusion as the ego gradually assimilates the truth. It daily balances and rebalances the maturing masculine and feminine energies by slowly releasing them from the parental complexes in which they are imprisoned. The inner partnership, as it moves toward a liberated creative dynamic, is constantly in flux. While the images may at first seem extreme, they are the language of the unconscious, the language of fairytales and myth.

Jaffa's mother, in the village in which she lived, was respected as a very civilized, cultured woman, a responsible and good mother. To her young daughter she was an evil witch. Jaffa's father was an artist whose "exquisite hands had never held a hammer." His gentleness created a loving, sensitive space to which his daughter attuned herself. She basked in the cultural heritage he brought to her. Jaffa's mother was also an artist, without incorporating into daily living any of the refinement that the love of beauty may bring —if that beauty does not mask a tyrant.

"I see my mother wearing ugly clothes," says Jaffa. "She is leaning over the kitchen table, her huge breasts hanging down. She has brought home excellent food. She is gobbling it down, shoveling it in. Her cheeks are full like a hamster's. She is talking, always talking—or whistling. She eats two-thirds of everything she has brought and leaves one-third for my sister and me to share. She seems to be eating me."

"At sixteen I couldn't stand it anymore. I couldn't eat. There was no space in me for anything. I was closed with no opening. I was ready to explode. For days I ate only dry bread. I began smoking and went out after school for martinis. I just wanted to die. I needed to be as unconscious as possible in order to survive. I collapsed one day. I couldn't understand why the doctor said there was nothing wrong with me. I found out afterward that my mother told him I was only simulating sickness, that I had eaten chalk. That compulsion to chew and drink comes over me even now when I am anxious."

Jaffa's mother lived in Europe during the Second World War. Like many people who have lived through war, she was quite silent about her experience. She wanted to forget. While Jaffa rarely heard a war story, her unconscious picked up the brutality and deprivation that her mother had experienced. Deprivation is brutality in perhaps its subtlest form. Both manifest in her dreams.

Two years before she began analysis, Jaffa had nightmares of wild dogs ripping off her limbs. The following is a major dream in a series of dreams about not having her own body.

> *"Arm or leg?" bodiless voices are calling out.*
>
> *My limbs are being roasted on my live body. Someone wants a piece of thigh and cuts it off with a knife. I myself have to eat a piece. Roasted flesh hangs off my bones, but I feel no physical pain.*
>
> *I am to hook a rug (a wall hanging), but I can't do it since I don't have arms or legs. Someone is starting it for me. Part of the left side is finished in a pattern of daisies in white, silver and pastel blue. I hope to finish it myself one day and to be*

able to use it. Right now I can't because my arms and legs are
"out of order."

Jaffa's father left his wife and two daughters when Jaffa was fifteen months old. Because she was her father's favorite, her mother
was vicious with Jaffa and fervent in her attention to Lara, Jaffa's
sister. Her cannibalistic attitude toward her older daughter is clear
in this dream. The arms with which Jaffa should reach out to grasp
reality, the legs on which she should take her standpoint are being
roasted, perhaps in the rage that exists between mother and child.

Even in this nightmare, however, the possibility of healing is
suggested. She must eat a piece of her own flesh, must incorporate
(literally, take into her own body) her own power. She must, that
is, give birth to herself, which is what the analytical process is all
about. Moreover, she is to hook a rug, which on a symbolic level
means her task is to assimilate the pattern of her life. The rug in
the dream is a wall hanging—not yet a place to stand—but already
it incorporates an image of hope, her favorite wildflowers. "I had
no standpoint then," said Jaffa, "but lots of float points—like the
rug on the wall."

Part of the left side, which is related to the unconscious, is
finished, suggesting that while the ego cannot consciously do
anything to establish a standpoint, the unconscious is hooking
whatever bits of life it finds into a recognizable pattern. All is not
chaos.

Seven years later in a contrasting dream, Jaffa was walking
through a meadow and found plenty of long threads in glorious
earth colors with gold and silver spun threads that could be
woven. Now instead of having her life hooked with little bits of
threads, she could take responsibility and weave the long threads
herself.

It was extremely important that she found these threads because, given her artistic environment, in which dismemberment
masqueraded as nourishment, she was tempted to turn her own
fragmented existence into a work of art to be hung on a wall. A
hooked rug offered itself in her earlier dream as an obvious hook
for her projections. What might at first appear as a healing image
could easily become, and indeed was at the time in danger of
becoming, a reification of her illness.

One aspect of Jaffa's struggle, which she was consciously slow to recognize, was to overcome the temptation to reify her life into a work of art, a reification that would make her forever the "still unravished bride" of her artist father. The violent bodily dismemberments repeated in many of her dreams reveal the ceaseless fight in the unconscious to release her from the dangers of her conscious attitude. The father who would save her from her mother's brutality was at the same time her jailer. This opposition between jailer and savior found its counterpart in the contrary roles of the mother at the conscious and unconscious levels. Consciously experienced as a tyrant, the mother in Jaffa's dreams appeared as the savage energy struggling to release her from the deadly aesthetic grip of her father. The dismemberment of her body in dreams was an attempt on the part of her unconscious to release her from the beautiful frieze her body was becoming under the steady aesthetic gaze of her apparently loving father. Thus in a later dream an image of bodily dismemberment is transformed into a fish she has prepared for her and her father to eat together:

> I am sitting on a bench with my sister. In front of us a body is roasting in an outdoor oven. Macabre!
> Then I am with my father on a country estate. I had prepared a fish which we were eating together. My father urges me to take some sauce; I stay with only fish.

Eating fish images the assimilation of suffering, an assimilation related to the myth of the slow descent of an eternal soul into the prison house of the body. In Jaffa's case, the eternal soul is her father's essentially disembodied vision of his daughter, a vision that cut her off from her own bodily energies, whose repression was mirrored in her mother's physical brutality. In eating the fish, Jaffa is attempting to recognize and absorb the energy of her own abandoned body roasting in an outdoor oven, a roasting mythically experienced in her mother's treatment of her. The father, for whom she has prepared the fish so that they can eat it together, would further hide from her the psychic meaning of her action by urging her to add some sauce. Jaffa, however, stays with the fish, a sign that her unconscious sees through the aesthetic screen to what her own real bodily needs are.

Jaffa is beginning, though still at an unconscious level, to recognize that she needs to assimilate and thereby transform her mother's raw energy by making it creatively her own. The shift in her masculine and feminine energies has unconsciously begun, though they are still largely trapped in the parental complexes to which, from the beginning of her life in utero, they were relentlessly bound.

In life, Jaffa had married twice. Both husbands treated her with the same violence that characterized her mother's behavior. She, however, was unaware of the degree to which her own chaste bonding with her father had evoked violence in her husbands. That is, in both marriages she was still unable and unprepared to deal creatively with her own repressed energy. Her marriages failed partly because they were largely contained in the parental complexes she brought to them.

At the time of the following dream she was in deep depression, recognizing the chasm that was developing between her husband and herself, a chasm exacerbated by the early bonding to her life-denying father. She could no longer endure her husband's sexual demands, nor could she make him understand what relationship in life and sexuality could be, at least as she then understood it. What she considered the repeated betrayal of herself she was determined to end.

The following dream enacts a further step toward the release she yearned for.

> My sister and I are walking on a muddy path through a forest. Walking is extremely difficult. Suddenly the trees look more luxuriant. We are approaching a very different part of the forest. I am relieved and breathe deeply.
>
> Suddenly the path becomes a wild, dangerous river. We turn around immediately to survive. On the way back, there is a hospital in front of which a man moves. My sister notices that his index finger is missing. Farther down we pass a hospital or apartment building. Behind one of the windows a woman (East Indian?) is pointing a gun. Quickly I run out of sight.

Jaffa and her sister—the two sides of the one mother—are together, walking now in a forest that Jaffa associated with her own life. "Not my mother's or my father's—my own." No sooner are they in the welcoming world of their own instinctual energy than their lives are threatened by a raging torrent. Ego and shadow sister are in danger of being consumed by the ferocity of their instincts, particularly since, in her waking life, those instincts are still largely imaged for Jaffa in her mother's violence. Jaffa, in life, was beginning to touch into her own repressed instincts.

As they travel back, they see a male patient in front of a hospital. In real life, Jaffa was attempting to stand firm to her own truth and put her own masculinity into action in organizing a study course for herself. While her masculine energy is still in the hospital, at least that index finger that has tyrannized her life is gone. It reappears, however, as a pointing gun held in the hand of a dark (an unknown part of herself) woman. The evil energy—that is, energy destructive to life—once personified in her personal mother is now beginning to manifest as impersonal, unknown energy closer to the archetypal level.

As the struggle for soul survival intensifies, the ego becomes stronger, but so do the forces ranged against it. Archetypal energy, whether positive or negative, carries awesome magnetic power. The unknown woman represents a hitherto unacknowledged feminine energy in Jaffa, an energy that will at first manifest with considerable rage (gun). The unknown woman is the mother's energy released from the complex and becoming at last Jaffa's own. The release thus announces itself in a shift from the personal to the archetypal mother.

Seven years after her dream of her roasting body without arms or legs, Jaffa hears a powerful voice in a dream saying, "Arms for all-embracing, legs for all-moving." The dream is releasing her body from the frieze of her father by filling it with the energy which she had once identified with her mother's rage. Her soul is at last being given its own proper body, granting it a standpoint in the world, a hold on reality. The Self, that is, is giving her new strength to counteract the once negative forces. Her arms are ready for "all-embracing," and her legs are strong enough for "all-moving."

This voice affirmed Jaffa's dedication to her inner work and opened her to a new level of trust in the healing process taking place. As the energy was released from the complexes, it became available to her ego and Jaffa was aware of capacities in herself that she had never recognized before. Such a strong voice from the Self often opens the way into the deeper secrets of the psyche. Once the ego is strong enough to endure the naked truth, the dreams move into the heart of darkness. Within the darkness lies the light that can set the soul free.

> *I "escape" into a bed with a woman to whom I am attracted and want to be loved by. I ask her whether that is okay with her. She says, "Actually, I am only comfortable with my friend Jeffrey." I accept it. Now we are friends with more distance.*
>
> *I am sitting beside my mother now. She offers me some underpants that I try on and then take off again. There is a feeling of shame because I am wearing only underpants.*
>
> *My mother points to a crow, which seems to be tame, and calls the bird toward her. There is a cat there, and I shudder, thinking it might catch the crow. The crow comes forward, and the cat lovingly licks the bird's wing feathers.*

This dream further clarifies Jaffa's problem with her mother. In the first section, when she yearns to make love to the woman, the woman replies that she is only comfortable with her friend Jeffrey. Jeffrey was her mother's maiden name. In associating with the dream, Jaffa said that her mother was never really married, never bonded to her father. Her idea of relating was to make Jaffa, Lara and their father responsible for her misery.

When Jaffa was a child, her chief goal in life was to be loved and accepted by her mother. The love/hate bond that existed between them was an incestuous love. Thus both of Jaffa's husbands were very much like her mother's power-driven animus. When Jaffa recognized how narcissistic her mother was, she also recognized that she and her sister were used merely to mirror their mother and fulfill, however inadequately, their mother's needs; hence began their profound lack of self-esteem. Because the child was expected to mirror the parent, instead of the parent mirroring the child, the young potential was stifled.

The "intimacy" with her mother is broken in the second section of the dream. Associating with the underpants, Jaffa remembered the horrid long woolen underwear her mother bought for her daughters. Jaffa used to stop in the woods on her way to school, step out of the long brown pants, leave the small white ones on and stuff the big ones in her briefcase. As an adult, she could never allow herself the luxury of delicate lingerie until she broke the power of her mother complex. In the dream, the transition begins when the mother offers her white underpants (which she never did in real life), but Jaffa cannot receive them from her. All she can feel is the shame of being partially naked. This echoes her early childhood fears of being naked in front of her mother. Even then she sensed the violence in her mother's sexuality and knew that her nakedness and Lara's excited her mother.

The last section of the dream, the lysis, points the direction in which the energy wants to move. Here, Jaffa's strong Celtic roots are echoed in Odin's bird, the crow. The spiritual energy symbolized in the crow is balanced by the instinctual energy symbolized in the cat. Jaffa expects them to be natural enemies. But the cat lovingly licks the crow. Transformation of the incest bond that links sexuality and violence between mother and daughter has begun in this dream.

When that shift reaches consciousness, a new relationship is possible between spirit and instinct. Instead of being enemies, the two energies can find a natural harmony; far from destroying each other they can relate. Spirituality and sexuality are like the two snakes in the caduceus of Asclepius, separating and uniting, each with its own strength, one harmoniously balancing the other.

Though Jaffa remained unaware of this larger archetypal action of the unconscious, she nevertheless received in the dream a glimpse of herself as her own person inhabiting her own creative energies. She saw herself free of the triangulated structure to which she had all her life been bound. In this glimpse of a lost or repressed instinctual life, she recognized an energy that her intellect could no longer rationalize or contain.

She dreamed of a circle of fire; her whole body became fire. Reflecting on the circle of fire, she remembered that Wagner's *Ring* had always fascinated her. In the opera, Siegfried kept covered by a leaf his vulnerable spot in the center of his back. The evil one, Hagen, tricked him, and when Siegfried lost his gentle green armor, he was vulnerable. Jaffa was suffering intense pain caused by vertebra behind her heart. So long as she didn't breathe too deeply, didn't take in too much life, it didn't hurt too much. She was beginning to realize through her body pain the depth of the cutting that was going on.

"I can't carry the weight of my head anymore," she said. "It's too heavy. For so long I have intellectualized my suffering. I see intellectualizing now as an excuse. I was so stuck in my head and

spirit that I smiled a smooth, secret smile and said, 'I'm grateful for
my suffering. This is how I've learned. This is my maturing.' Head
stuff! Totally ignoring my body! This is such a grand stand I've
taken. Quite arrogant really! Let her suffer! Let her burn in the
fire! I didn't know what real suffering was. I had gone through
everything with my body closed down. I didn't want to look at
anything, didn't want to suffer. Now I see what it really was. My
life before was just headlines, no substance. All I wanted was
coziness for everybody. I accommodated to everything for peace.
Now I want freedom to live my life."

The transformative fire brought up associations with Wagner's
Brunnhilde. Brunnhilde, favorite daughter of Wotan, saw what
human love could be and turned against the perfectionist values of
her father god, Wotan, in favor of the human hero. Her enraged
father put her on a rock forever. But Brunnhilde persuaded him to
encircle her with a ring of fire (passion), a ring which only a hero
could break through to release her. Wotan agreed but with a price:
if a man dared to come through the fire to awaken her, she would
no longer be a Goddess. She would become a human being.

The Brunnhilde image is evoking not only Jaffa's mature feminine consciousness but her focused, assertive masculinity as well.
Having achieved a temporary plateau in the development of her
feminine side, the Self now guides her to growth in her masculinity.

*I walk through my home town on a badly lit road. I could have
reached my goal on a different road with more traffic, but I
chose a back alley. I sense danger. A man follows me, becoming even more creepy when he calls out my name. He must
know me and have observed me for a long time! He must have
planned his attack cleverly! An accomplice of his is now approaching me from the front. I remain conscious of the danger
but don't panic. The first man now grabs me around my ribs in
a sweet-sour way. I don't fight, don't run, but know I must
protect myself. I see a car parked with three women inside and
slowly walk toward it. The men allow me to go to the women.
I guess they must after all be harmless. I ask the women
whisperingly to secure my protection. All three agree silently.*

*Later, at the three women's house, two of their fathers are
visiting. Against one wall the first of the two attackers sits and
paints! I am astounded, for I thought he was a criminal! The*

*other father is sitting at the table gobbling down food like a
madman. I think it is a pity to gobble and not to enjoy. Hot
hunger! The women now tell me that the first father is quite
harmless and known for that.*

*I think I should look him in his face and de-harm him for
myself, best upside down. I imagine how either I myself, or he,
would hang on the balcony railing and how we would, in this
way, look into each other's eyes and recognize one another.
SHOCKED!*

Slowly, inevitably, this dream drives the sword home. Having
chosen to leave the collective road, the dreamer is moving through
the back alley where she meets her assailant and his accomplice,
who know her well. When she is grabbed in "a sweet-sour way,"
she experiences the attack exactly as she experienced the hands of
her husband—cold, intrusive, violent in the sexual act. The assailants either hold the power, or she projects her own power on
them. As the violence closes in, there is danger of violence, but she
does not fight or panic. Instead she slowly moves toward the protection of women in the nearby car. The assailants allow this.

This moment of transformed action—where the ego stands
firm, doesn't panic, faces the rapists head on and realizes they are
now "harmless"—can only come after months or years of hard
work. In the early months of analysis, the weak container would
try to run from the danger or fight it, thus setting up the very
dynamic that would end in violence. When soul and body are in
harmony, the body supports the ego, the ego can face the assailant.
The face we turn to the unconscious is the face that is reflected
back to us. So long as we keep running, it chases us and sometimes
trips us. When we turn around and face it, its monumental terrors
can be dealt with, detail by small detail.

In the protective presence of her feminine energies, Jaffa faces
the power drives she has been running away from all her life.
While she does not have a chronic eating disorder, she does under
stress gobble food, smoke cigarettes, rush from one thing into
another and then fly out for more books. The "other father," gobbling his food like a madman, personifies the unconscious wolf
energy that does not know what it wants but consumes everything
in a crazed desire to be filled with something. Undermined by
powerlessness and emptiness, it blindly lashes out, gobbling, not

digesting anything. This father resonates with Jaffa's early memories of her mother gobbling at the kitchen table, eating her up. The negative animus is the addict that consumes the feminine.

The other father is painting. The dreamer is astounded that he is not a criminal as she imagined. Here is the core of what Jaffa will deal with. Both her father and mother were artists when they married. Her mother's creative powers, without a strong ego to protect them, were swallowed by the madman gobbler whose negative energy, fired by the misappropriated creativity, became totally destructive. The two sides of that creative fire are also juxtaposed in the criminal artist. Now Jaffa has to face the fact that her beloved father may not be blameless. His perfectionist standards in his own work and his support of everything she does rob her of her own creative fire. She is paralyzed when she begins to paint, even as her mother, as artist, was paralyzed in her marriage, her own creative energy gobbled up in rage. It is thus her mother's rage she must redeem by recognizing that rage in herself. In the last section of the dream, the dream ego realizes Jaffa must look this situation squarely in the eye but upside down.

This image is related to The Hanged Man in the Tarot pack, who

> *augurs the need for a voluntary sacrifice for the purpose of acquiring something of greater value. This might be the sacrifice of an external thing which has previously provided security in the hope that some potential can be given room to develop. Or it can be the sacrifice of a cherished attitude, such as intellectual superiority, or unforgiving hatred, or a stubborn pursuit of some unobtainable fantasy.*[1]

Jaffa is now faced with an image that suggests that her idealized father was neither the God she imagined nor the criminal. She imagines either him or herself suspended, as indeed her life is now suspended, without the perfection of her father at the center. As Jaffa looks into the father's eyes, she will see her own masculinity, her own creativity, her own capacity for action, like her mother's, hung, feet in the air, upside down. The situation cannot be faced directly yet, for to face it directly would be to short-circuit the soul process, and to short-circuit the soul process is to be electrocuted. This is a soul problem, not a behavioral one.

One of the tragedies of human relationships is that very often one partner cannot respect the soul process of the other. What is rape for Jaffa is not rape for her husband because he does not have her trauma. Ripping aside the veils is rape when one partner is not ready.

Jaffa is being called to make a sacrifice. What the sacrifice is she does not know. It has to do with what is most sacred to her. It has to do with making herself vulnerable to the new possibilities life may bring. It has to do with forgiving the enemy mother who in psychic reality mirrored, in her violence, Jaffa's repression of herself. Release from repression, that is, is less a slaying of the evil witch than a transformation of her negative energy through creative assimilation. It is releasing Pegasus buried in Medusa. The father hanging upside down so that she can look him in the eye contains the potential recognition that her upside-down father is what in part her mother is.

Two months later, after immense efforts to change her standpoint, Jaffa dreams that her suitcases are packed but still in her father's apartment, exactly as the apartment was twenty-five years ago. As the dream develops, the reason for no immediate radical change becomes clear. Chaos threatens:

> My sister, as a baby, chatters uninterruptedly. My mother talks of "putting the kleenex away" after having made love to me in order to keep it secret from my little sister. I am strangely aware of her assumption of "intimacy" between us.
> Then one word—AGAMEMNON.

Again the collusion of mother and father complexes is apparent. Obviously, father is happy to have Jaffa stay in his house (power) forever. "The suitcases are my soul that I put down in my father's apartment and left there," Jaffa said.

The second part of the dream stunned Jaffa. Whether physical incest actually took place or not she does not know. The dream at least suggests that Jaffa's youthful psyche experienced her mother's attitude toward her as an intrusion, a deviation from a healthy mother–daughter relationship. The baby sister who "chatters uninterruptedly" is that unconscious, innocent part of the child that cannot believe the violation is happening. Denial is the only defense the child has against the impossible truth.

Jaffa's strongest initial reaction to the dream was an all-consuming resentment of her mother's assumption that her daughter would make love to her. Her "absolutely not" in response to the dream contained all the energy that blocked out the act, an act that would consciously require far more processing before its creative possibilities could be absorbed. Those creative possibilities lay not in any actual relationship between Jaffa and her mother but in Jaffa's learning to mother herself.

When one being is invaded by another—whether it is body or soul that is raped, or both—the symbolic language of the dream is the same. The inner world is so devastated that the trauma may be split off, isolated in the unconscious, while an unaffected part of the psyche chatters incessantly, camouflaging the truth. That truth, however, resides not in the trauma of incest or rape but in the final recognition that energy repressed will first explode in unacceptable ways before it finds the channel of its positive creative flow.

As Jaffa worked on this dream over the next few months, she realized that there had indeed been an incestuous overtone to the beatings. The mother would become so excited and strike so hard on the child's buttocks that the imprint of the hot hand remained on her, in her, all day.

Then the one word, "Agamemnon," delivered a blow even deeper than the incest section of the dream. When she looked up the story in Edith Hamilton's *Mythology,* she found that Agamemnon sacrificed his daughter, Iphigenia, and years later was killed himself by his wife's lover. The words that Jaffa underlined were "a mother's love for a daughter killed by her own father."[2] She took "Agamemnon" as a command, as if her psyche were to say, "Look at me. There's more here than spirit. Demystify spirit." Incest energy with the mother had to be understood as the constellation of that energy which, when absorbed, would release her from the killing love of the father.

Jaffa realized that, by making her his queen, her father had not allowed her to live. In fact, he had talked Jaffa into giving up the man she loved and staying with the man she first married. "If I had gone off with my lover," she said, "Father would have been threatened. 'Come to me,' he says, 'Come to me.' He sacrifices the woman I am to his image of the perfect woman for *his* salvation. I became a willing victim to the extent that I sacrificed my body. What father did to me, I did to my body." Jaffa's growing understanding is redeeming the negative mother at work in herself.

There is that other factor that must be kept in mind in working with this dream: Jaffa is an artist and her creativity is grounded in the matrix of her being. So long as Jaffa needed to abreact her anger, I left the matrix alone so that it would not be contaminated. Jaffa, in the immediate sense, is the product of her accidental life circumstances, as are we all. These accidental circumstances must, therefore, first be dealt with in order to make a clearing in which the archetypal or creative matrix of her being can appear. There is always some danger at the purely personal level that she could be trapped in the chattering child, imaged in her sister, who can only deny the experience of incest instead of moving into the adult who seeks the meaning and gives it form in her art.

When Jaffa began to take full responsibility for her own life, she worked patiently at finding a new home for herself and making time for her studies. She relied on her own sense of discipline and willpower. Something, however, was missing as is clear in the following dream:

> *The Queen Mother is in a wheelchair.*
> *At a castle ruin: I am walking toward a kind of jacuzzi (old bathtub, round, made of wood). I hesitate when I see my father in the tub with a woman. Then I feel an urge to find out more about the woman. I had somehow been aware of her having a son about fifteen years old. Now she seems to totally ignore the fact that she is apparently sitting on top of her son in the water. I cannot do anything but am alarmed and extremely concerned. Finally she stands up, completely unconscious, feelingless. Now I can see that indeed she had been holding her son under water all that time. He has shrunk to the size of a fifteen-year-old baby. He seems without any life, even though soft (not dead but stiff). It is a horrible sight. I cannot help. I walk away slowly. Should I call for help?*

The mother complex is now crippled. As the old queen crumbles, it is natural that the castle (the authority) of the complex would be in ruins. In that ruin, however, is an old alchemical bathtub, a feminine container, wooden and round, which is the creative feminine at the core of the mother complex. Yet, in that creative place are the father and the unknown woman who sits feelingless on top of her fifteen-year-old son who has shrunk to the size of a baby. He is not dead although he seems to be.

Fifteen years earlier, Jaffa, at her father's request, said goodbye to a man she loved, a man whom she associated with her creativity. "It was a time of death," she said. "Everything around me died. I could concentrate on nothing." Her father's anima, his soul, who loved painting, had been sitting on top of Jaffa's creativity for fifteen years. Everything about the tub—old, wooden, round, holding water—suggests the creative matrix, but Jaffa is not in the tub and her creative masculine is being held down in the un-conscious by an unknown woman.

Here is a very different kind of patriarchal woman—more subtle but no less destructive. "I love you so much, I know what is best for you" is her message, and it has nearly drowned Jaffa's creative spirit. Thus, although the mother complex is in ruins, rage reduced to the impotency of a wheelchair, the father complex remains. Jaffa still needs the energy locked up in the mother complex to release her from her father complex. The Queen Mother in a wheelchair, now understood as Jaffa's own crippled energy, needs that energy, creatively transformed, in order to release herself from her father's anima. Not surprisingly, therefore, in the dream she is still trapped, not knowing what to do: "I cannot help. I walk away slowly. Should I call for help?" In this dream, the dream ego is so shocked it does not ask for help.

The following dream suggests that Jaffa is seeking help in the wrong place.

> My son is sitting on the couch of my father's living room. In front of him, on the floor, a white (!) Negro doll (size of a two-year-old child) is standing. She can talk. My son says to her, "I am not your grandmother!"

Her young masculine energy is now in her father's living room. Her young femininity (deficient in instinct—Negro doll, but white), which was crippled into a doll-like puppet by the age of two, is able to talk, but the boy rebukes her. Perhaps she was looking to him for understanding, for nourishment, for all that she needs to look for in the Great Mother. This would be the old pattern repeating itself: the starved, ungrounded feminine projecting strength and caring on the masculine. Then the masculine grows fat while the feminine remains anorexic (which was precisely what was happening between two of Jaffa's children). The dream seems to be warning Jaffa not to make her son into her loving mother in real life and not to indulge herself in a doll-like femininity that would feed on her creative masculinity. It needs all its own strength to mature.

In the following dream a vibrant creative energy is beginning to manifest.

> *My husband has taken his car apart.*
>
> *At a lake: I see some people on a strange kind of lift, just jumping off onto a platform and from there onto land. They are older people. Then I find myself high above the lake lying flat on my stomach on a small flat lift. I am lying quite still and do not get dizzy. I am spiraling downward and land safely.*
>
> *Unexpectedly, I walk through a village in which all the inhabitants are participating in a funeral or memorial ceremony. Everyone is dressed in black. People have camels and cows with them; I am trying to squeeze through. Egypt seems to have a deep importance.*
>
> *I am conscious of the presence of magic: first in the form of a man and/or his voice which enables me to figure skate, even though normally only my sister can do that. Then the magic seems to come from a cat.*
>
> *I return from a hike with my father to the center of town. He steps into an empty bus. I want to follow him. As quick as a wink the doors shut, the bus takes off, and I am furious!*

A car is a metaphor for the way our energy moves through life. Our body is our most immediate means of locomotion. As patriarchal rigidity is dismantled in the musculature of Jaffa's body, the shifting of the energy patterns is at times excruciating.

In part two of the dream, the lift is like a crane holding a platform that comes spiraling and safely down, first over the lake, then over the land. It reminds Jaffa of joining hands with her sister and swirling like two dervishes until they found the still point at the

center and spiraled around the outside without becoming dizzy. As
T. S. Eliot puts it,

> Except for the point, the still
>   point,
> There would be no dance, and there is only the dance.[3]

At the still point, spirit embraces soul. Soul is in time, in matter.
Spirit penetrates soul, bringing meaning to what might otherwise
be endless, meaningless time. Their union creates the dance that is
a celebration of all that lives. Jaffa in the dream is being released
from the complexes characteristic of a triangulated child through
an influx of archetypal energy that breaks the chains of the personal.

The dance of celebration is further developed in the third part of
the dream. Something has died but something new is being
born—and the dream ego is "trying to squeeze through." Egypt is
very important to Jaffa because as a child she escaped from her
depressed personal world by entering the archetypal world of the
museum where Egypt lived in her imagination. She loved the ancient beauty, the power of the pyramids, the regal faces, the ma-
jestic forms. She loved the jewelry, the whole milieu of sun energy
that brought her close to the divine.

As she reconnected with that archetypal world of her childhood,
she developed a love for belly-dance music, which evoked a sen-
suous, sacred energy that brought her into touch with the feminine
power in her body. Isis, the Black Madonna, is in that energy.

The powerful Black Madonna energy finds a partner in the next
section of the dream. Masculine energy in the form of "a man
and/or his voice" infiltrates the atmosphere with magic, and Jaffa
is able to figure skate. "I love to watch figure skating," she said. "It
is embodied spirit moving." All the lightness, the magic, the grace
she once projected on her sister she is now claiming in herself. And
with that thought, the magic she associated with a man seems to
come from the feminine energy associated with a cat. Light enters
matter.

Where does the energy want to go? The lysis makes that clear.
The energy that is personified in the father gets into a bus, and the
ego still wants to follow. "Quick as a wink," the unconscious shuts
the door between them. The ego, furious at being left alone, has to

accept the cut she has not the conscious strength to make. Father, of course, will sometimes return, but right now, Jaffa has to allow her own masculinity to grow without projecting on her father or modeling herself on him. This episode is a splendid example of "the fullness of time" having arrived and the unconscious taking the action which the dream ego is not yet able to take. Jaffa in the dream is being released from both parental complexes through an infusion of archetypal energy. Thus she is discovering her own center, that still point around which her own creative dynamics revolve in harmony. She is released from the artists in her parents which blocked the artist in herself.

In a later dream, Jaffa and a male friend are visiting a married couple who are preparing dinner for the four to share. The husband is mixing spaghetti with the chicken his wife is cutting up. Jaffa likes Italian men because "they are not threatened in their masculinity. They can do what they need to do and work with a woman doing what she needs to do." In the dream each is independent, sharing without burdening the other. The dinner the four will eat together has feminine and masculine components blended but each defined. This dream, simple as it is, points to uncontaminated masculine and feminine energies uniting while holding their uniqueness.

Life has moved in many directions since Jaffa had these dreams. Covering a span of seven years, they make clear the dark foundations that have to be renovated in order to create a secure base for the new structure. While that structure is taking shape, the dark incubation period of healing requires a temenos, a sacred inner space. The depth and breadth and height of the process can only be suggested. Each of us travels his/her own path, but recognizable patterns emerge. Reviewing her dreams, some of which are recorded here, Jaffa said, "I see a gaping wound with a thread of healing going right through."

Jaffa's "gaping wound," commonly called the "healing wound," is the wound through which the God or Goddess enters. It is the place made vulnerable, made open, to the infusion of archetypal energy. Through the interaction of conscious and unconscious, Jaffa is shaping her own creative dynamics toward the equilibrium which is conferring upon her an identity of her own rather than a false identity borrowed from her unhappy parents. Far from slaying the dragon-mother, she is, in fact, redeeming her.

Her struggle, it would appear, was (and still remains) less with the father than with the mother. Even as the puer, in James Hillman's rendering, is understood in relation to the senex, so also the puella ("Daddy's little princess") must be understood in relation to the mother, whom she is struggling to surpass. In struggling to redeem her mother, she thereby releases in herself what in the mother remained dark and hidden. Essential to a creative resolution of the conflict is a recognition of the parents' interaction on a psychic level. They have imposed an unconscious pattern of negative bonding on the child. In Jaffa's case, the bonding between the parents was presumably broken by divorce. That bonding, far from broken, becomes all the stronger in the child whose own life has for its destined task the healing within of what was broken without. In the ongoing healing of the parental image at the archetypal level lies the wholeness which is the goal of the individuation process. Surrender to the archetypal parents, "father–mother of all higher consciousness"[4] is, Jung writes, "a confession of man's subjection, his imperfection, and his dependence; but at the same time a testimony to his freedom to choose between truth and error."[5] That surrender, reached by Jung at the end of his life, remains for Jaffa a far-off goal propelling her in ways that she does and does not understand.

1.   J. Sharman-Burke and L. Greene, *The Mythic Tarot* (New York: Methuen, 1986), p. 59.

2.   E. Hamilton, *Mythology* (New York: NAL Penguin, Inc., 1969), p. 240.

3.   T. S. Eliot, *Four Quartets,* "Burnt Norton," lines 66–67.

4.   C. G. Jung, *Memories, Dreams, Reflections* (London: Collins, 1963), p. 386.

5.   Ibid.

What's the Matter with Mother?
Patricia Berry

IF THERE IS any concept that we in psychology have overused, it is that of the mother. And we have blamed her extensively. At one time or another, in one way or another, we have used her to explain each of our pathological syndromes: our schizophrenia as a double-binding by her; paranoia, an inability to trust because of her (a need to tie our thoughts into rigid systems, in compensation for her lack of order); hysteria, a tendency to over-sensitize without feeling, because of the wandering womb (*her* womb) in our bodies.

In light of the frequency of these explanations, I began to ask myself—so what's the matter with mother? What's the matter that makes her so useful, particularly in psychology's explanations?

In order to explore this question, let us begin by turning it slightly to what mother's matter is—what the content of mother is. And let us focus on the Great Mother of our Western mythological tradition, as described by Hesiod in his *Theogony*. In the *Theogony* Hesiod honors the Great Mother Gaia, Earth, as the original divinity and progenitor of all the other divinities—all those many forms of our psychic possibilities, forms of psychic awareness. For all these, Gaia lays the original ground.

According to Hesiod, first there was Chaos, a formlessness, a nothingness. Then there was Gaia, Earth: the first form, the first principle, a something, a given.

But inasmuch as Creation takes place continuously—every day our psychic experience is created, our emotions and moods are given form—rather than tell Hesiod's creation tale in the past tense, we might more accurately tell it in the present: first there *is* Chaos, and then there is Mother Earth. Within our experiences of chaos, at the same moment there is contained a specific possibility of form. Or, each chaos mothers itself into form.

Now this view of chaos is different from our traditional linear notions, in which form is imposed later upon chaos from without or down from above, conquering and replacing the chaos.

To view this tale, however, as I am attempting, would be to see it as an image—i.e., more as a picture than as a narrative—so that the facets of the event (the chaos and forms or earth) are given all at once. Some interesting things turn up in this image picture that don't show up in sequential narrative. For example, this way of looking sees chaos and the forms as co-present: within chaos there are inherent forms. Each moment of chaos has shapes within it, and each form or shape embodies a specific chaos.

Of course, this way of looking at things also has implications therapeutically. For example, here it implies that one must not rid oneself too quickly of chaotic feelings (by abreacting or primal screaming them), because then one would also lose the forms. Better would be to contain, and even to nurture, the chaos so that its shapes may exist as well. (The image further suggests that our forms cannot rid us of chaos, for where the forms are is also where chaos is.)

I can support what I have just said with matter. For mother, this mothering ground of our lives, is connected with the word *matter.* Mother and matter (*mater*) are cognates. And matter has been viewed in two ways—almost as though there were basically two sorts, or levels, of matter.

One level is considered as a universal substrate. And as such it exists only in abstraction. In itself, this matter is unknowable, invisible, and incorporeal. Matter in this sense is itself a kind of chaos or, as Augustine describes it, an absence of light, a deprivation of being.[1] So this view of matter holds it to be nothingness, a negativity, a lacking. Now the second view builds upon this first view.

The second sort of matter is not only the most nothing, but in addition the most something—the most concrete, tangible, visible, bodily. Augustine calls this matter "the earth as we know it" and contrasts the heaven, which is nearest to God, with this earth that though most concrete is nevertheless nearest to nothing.[2]

There is within the idea of matter a paradox. Matter (and by extension mother earth) is both the most something *and* the most nothing, the most necessary (in order that something can happen) and at the same time the most lacking. With this combination of qualities, matter and mother have of course had a rather hard time of it in our Western spiritual tradition. Mother/matter is the ground of existence and yet doesn't count—she is nothing. Archetypally, she is our earth and at the same time is always lacking.[3]

When we get close to our "matter," our lower substrates, our roots, our past, the ground from which we came, our lower physical nature, our cruder emotions, it is not surprising that we feel something unsettling, something inferior, chaotic, soiled perhaps. But these feelings are given with the very nature of mother's matter.

Let me tell you of an experience Hesiod had. In the beginning of the *Theogony*, Hesiod tells of his conversion to poet, to a man who praised the Gods. As he tells it, he was out tending his flocks when suddenly the Muses appeared and berated him for his lowly state. They evoked in him a sense of shame for being only a man of the earth. Hesiod became then a poet who praised the Muses, but he never gave up being a man of the earth (a farmer) nor the earth as his subject. He became instead a more complicated farmer, one who now sang the praises of an earth that felt to him shameful.

Now this would seem peculiar: that a man who was shamed, who was called a fool for being merely of the earth, would turn now to praise this very earth for which he felt shame. Or is it that the experience of shame is connected with the experience of earth, and perhaps shame is a way that may even lead one to the experience of earth?

Shame is a deep bodily reaction that cannot be controlled (at least very effectively) by the mind. And so shame points to something beyond the will—something of power beyond the human, which we might call the divine. Hesiod was led to experience the earth as a psychic earth that though shamefully of himself was yet, because of his very shame, more than himself. Within this psychic movement, earth became a divinity. No longer a mere flat expanse on which to pasture his sheep, as a Goddess she became an earth of

many levels upon which his soul (his Muses) pastured as well. For
Hesiod she was no longer "nothing-but" a physical ground, a
neutral ground without quality; because she was experienced as a
divinity she was experienced psychically, so that her matter mat-
tered to and in the psyche.

Had it not been the experience of earth that the Muses wished to
evoke in Hesiod, they might have approached him in another way.
They could have brought about his conversion through a visionary
experience of great beauty in the distance; they could have asked
him in an uplifting moment to lay down his staff and follow them,
or whatever. But what was given was the experience of earth—for
Hesiod was to be a poet of the earth, and from this earth the entire
Theogony, in praise of all the Gods and Goddesses, was to be
sung.

Let me offer you a Navajo chant that expresses something of the
connection between shame and earth. It goes:

I am ashamed before earth;
I am ashamed before heavens;
I am ashamed before dawn;
I am ashamed before evening twilight;
I am ashamed before blue sky;
I am ashamed before darkness;
I am ashamed before sun;
I am ashamed before that standing within me which speaks with me.
Some of these things are always looking at me.
I am never out of sight.
Therefore I must tell the truth.
I hold my word tight to my breast.[4]

"I am ashamed"—who has not had that feeling when faced with
the wonder of the earth? But this sense of shame occurs too when
other aspects of 'earthy' feeling appear. This happens in analysis
when the 'chthonic' is constellated: the bug-eyed, toady, twisted,
grotesque, slimy, or hulking creatures that bring us startling
recognition of ugliness and deformity. Strange that we should feel
these creatures as *de*formed, arising as they do from such natural,
earthy levels of the psyche.

We generally try to repress these creatures. If that doesn't work
we try second best: to rush them through their transformations as

quickly as possible. With a kind of desperation we paint, model, and carry on active imaginations. The principal difficulty is that—in the hurry—we may lose the experience. Because these shameful creatures of the earth carry the experience of earth, we lose something of the very earth we are seeking when we transform them too smoothly. It is a funny psychological fact that being soiled is intimately connected with the experience and benefits of soil.

Fortunately for our mythological tradition, Hesiod's shame connects him to this earthy sustenance and generativity, so that out of her—out of Gaia—proceeds his *Theogony*. Out of her comes the starry sky, the mountains, the depths, the sea.

Strangely enough, all of those so-called masculine regions (starry sky; mountains–Olympos; depths–Hades; sea–Okeanos, Poseidon) have come out of her and are part of her basic matrix. Moreover, she creates her own mate, Uranos. As this Uranos sky is a phallic force proceeding out of earth, we can see it as earth's original hermaphroditism. Within the feminine as void, within her as passive, lies a sky-like potentiality. Hence to get in touch with earth is also to connect with a sky that proceeds from earth, and the seeds that drop create a kind of original self-fertilization. Not one without problems. But for the moment it is enough to note that sky, mountains, depths, and generations all have their beginnings in primal earth.

In early worship black animals were sacrificed to Gaia Earth.[5] Let us speak for a moment about sacrifice. The very word *sacrifice* means "to make sacred." Thus it is the "black" that is sacred to Gaia and may help keep her sacred. Black: the dark, the depressed, grieving over losses, the inexplicable, the shadowy, the sinful (we might now say).

We now have another hint as to how we may get in touch with Gaia Earth, i.e., through feelings of depression, black moods, losses, and lostness. As shame is a way into the experience of mother earth, a related way is the feeling of one's darkest nature and hopelessness—limitations that do not change, complexes that have marked one's personality and will always be as they are, since they are the *ground* of personality, unique and individual. To attempt to lighten these experiences, to get away from these complexes, or to whitewash them with explanations, to rationalize them would then also be to lose one's possibilities for psychic body, for earth. These limitations in fact *are* psychic earth.

Depth psychology serves this ground of the mother in many ways. One is by giving support to the human sense of shame and infirmity, the incomprehensible, the rejected. Psychology not only draws support from the mother's dark depths but in turn worships these depths by creating of them a theogony of phenomenological descriptions, systems, and pathological classifications, much as Hesiod created his theogony.

And this sense we have of something as pathological cannot be explained away as only due to society, or only because of our parents or the faulty interaction in our families. An idea of pathology, of something amiss, exists in every society. So it would seem to be an archetypal, primary experience. Though of course the designation of *what* is pathological may vary, nevertheless the archetypal fact of it remains constant, through the ages and from culture to culture.

By deepening the experience of pathology, we may deepen our recognition of the Mother, the Earth. By this I do not mean experiencing pathology in projection, as something out there. If pathology is archetypal, then by definition we must experience it in ourselves, much as we would any other archetypal quality— anima, animus, child. As meanings they begin in ourselves.

Another of the qualities of mother Gaia is immovability. Gaia made things stick. She was the Goddess of marriage.[6] One swore oaths by her, and they were binding.[7] Mother/matter as the inert becomes now mother as the settler, the stabilizer, the binder.

In psychotherapy we still can find this idea of Earth, earth as that which will settle down a youth who is too high-flying, or a woman who doesn't take responsibility for her home, or a man who is too intellectual. What these people need is earth, we say. The young man we may send off to work on a farm for the summer or urge him to marry. The housewife we may tell to pay more attention to her homelike activities, to put up her own preserves, or work in the garden, or take up knitting. The intellectual we tell to get down to the practical and live life, even at the expense of his 'bright ideas' and fantasies.

What we are attempting to cultivate in the psyche of all these people is some ground in which things "matter," happen, become substantial—something into which their life experiences may etch. We are trying to develop the mother within them, their *prima materia* into a supporting matrix, some basic substrate in which psychic movements may take form and gather body.

The curious thing is how literal these therapeutic prescriptions for earth become. The analysand must actually, literally, do some concrete activity that everybody would agree is "earthy." And yet we all know that when people are even physically involved with the earth, they haven't necessarily what we mean by psychic earth. A person can grow his own grains and at the same time spin in a mental and emotional space with very little psychic grounding. So it isn't really just physical earth that connects us to the divinity of Mother Gaia, but psychic earth, earth that has become ensouled with divinity, psychically complicated and, like Hesiod's, touched by the metaphorical Muses of soul.

But there is this apparent difficulty in speaking of any kind of earth, because something about the nature of earth makes us take it more literally than we take the other elements. If a person lacked air, we would never send him off to learn to fly an airplane.[8] Or if a person's dreams showed that he lacked water, fluidity, we would hardly send him off to learn actually to swim. But when a person is lacking in earth, we tend to prescribe something rather obviously connected with the earth, like taking a cottage in the country, making a garden, or chopping firewood.

Don't get me wrong. I'm not saying that the Muses of metaphor cannot appear in these activities. I'm only saying that they needn't necessarily. The more we insist on enjoining these quite literal earthy activities, the more we may be blocking the appearance of the Muses and a genuine metaphorical earth arising from within the person, where it makes matter (substance, containment) psychologically.

Depth psychology would seem a discipline in which this re-worked and more metaphorical sense of earth is quite pronounced. It is a field in which we work a good deal for the benefit of, and in keeping with, the metaphorical ladies of soul. And yet even we find ourselves caught in the trap of earth literalisms. Perhaps it appears in the feeling that our particular orientation is *the* way—and certainly it begins with our persuasion as to what is most 'real.' For what's 'grounded' and what's 'real' tend to be habitually inter-related.

In Jungian psychology some of us see as most real our personal

mother, our childhood, the breasts we actually nursed from as infants. Others of us see what is empirical as most real—those
grounds that can be measured and tested. Still others see the social
as most real, and so we strive for 'genuine' personal interaction
and require group therapy. Others may see synchronistic events as
most real.

But whatever we take as most real (and partly dependent as
Jungians upon whether we inhabit the earth of London, San Fran-
cisco, New York, or Zürich) is what we are using as our mothering
ground. And this grounding is extremely important: it is that
which gives our thoughts fertility and substance, our therapies
body and results. It is what nourishes our psychological endeavors
and makes them matter.

Yet we must not forget the other side of mother's nature (her archetypal being as lack, absence, deprivation). So however hard we
work at grounding, each in his or her own way, we never feel this
grounding complete. Always hidden in the very ground we are
working is a gnawing sense of lack.

In other words, what we assume as most real, as our mother, is
at the same time that which gives us a feeling of unsureness. And
so we compensate this unsureness with insistence. We insist that
one *must* go back and re-experience childhood, relive the good and
bad breast dilemma, for this would give the grounding and the
body that is needed. Or we say, if Jungian psychology is not to be
lacking, it must be tested and proven to the world. Or, enough of
all this flying around in the air talking about synchronicities, we
must get down to where people really live with others, in personal
emotions and real-life entanglements.

When one orientation fights another, the dispute is fairly serious, for each of us is defending the incompleteness we depend
upon as our mother—the ground that has given, and is giving, our
activities sustenance. But because we fear her nature as lack, we
strive for more support by substantiating her ever more surely. As a
solar hero, one fights for the death of the mother's ambiguity by
fighting to the death for this increased grounding and substantiation of the mother. Thus identified, one casts aside other, less
heroic, modes that would allow the incompleteness of mothering
ground to connect with the Muses of metaphor, for whom lacking
ground is fertile ground indeed. Metaphor depends upon this sense
of lack, this sense of the "is not" with every "is."[9]

We must ask how it is that this literalizing tends to occur with earth. One explanation lies within the myth. We have mentioned how Gaia created out of herself not only the world but even her own spouse, Uranos. Every night Uranos, the sky, spread himself down over Gaia in mating. But the children thereby engendered he kept imprisoned in the earth, which gave Gaia, earth, great pain, the more so with each additional child, so that by the time the twelfth child arrived (twelve being the completion of a cycle), she plotted an end to this ever-increasing burden. And so she crafted a sickle to castrate Uranos.

This motif of the child trapped in the earth suggests a way of looking at the problem of literalization. A child, a new possibility, is born, but then this child is trapped in matter. It is imprisoned in the earth (making this earth only physical, only literal matter). So the spirit of the new offspring, or the psyche or soul of it, is buried in an earth that is merely material. Interestingly enough, according to the tale, this materialism gives the mother Gaia herself great pain. She is burdened with each successive offspring buried within her. She is forced to carry what has been projected into her (as literal plans, goals, whatever), thereby losing her more metaphorical possibilities, that part of herself that is insubstantial.

In the myth the mother eases her burden by turning her destructive potential against this concretism. We might call her in this role the negative mother. She plots castration and devises the means for it. The sickle she invents, however, is fashioned of iron, that metal so important to the building of civilization. So her destructive act is not without benefit and expresses her pain over the way she as earth is being used.

It could be that when we put too many of our children, our possibilities, into concrete explanations and literal programs, burying their meanings for the soul by living them materially, we are not at all propitiating the mother. We are offending her and causing her great pain. We might, therefore, re-examine some of the negative mother phenomena that appear in dreams and fantasies to see if the negative mother, the castrating mother, isn't attempting (with her belittlement of us, the insecurity and inadequacy she makes us feel) to relieve herself of the concrete demand, the materialistic burden we have placed upon her. What we experience as 'castration' of our powers in the world might be that which can move us into a more psychic view of matter. In a curious sense, the effect of the mother's negativity may be to return us to soul. By destroying the superficial surface of that earth upon which we stand, our literal projections into and upon earth (achieving more and more, establishing ever more solidly—our materialism), perhaps she is giving opportunity for a deeper ground, a psychic earth beneath the level of appearance and in touch with the Muses.

Now let us look at the children trapped in the earth in another way. Let us see them as the children 'in us' who wish to remain as children buried within the mother, within the concrete. There seem several ways we could do this.

One way would be to identify with the child and then to project a goodness, an all-embracing lovingness upon mother nature. Then because mother nature is all good, I-the-child am also good, innocent, helpless, without shadow and indeed without much body. I feel no shame—there *is* no such thing as shame—I am innocent. This state might resemble Hesiod's state before the Muses and before he was called upon through his experience of awkwardness, separation, and shamefulness to worship the mother. Insofar as a child feels no shame, he/she is also unable to worship.

Another possibility would be for the child to reinforce his or her state as child by seeing the mother as all bad. This would be the nihilist perspective and just the converse of seeing the mother as all good. It too would deny the mother's possibilities as psychic, complex, worked earth. This child, scarred by the world's harshness, remains forever the unloved child, but nevertheless still the child.

Another way in which to remain a child buried in the earth is by dividing experience of the mother in two: good mother/bad mother, good breast/bad breast. Although the opposing aspects of the mother are expressed, they have been separated and literalized, seen as nothing-but good here and bad there. And because they are literalized, they tend to be projected into the world as realities out there. This substantiation and projection give them extraordinary power so that I-as-child find myself overwhelmed. Unable to cope in a world so loaded with goods and bads, rights and wrongs, the child languishes ineffectually. Because the world is so important, the child becomes unable; the world's ambiguity becomes the child's ambivalence.

Most often, however, our child abandons his pattern at this

point and moves into the neighboring one of hero. Then the darker attributes of the mother appear as the dragon to be heroically slain. Child-turned-hero now girds himself and charges off to do (what turns out to be a rather continuous) battle with the dark mother now become monster.

When heroically opposed, the mother turns monster. The religious sense of her is lost. Her nature as non-being, absence, lack is no longer part of her mystery—that which makes her greater than our own narrow senses of life and achievement. Rather, she becomes a contrary force to rule over and conquer. Her earth becomes replaced by our egocentricity, our illusions of competence, self-sufficiency, ego capability. We deny the earth's divinity and exchange her ground with its complexities, its twisted chthonic creatures, and shame for our goal-directed, clean, ever self-bettering fantasies of goodness, health, and achievement.

The nature of the hero is to take literally the mother's negativity. Her nature as lack, non-being, becomes a real something, an enemy to be fought; her femininity and passivity become a succubus to that heroic life fixed upon progressive achievement. The result is a heroic over-achievement and over-production, which must be countered by equally literal prophecies of doom and destruction. The mother as lack, as negative, returns in prophecies of ultimate, literal catastrophe. Because the earth is taken so literally, its negative reappears in the forebodings of an equally literal destruction.

The hero's mother-complex is characterized by his struggles to be up and out and above her. And because of his heroic labors to free himself from her, it is he who is most surely bound to her. Better service to the earth mother might be to assist her movement down to the deepest regions of her depths. For the mother's depths are the underworld. Gaia's original realm included both the upper realm of growth, nurturance, and life and the underworld realm of death, limitation, and ending.

We must describe a bit of this underworld to appreciate how astounding it is that this realm was once part of our mother's earth.

The underworld is a pneumatic, airy realm. The beings there, called shades (skiai) or images (eidola), are insubstantial like the wind.[10] It is a realm in which objects cannot be grasped naturally, i.e., taken literally, but only felt in their emotional essence. Ulysses, for example, in his visit to the underworld, yearns for his

mother, but when he attempts physically to embrace her finds she
is only an immaterial shade. It is a realm of the non-concrete, the
intangible.

And yet an essence of personality is preserved. Cerberus is said
to strip away the flesh of persons who enter, leaving only their
skeletal structures, those essential forms on which the flesh of each
life has been modeled. This sense of essence is also shown by the
repetitions that some shades enact (Ixion on his wheel, Sisyphus
and his stone, Tantalos and his everlasting hunger and thirst).
These repetitions may be viewed symbolically as the characteristic
pattern of each individual personality.

The underworld is colorless.[11] Even the shade of black does not
appear except in the upperworld sacrifices to it;[12] hence we emphasize the experience of blackness in connection with Gaia, for
black is our upperworld experience of the underworld, our way
into it. But once there, one is, so to speak, deeper than one's emotion. One is beneath the depression, the black mood, by having
gone down through it to the point where it no longer is. When we
no longer cling to the light, blackness loses its darkness.

In the underworld one is among the essences, the invisible
aspects of the upperworld. The word *Hades* means the invisible or
the "invisibility-giving."[13] It is that realm deep beneath the concrete world and yet somehow within it, in the same way that the
seed is within the full-grown plant and yet is its inherent limitation, its structure, its telos.

But there came to be a split between the upperworld aspect of
Gaia's earth and its underworld aspect. Her upper realm became
Ge-Demeter while the under realm became Ge-chthonia and
relegated to Persephone.[14] The upperworld became a Demeter
realm of concrete, daily life, devoid of the spiritual values, the
sense of essence and the dark (and beneath the dark) carried by her
underworld daughter, Persephone. For reunion with this underworld daughter, Demeter suffers inconsolably. And we, without a
religious sense that includes and connects us with the earth's
depths and essential insubstantiality, suffer as well.

In our efforts to establish a solid 'real' world and to make the
mother carry our concreteness, we have lost an aspect of her
grounding—a grounding that has not so much to do with growth
in any of the more concrete senses of upperworld development.
More psychologically fertile is our invisible mother in the under-

world: the Persephone who rules over the soul in its essential, limiting, and immaterial patterns; and that original mother of all—Gaia—she who is Earth and yet, without contradiction, that deeper ground of support beneath the earth's physical appearance, the non-being beneath and within being. Our fruitfulness—our fecundity, our sense of what 'matters'—has its roots in our very unsureness, in our sense of lack.

1. Augustine, *Confessions*, 12, 3.

2. Ibid., 12, 7.

3. It is interesting to note in this regard that Theophrastus describes green, the color of nature, as "composed of both the solid and the void. . . ." Cf. G. M. Stratton, "Theophrastus on the Senses," in *Theophrastus* (Amsterdam: E. J. Bonset, 1964), p. 135.

4. Told by Torlino, trans. Washington Matthews, 1894.

5. L. R. Farnell, *The Cults of the Greek States*, vol. 3 (Oxford: Clarendon Press, 1907), p. 2. This sacrifice of the black animal (in Gaia's case, the ewe) was typical for Hades and other Gods in their chthonic, underworld forms. So we must realize that Earth Gaia is as much at home with the dead and the underworld as she is with the seemingly more life-sustaining activities of agriculture and vegetation. For her there is no real contradiction between life and death, daily world and underworld.

6. Farnell, p. 15; cf. also W. Fowler, *The Religious Experience of the Roman People* (London: Macmillan, 1933), p. 121.

7. Farnell, p. 2.

8. From J. Hillman, *The Dream and the Underworld* (New York: Harper & Row, 1979), p. 77.

9. As pointed out by R. Romanyshyn, Conference for Archetypal Psychology, University of Dallas, 1977.

10. F. Cumont, *After Life in Roman Paganism* (New York: Dover Press, 1922), p. 166.

11. C. Kerényi, *The Gods of the Greeks* (London: Thames & Hudson, 1961), p. 247.

12. Cumont, p. 166.

13. Kerényi, p. 230. Cf. also H. J. Rose, *A Handbook of Greek Mythology* (London: Methuen, 1965), p. 78, where he suggests that the name *Hades* may also be derived phonetically from "the Unseen."

14. Whereas Demeter, like Gaia, appeared imagistically as the ripened or ripening corn, she never appeared in connection with the seed in the ground or with underworld figures as did Gaia; cf. Fowler, p. 121. This absence of Demeter's underworld aspect makes an underworld Persephone "necessary."

The Bad Mother
An Archetypal Approach
James Hillman

I.

WHAT FOLLOWS TAKES up again a well-worn theme: mother and child. The mother archetype, the child archetype—depth psychology founds itself, and founders, usually, on these rocks. That life and depth psychology begin with mother and child says that we are in the rhetoric of beginnings, of foundational questions. That the theme is so wellworn says it has become unconscious again, laid smoothly in a groove, a grave. We do believe we know pretty much about it; read the psychological literature from Freud and Jung through Wickes, Neumann, and Fordham to Berry: we all do believe we know what's the matter with mother.[1]

If we can find a new twist in this basic theme and if, in particular, the bad mother can be revisioned, then we may be revisioning the basis of psychology and even life itself. Finding that twist is what we are all about. We start with four assumptions.

First, there is an archetypal *experience* of bad mothering that badly needs to be understood as a psychological phenomenon in itself apart from norms about good and bad behaviors or acts of mothering. Even so-called good mothers experience themselves to be bad mothers.

Second, we can analyze this archetypal experience of bad mothering apart from empirical cases, phenomenological protocols, and sociological surveys. There are also archetypal structures in experience, and these may be scrutinized by an *archetypal method*.

Third, we assume there is an inner child, an archetypal child *imago,* affecting each of us and so affecting every mother and mothering act.

Fourth, we can distinguish between the archetypal contents of mother and child as contents in a tandem and the archetypal structure of the *tandem as such.* Mother and child are not only each what they are, but they are as they are because they are locked together in a tandem which affects the nature of each.

We therefore need to look more closely at tandems if we want to understand any contents, such as mother and child, that are embraced by a tandem. These tandems—and I use this term for dyads, pairs, couplings, polarities, syzygies—whatever their contents, are affected by patterns of oppositional thinking such as dark/light, alive/dead, order/disorder, true/false, presence/absence, vertical/horizontal. Philosophers have elaborated further basic antinomies and have dissected oppositions into different sorts (contradictions, contraries, complementaries, etc.). Structuralists have located various kinds of oppositions in social practices and linguistic structures.

The mother–child bond, simply because the bond is a tandem, is subject to the influence of oppositional thinking, or "oppositionalism." This fact complicates whatever we say about our subject. Even if oppositionalism is not the only way in which reflective thinking proceeds (one can reflect in images, with feeling moods and by playing), nonetheless oppositionalism does affect the individual patterns and thinking about these patterns in any particular dual relationship between male and female, superior and inferior, young and old, and within the mother–child relation as well. Later we shall attempt to free the tandem from oppositionalism, but for now it is important to recognize that human behavior is subject to the transhuman structuring of archetypal configurations such as the tandem.

By placing the tandem relation in the foreground, I have reversed the usual approach of psychology which generally considers the mother-and-child prior to every other rubric. I want to show, however, that it submits to a category beyond itself. This 'meta'-physical approach to an empirical problem—the experience of bad mothering—is a contribution of the archetypal viewpoint to psychology.

A meta- or superordinate factor appears also in the biological approach to the mother–child bond. It too imagines the tandem, called "bonding," to be the determinant factor to which both infant and mother submit. Baby songbirds stretch their necks upward and open their mouths to reveal the yellow signaling spot which, anticipated by the mother's inborn release mechanism, releases the food in her beak into their throats. Lactation in the human mother coterminous with the search for the nipple in the neonate is a further example of superordinate bonding—a coordinated pattern, delicate, complex, and of enormous durability, holding mother and child together in a single pattern of behavior which, following Jung, we may call an archetypal image of instinct.

Lactation is not a simple mechanism; mother and child are not unvaryingly in the service of that function. They each bring with them their individual idiosyncrasies. In the relation, as contents they affect the relation—of course. And psychology usually locates the psychic structures that modify bonding within the mother per se or the child per se and their idiosyncratic interaction. I wish to add a dimension by locating the psychic structures which influence bonding within the phenomenology of tandemness. My point is that at any moment of mothering, or of 'childing,' archetypal twoness is at work, necessitating a rich phenomenology of ambivalence, bipolarity, tension which constellates oppositions of various kinds. Here, *in the tandem*, and not merely in the mother or in the child or in their superordinate instinctual interaction, the major psychological problems of motherhood and childhood begin.

The oppositionalism influencing tandems may take several forms. I shall single out one for our consideration: the child is imagined to be good, the mother bad.

II.

Unmediated reactions of mothering are complicated by mediated ideas, or fantasies, about good and bad mothering. These fantasies differ from culture to culture, but whatever their content, fantasies remain constant norms in governing the conscious role-model of mothering. These directive and corrective fantasies working within the mother as guilt have a major impact upon her child. A

child grows within the shadow of the mother's guilt about mothering as much as within the mothering itself. The guilt regarding
'how to be a good mother' usually derives from the archetypal
Mother, imagined either as a woman's actual parent, her grandmother, or as normative ideals held up by the culture.

Owing to that either/or accreting to the tandem, tensions in the
mother–child relation tend to be placed on one side or the other;
either the mother is wrong or bad, or the child. Even if the symptoms—such as crass autistic or motoric disorders—appear only in
the child, the actual human mother will assume guilt for them on
herself because of the archetypal ideal. The actual mother thus
feels herself to be a bad mother.

The tandem itself reinforces this appraisal. If she is bad, then the
child is good, offering a magical way of cure by belief in its
goodness. This is of course a vicious circle, since the more good
the child, the more bad she must be. The archetypal fantasies of
the Divine Child, good, strong, and laughing, create an inevitable
sense of herself as negative.

The archetypal tandem influences psychological theory, too.
Many schools have been caught in the same pattern of thinking as
mothers. The blame for the human condition is still laid upon the
mother, her breasts, her habits during pregnancy, her caring during the first nine months, and so on. If the mother is held to be responsible, it of course implies that those who think this way have
occupied the position of good children. Perhaps one reason why
the theory of blaming the mother is so popular and perduring is
that it allows us psychologists the privileges of innocent childhood.
The altar at which much of psychology worships is the shrine of
the Negative Mother.

So, psychology finds a mother 'never enough.' If she is always
present, then she is said to foster weakness, pampering, and
dependency. If she nurtures with warmth and closeness, then she is
called smothering and devouring. If she desires much for her child,
fantasying its future from the reserves of her spirit, then she is
dominating its life with her goals. If she is farseeing, intuitive, and
detached, then her prophetic wisdom is that of a witch. If she
delights in life and the pleasures of the senses, then she is either
seducing her children or depriving them of their lives by living so
voluptuously her own. Whatever the style of motherhood, it seems
cursed. What can a woman do? Whatever pattern of existence is

hers, it becomes victim of the negative cast thrown by the archetypal factor of the negative mother. All the while she strives to enact the model of the good mother—being present to her child, nurturing, protective and attentive, sagacious in judgment, carrier of tradition, sensitive to the values of small signs in the bonding—inwardly she is haunted by feelings of inferiority and failure, or she defends brightly against her badness.

III.

We are now ready to examine this experience of badness from three perspectives and to offer solutions to it. We may say first that the bad mother reflects the *negativity in the archetype* itself. The phenomenology of the negative mother has been laid out in detail by the Jungian school. Jung's work on the symbols of the maternal libido (1912) presents the mytho-pathological background of the negative mother and deliverance from her through battle. In 1938 Jung composed his insights into a major essay on the mother archetype. (See elsewhere in this volume.) This has been followed by Neumann's mammoth studies of the symbolic manifestations of the negative mother and their psychological effects. Their work was supplemented by Esther Harding, and by H. G. Baynes and John Layard in England, and by the London school of Jungians, especially in regard to infants and in relation with ideas of the mother–child relation absorbed from Melanie Klein, Anna Freud, Bowlby, Winnicott, Fairbairn, and Guntrip.

In this plentiful literature, two dominant ideas stand out. First, the human mother is not the same as the archetypal imago, although she is influenced by it and is perceived by her child by means of it. Second, the archetypal imago has a dual nature, two sides, positive and negative. Symbols and metaphors express this dual nature. The ocean that is source of life also represents drowning in its dissolution. Earth both supports us and buries us. Containers (jars, boxes, houses, institutions, cities) protect and also suffocate. The transforming vessel (alembic, oven, bathtub) serves both the need for temenos and for narcissism. Those animals said by Jungian literature to represent the mother archetype show the dual nature most clearly. The hugging, shaggy, loving bear is also a clawing, crushing monster; the patient cow with its cud and udder is also stupid, self-satisfied passivity; the nurturing wolf is at the same time ravenous greed.

Jungian psychology considers the dual nature of the mothering experience to be archetypally given and therefore irreducible. You cannot have a good side without the other. The moment mothering is constellated, both sides are constellated. Nor is it possible to convert the negative into the positive. The empirical mother's experience of her badness is an intimation of the archetypal reality. Kali lurks eternal, so there will always be urges to destroy the child. Child abuse, even an instinctual delight in it, is given with the archetypal nature of mothering. The full experience of mothering calls forth the urge to destroy the child, to feed off its life, to turn it to stone, drive it mad, abuse or abandon it. This side of mothering appears in the stepmother of fairytales.

Jungian therapy aims at making this shadow, this bad side, of mothering apparent to the individual patient who is trying to deal with her feelings of hatred toward her child and her inferiority in regard to her only-positive ideal of mothering. By recognizing her fealty to a principle in which a dual nature is always present, she is less likely to fall into a vicious oppositionalism with her child (leading her to enact the cruel, negative mother in sinister punishments or passionate outbursts).

By shifting badness away from personal identification and locating it in the negative side of the archetypal itself, a Jungian therapy can alleviate torturing self-recriminations. Badness may not be condoned by this shift, but at least the patient can see its archetypal necessity. For archetypes are the superhuman carriers of collective consciousness, and so they help the ordinary human carry the superhuman burdens of life. (Archetypes all have a mothering function.) As a universal human event, bad mothering belongs to any mother and to the Great Mother. This archetypal perspective leaves a mother less alone with her badness and, so, less driven to repress it and then forced to act it out.

Second, the bad mother, as an archetypal phenomenon, *entails the good mother* with it. If the first perspective located the experience in the negative side of the archetype, the second perspective re-locates the negative itself in the conjunction of opposites within the archetype. Instead of opposing negative and positive

sides and oscillating between feelings and behaviors called good
and bad, we here understand duality to mean that there is always
good within the experience of bad.[2]

Here I turn to the Buddhist idea of *sunyata*, metaphysical emptiness or void. Against this background, the feelings of inferiority
and failure—that one has nothing to give, that one is devoid of
values, of love, beauty, and the positive virtues of mothering—
take on a deeper significance. The guilt toward a fully positive image of mothering is emptied out, voided. This voids the
positive image itself so that a mother can see through its idealized
delusional aspect. This emptying out allows the guilt to shift. No
longer is she bad because she failed the idealized image of the good
mother. Now the idealized image itself, taken from her mother,
her grandmother, her culture, shows its own vacuity. The idols
fall; the supportive saints fade. She awakens to see that good images have bad effects. And, as the good reveals its badness, so the
deepest experience of her badness (her inferiority and failure)
proves to be where her goodness actually resides.

I mean here that the sense of badness about her mothering is
actually where she is close to that ground of being, the Great
Mother, whose support appears exactly when she feels let down
by all normative fantasies, all goodness gone. Where nothing sustains her, she finds Nothing sustaining her. The *sunyata* as a metaphysical void becomes manifest in the absence of her personal will
to do good and be right. In this emptied condition she can be nur-
tured by moments of not being anything other than she is.
Unmediated reactions affirm the bonding.

Guilt too then finds a new location. Guilt—which forces literal
actions of directing and correcting this or that instance of badness—becomes the inner voice of *sunyata:* "I fail because failure
is inherent in all my willed actions." They can succeed only when
they come from the ground of emptiness, when I am grounded in
an undefined, emptied-out mothering, beyond all positivistic, tech-
nical notions of it. I abandon the search for *how* to be a mother.
Sustaining itself sustains; in my absence everything in the world
beyond me and outside of me carries my child. My very negativity is the *via negativa,* not only of mothering, but mothering too
becomes a soul-making, a psychotherapeutic activity. Mothering
becomes deliteralized from only the actual care of an empirical

child to a path of deepening awareness into the sustaining goodness of the world.

Psychotherapy leads into *sunyata* by letting go—not only of
idealized norms but letting the bottom fall out of therapy itself. Its
corrective, constructive search fails. An utterly non-supportive
therapy. One falls into the lap of the bottomless ground. For only
the abandoned child can be found by the mothering wolf. It is the
abandoned child who discovers *sunyata*.

Before proceeding with my main concern, the third perspective—the bad mother in tandem with the good child—we need to
recall that child, like mother, carries symbols on its back. Child,
too, is an archetypal metaphor, indicating both an actual young
person and an aura of impersonal symbolic connotations. And, as
mother can be abstracted into positive and negative, so child can
be divided into the oppositions of childlikeness and childishness.
Oppositionalism haunts the discourse of psychology.

According to the studies of Freud, Jung, Kerényi, Neumann,
Brown, Campbell, and Bachelard on its archetypal phenomenology, we find these qualities and expectations in regard to the child.
Futurity: the release of hopeful fantasies forward in time or
beyond time; redemption of the present by rebirth into the future.
"And a little child shall lead them." *Growth:* maturation as a
developmental process with increase in size and differentiation of
function. *Simplicity:* the child as primitive, natural energy, an intense seed of being. *Origins:* the small beginnings of any process,
whether as beginning in a world beyond with innate knowledge of
that beyond or in this world as the freshly novel and unpredict-
able. *Amorality:* the dedication to pleasure and polymorphous
perversity, close to the animal and insane, and thus in need of bap-
tism, initiation, and education. *Dependency:* weakness, exposure,
abandonment—feelings which churn out the omnipotence wishes
of heroics, magics, and make-believe of many sorts. *Joy:* a delight
where self and world are fused, "the archetype of simple happiness" (Bachelard).

We are obliged to remember these archetypal implications of the
child in discussions having to do with actual children and
childhood. We must be careful in what we say about actual children until we can see them, and we cannot see them very clearly
until we can see the notions that govern our modes of seeing, the

archetypal projections that arise whenever the child imago is constellated. The history of ideas in depth psychology about children
shows that they, like primitives, animals, artists, inventors, and the
insane, have been forced to carry every sort of discarded and
fantastic piece of the psyche that the 'normal,' 'civilized' adult has
excluded from his or her domain. By definition children are the archetypal minority group, whether idolized as perfect from the
beginning or denigrated as bits of untamed nature needing a
discipline to convert them to adulthood. We cannot see them for
what they are until we can see what we consider 'childish'—i.e.,
undeveloped, infantile, minor, dependent, immature—in our own
minds, until we have taken back from children and childhood a
variety of potentialities we as adults have disowned and placed in
the special world called childhood.

Let us list these attitudes and behaviors of that special realm
that supposedly belongs to children: spontaneity, creativity, play-
fulness, fantasy, wonder, curiosity; emotional vivacity in place of
conceptual abstractions; need for sensual pleasure and immediate
gratification of desires; thought processes that overcome natural
laws, or what often is called magical thinking and a magical sense
of concrete objects and actions; history as legend rather than as
factual past time; shyness and shame in place of mannered de-
corum; an eidetic imagination leading to easy familiarity with
make-believe voices, faces, figures, and with animals and ghosts;
rhetorical joy—hyperbole, sing-song, alliteration, rhyme, onomat-
opoeic and apotropaic noises, story-sequences, and the love of
story. All this in one word: imagination.[3]

These traits, this imagination, belong to the child archetype and
not literally to actual childhood and children. The literal identification of an actual person with an archetypal personification is
the psychological error wherever we find it: femininity literalized
and expected only from women, senex literalized only in old
people, the dark shadow literalized only in dark ethnic groups.

Now, to the third perspective: the bad mother *arises within the
tandem* with the good child. We shall no longer be speaking of the
bad mother as a self-contained figure as was the case in the first
two perspectives—both based on ideas of negativity within the
single archetype. Now we look at the tandem that is superordinate
to either mother or child and affects both. The tandem has this effect: qualities that the actual child receives from the archetypal

projection impoverish the mother of those same qualities. Stated most extremely: what the child has and is, the mother has and is not.

Although coming into motherhood may expand a woman's existence in the directions found in the mother models of myth, culture, and family tradition, still, owing to the tandem with the child, motherhood also restricts her to a more singularly adult existence. She is expected to move away from imaginative attitudes and spontaneous behaviors that belong to the child archetype. She feels herself no longer allowed to be immature, undeveloped, infantile. The mother becomes separated from her actual child owing to her separation from childishness. She may resent her actual child for retaining qualities of which she is now deprived simply by her position in the tandem. Or, she may attempt to recover these potentials by clinging to her actual child. Basic structures of bad mothering—rejecting her child, resenting her child, dependency on her child, and fostering dependency from it— derive from the empirical mother's relation within the tandem.

Moreover, she loses the ability to imagine a way out. Having lost the child, she has lost imagination which would be the very way back to it. For instance, the radical change in sexual feelings after childbirth (a complaint of husbands about their wives) can be partly understood as an archetypal change, a shift in myth and a shift into a new tandem. The woman has lost her child by giving birth to it. She has become separated from her polymorphous perversity, curiosity, and spontaneity—the playful ground of sexual joy.

IV.

We are now able to draw conclusions for defining the 'bad mother.' So far I have restricted these observations to the experience of badness, without defining the content of badness beyond the acceptable conventions—such as, the bad mother rejects, demands, pampers, is guilty, self-centered, and the like.

I have refrained from defining the content of badness because a psychotherapeutic approach has to be assiduously careful about norms. Once we define just what a good mother is—nourishing soul, sheltering body, fostering spirit—we have only added to the

guilt from which a mother already suffers for failing to live up to
these norms. Norms in therapy become counter-productive to
what they aim to establish. Norms are addressed to the will; they
give it standards, and they lodge themselves in the superego. Yet it
is precisely because the patient cannot redress her plight by will
that she comes to therapy. The woman already has the best of
norms which only make her feel worse. For psychotherapy, the
issue is rather an analysis bit by bit of the experience of badness—when does she feel bad, what is her 'lack,' what are her
'bad' acts, how are they performed, in what mood, to which child,
how does she self-correct, on whom does she model herself? And,
who tells her she is 'bad': what voice? We look at the experience,
its lived phenomenology, its images and voices, its mythical patterns.

The phenomenology of the experience of badness suggests images of its archetypal nature. But again we must be cautious—and
now for a theoretical reason. If the mother is a figure *in a tandem*,
then we cannot adduce negative mother experiences only from the
usual mythical stereotypes: Kali in India, Yamamba in Japan, Baba
Yaga of Slavic or Frau Hölle of Germanic folktales. Plenty of child
abuse here. These loathsome ladies bake children in the oven or
eat them alive. They poison them, put them to endless sleep, turn
them to stone. They do indeed frighten the daylight out of them.
Plenty of grounds here for anorexia, dyslexia, school refusal,
mutism, and eruptive violence.

Yet we may not draw our definition of bad mothering from these
ladies, because these terrible devouring petrifying negative mothers
are self-enclosed prototypes. They stand alone. They are not
figures in tandem. So, just here, an archetypal approach differs
from that of Neumann, Harding, and other Jungian therapists.
They tend to read human behaviors in terms of single archetypal
figures, reading myths with monotheistic consciousness. For them
it is usual for an archetypal figure to be one and alone: The Great
Mother, The Negative Mother, The Divine Child, The Puer Aeternus, and the like.

Myths, however, take place in a polycentric field of persons.
Myths are not merely tales about these persons but tales about
their structural complications, their psychological relations. Mythical figures are in plots, as Aristotle calls myths; and human actions reflect not only the individual figures but also the *pathos*, the

sufferings occasioned by the plots. In other words, to study how human nature performs its *imitatio* of the Gods, we cannot confine our scrutiny to mythical figures; rather, we have to analyze, take apart, the interlacings of their plots.

Roasting a child in the fire—that content—is not in itself bad mothering. When Demeter roasts Demophoön it is one thing, and should the witch roast Hansel it is another. Good and bad depend here on the plot, the structure of the mythos.

Not that structure is prior to figure, prior to content—just to go on for a moment with archetypal theory. Rather, figure and structure are coterminous.[4] The very term *mother* takes its significance partly from the tandem with *child*. Mother is subject to a psychologic of relationship which is primordial as the figures of the relationship. Mother isn't just mother: she is always in a plot with the child—now called "neurotic interaction"—and this determines bad mothering as much as does the singular figure of the Terrible Mother. A psychological structure is a relation, a *con*figuration or plot.

This primordial complication of the tandem, this plot, is one way I understand Jung's emphasis—and Heraclitus's before him —on opposites. Figures and symbolic contents do not alone determine what happens in soul. They are subject to the tensions of relations which, when thought about abstractly, become "opposites." I prefer to derive opposites from tension, from plots, logical thinking from dramatic thinking, rather than the other way around. I really do hold that psychological relations precede philosophical conceptions in time and rank. Moreover, where the tension of opposites requires a language of overcoming, transcending, and conjoining, tandems and plots affirm relationships from the outset. We are always conjoined.

That we are always conjoined suggests a ground for the phenomenon of conscience. *Conscientia* is the Latin word for the Greek *syneidesis*, which, like "conscience," means 'with-knowing,' 'together-knowing,' an *eidos* shared in relation. The guilty feelings of bad mothering point therefore beyond their location in the subjective ego or superego; guilt derives complexly from our tandems, not simply from our persons. 'Bad' feelings express the *agon* and *pathos* of the plots we are subjected to, those tensions of relations within and between the souls of human beings as well as between the human soul and the world soul. The tandem always forces us

to consider an Other. Guilt reminds of this other, and conscience is
the precondition of any individualism; the sense of badness is the
price one pays for that neglect of the tandem-reality of human affairs which we nowadays call Ego.

Whether we call these complex tensions *plots* or more particularly *tandems*, they organize events in definite patterns, sub-
jecting human events to the priority of the image. An image is the
intensification, the epitome, of the plot, because in it, structure
and content, relations and figure, myths and persons commingle.

This view has immediate therapeutic bearing. An actual mother,
seeking to rectify her sense of badness by modeling her dilemmas
with her child on any single symbolic mother figure, cannot be sufficiently relieved. Not she, but the model, is inadequate; her problems derive from the relation itself. She is right in saying that her
problem appears only when she is with her child. She is suffering
from the psycho-logic of the tandem which sets up badness as part
of its plot.

Thus, bad mothering takes its definition from the oppositional
effect of tandem logic. The dramatic tension with her child reduces
to separation from it and loss of it. As child is equivalent with imagination, her language becomes unimaginative, imperative,
abstract. As the child is growth, she becomes static and empty,
unable to react with spontaneous novelty. As the child is timeless,
eternal, she becomes time-bound, scheduled, hurried. Her morality becomes one-sidedly responsible and disciplinarian. Her sense
of future and hope is displaced on her actual child; thereby post-
partum depression may become a chronic undertone. As her actual
child carries her feelings of vulnerability, she may over-attend to it
to the neglect of herself, with consequent resentments. Also, her
thought processes become restricted to adult forms of reason so
that the ghost voices and faces, animals, the scenes of the eidetic
imagination become estranged and feel like pathological delusions
and hallucinations. And her language loses its emotion and incan-
tational power; she explains and argues.

Therapy derives from this description. And the first step of
therapy is to view the tandem itself imaginatively, from the pole of
the child rather than from the adult pole of oppositionalism,
moralism, and hopelessness which immediately turns tandems into
problems: good breasts and bad, positive and negative mothers,
left and right brains. To experience a tandem as an opposition is

already to be separated from the child. From the childish pole, the
tandem is a seesaw, upsidaisy/downsidaisy, the eternal game of
pushme/pullyou, offering endlessly pleasurable incentives.

So therapy with an actual mother is rapprochement with her archetypal child of imagination—through re-kindling fantasies, re-
finding pleasures, releasing spontaneity, re-awakening dreams. It
brings back the voices, the animals, and ghosts. Things take on
names and faces. Therapy turns again to children's story, beginning with the patient's childish stories now going on, their shame
and silliness, and the story of the patient's childhood. The mother's
therapy begins in the tandem with her lost child of imagination,
and her therapist is her actual child. Though mothers know this
and practice it playing with their children, even a momentary experience of bad mothering can set a woman back into the adult
posture, its separation and loss. The movement in and out of imagination itself becomes a tandem.

V.

I have offered three perspectives to the bad mother experience and
suggestions for therapies implied by those perspectives. First, we
saw the experience against the archetypal figure of the Terrible
Mother. This perspective considers the experience of bad mothering to be given with the destructiveness of the archetype and
therapy to be awareness of this archetypal necessity. Second, we
saw the experience against the emptiness of *sunyata*. This perspective considers the depths of one's failure to be the deeper ground of
mothering. Therapy abandons supportive norms of good mothering in order to stay with the bad experience in which the deeper
good resides. Third, we placed the experience within the
mother–child tandem, claiming that bad mothering results from
the impersonal logic of oppositions that accrete to tandems.
Therapy is the recovery of the separated and lost child, the
recovery of imagination.

A word in conclusion about my archetypal method. Rather than
presenting a basic anthropology of the mother–child relation in
terms of positivistic research or positive philosophical values regarding goodness and badness, I have attempted to enter that relation by staying with bad mothering as a primary datum. As an

ever-recurring, ubiquitous, and emotionally important experience,
it is assumed to be archetypally necessary. Positivistic approaches,
as they harden their research results and strengthen their evidence
into norms, make it harder for the individual woman to find
necessity in her deviation from the norms that become more and
more normative, leaving her less and less room for her increasing
sense of badness. Positive research results tend to force practi-
tioners to see 'bad experiences' normatively, as pathologies, literally bad, to be done away with. The positivity in the method
demonstrated here is therefore therapeutic rather than normative.
Bad mothering finds place as an archetypal necessity in all three
models. The method intends to result in an archetypal understanding of bad mothering which, like all deep pathologizings
given with human life, belongs to the fundamental psycho-logic of
human relations that are set within the cosmoi of archetypal patterns, patterns that force both necessity and compassion upon
us.

A Coda on Education

Education of children, as Jung said in his lecture on this subject in
1924, begins with the education of parents and teachers, and it
begins in lower education, not higher; in retarded, not advanced;
with lowering our sights and their standards, down on all fours,
with fingerpaints, with drums, with bare feet; with slower days,
not longer hours; with tasting, not testing; with nonsense instead
of jargon. Too much Rousseau and the sentimental education?
Too much Rudolf Steiner, Free Schools, and hippy-happy kinder-
gartens? Don't get me wrong: I am talking about *us*, adults—not
what children should be doing.

If nonsense rhymes and fingerpaints seem too childish, look at
what we do now with the child—pouting resentments and junk
food, passive-aggressive sport violence in front of the television,
buckets of popcorn, buckets of beer. The adult household with its
apple toys, home as a radio shack, a fantasy island or closet of col-
lectibles, its gamerooms, its gimmicks and gadgets for building
bodies as the imagination cheapens and blow-dries. Mary Kay and
supermarket paperbacks. Meanwhile, growth, originality, and initiative, those primordial forces of the child, are consumed by that

hyperactive omnipotence fantasy called "development"—whether personal, mystical, or financial, the project of oneself in space.

Nonsense rhymes and fingerpaints mean that I am not recommending the replacement of trashy child*ish*ness with higher forms of child*like*ness, such as Bachelard's reveries toward childhood, Jung's divine child, Blake's innocence and delight, the Platonic child of wonder in the cosmos. A therapeutic education must beware of the ennobling course. Therapy is an education that works with equivalences, not conversions. It's a business of straight barter. We can't turn sinners into saints or dimes into dollars without short-changing the shadow. So, in exchange for fingering the pushbuttons, fingerpainting; instead of television's nonsense language-game, Lewis Carroll; instead of Kodachrome, Easter eggs. The primitive barter of stupidity for simplicity— beginning where it's at.

Education, however, cannot stop where it starts. By definition, education must 'lead out.' It leads simple fantasy into imagination. The fingers themselves and the tongue, twisting along in its syllabic chant, want more than repetitions. The fingers and tongue find novelty by sophisticating fantasy into imagination.

We have come to that old conundrum, the difference between fantasy and imagination, and we can locate this difference now in the mother–child tandem. Fantasy is the activity of the motherless child; imagination is mothered fantasy: it is purposive, responsive, thoughtful. It mothers because it is child-focused—focused on the imagination. The key word of imagining is therefore not free but fecund, and its aim therefore is not exploring only but furthering, and the elation of fantasy is contained by consistency and carefulness. Child and Mother, both. To be led out to this Both, we must make another psychological equivalence, exchanging the actual child as focus of education for focus upon imagination of the adult. We take childhood back in. This recovery of childhood from children gives them their chance at poise, dignity, and sobriety, their desire for reason and for duty, as we return to the closet of our childishness. This move is primary because the fantasy of educating imagination has all been put on actual children— what they should do for us. They have had to do what we as adults are not allowed (except in asylums and in that national asylum, California, the golden state of childhood), leaving us with an undernourished, deprived, mute, abused, and violent childishness, fit for Pacman, *Star Wars*, and Halloween—amusements of the adulterated mind.

This adulterated mind is the ultimate bad mother. By forcing childhood on children, we become bad mothers each of us. Each of us a 'mothuh'—and this whenever, wherever, we take recourse in a non-imaginative response, in language, in administrative policy, in human relations, in shopping.

Daily encounters with the city of the world are imaginative moments to the child's mind. To the imagination, events are stories, people are figures, things and words are images. To the imagination, the world itself is a mother, a great mother. We are nestled in its language, held by its institutions, nourished by its things. The great mother-complex that so afflicts our Western psyche—its dread and fascination with matter, its denial of dependency that we call Free Will, the oral craving of consumer economics as cure for depression—cannot be resolved by personal therapy alone. Personal therapy as cure, and that notion of cure itself, is an apotropaic defense against her—banning the city from the consulting room. The little mother of the consulting room can take care of us for a while, but outside lies the great wide world, and only the great wide world can cure us—not *of* the Great Mother, but by means of her, for the word *cure* comes from *cura,* 'care.' Like cures like because likes care for each other. The city itself mothers us once we recover the child of imagination.

We need but remember that the city, the *metro-polis*, means at root a streaming, flowing, thronging Mother. We are her children, and she can nourish our imaginations if we nourish hers. So, the *magna mater* is not the *magna culpa*. The actual blame for it all— the whole caboodle of downtown and the budget, of illiteracy and rearmament, ethical decay and ecological poison, the cause of the withering of our institutions: government, schools, family, trades and services, publishing and language—is the neglect of the city. And the city can be restored as mother by the child of imagination. Without that child we cannot imagine further our civilization or further our civilization's imagination, so that civilization itself becomes a bad mother, offering no ground or drink to the soul. Of course the individual mother feels a failure. The experience of bad mothering is given with the civilization itself when the education of imagination is neglected.

So, to end where we began, with a classical, cyclical close appropriate to the rhetorical mode of the archetype we are invoking, the interminable mother: yes, restore the child to the mother, the imagination to the institutions of education, including psychotherapy—more, to the whole city of the world—and indeed you revision the foundations of daily life.

1. Cf. P. Berry, "What's the Matter with Mother," in *Echo's Subtle Body* (Dallas: Spring Publications, 1982).

2. Ibid.

3. Cf. C. Downing, "To Keep Us Imagining: The Child," in *The Goddess* (New York: Crossroads, 1981); also my "Abandoning the Child," in *Loose Ends* (Spring Publications, 1975).

4. Cf. Berry, "An Approach to the Dream," in *Echo,* pp. 63–64.

Mother and Child
Some Teachings of Desire
Mary Watkins

4/26/86

MY DAUGHTER RACHEL is now a few months past her first birthday. Her rage at me is like a clear, shrill siren. Before her first birthday she showed some bouts of anger at being constrained: being diapered, being in her highchair. But as soon as she could begin to walk a few months ago, her anger concentrated into tantrums that can sustain themselves over several minutes. Interestingly, the cause seems always to be the same. She will have a direction she wants to go in, something she is interested in, involved with, when often for reasons of practicality—my wanting to get somewhere else or do some other thing—I interrupt her. With her whole being she protests. She lies on the ground—mud puddles or kitchen floor do not deter—begins to scream and kick her feet. If I try to pick her up, her body straightens like a board and loosens my grasp. I relinquish her to the floor, along with whatever or wherever I was hoping we might do or head. I sit beside her, until I can hold her, and together we can go on her way or mine. (Though to be truthful, the tantrum leaves her more malleable, more susceptible at the end of it to *my* control, *my* direction.)

My initial shock at such a hearty display of rage at me from this dear one has turned to respect, a kind of awe. Her spontaneous rage, autonomous of her control, seems bent on teaching me not to interrupt her, to allow her to follow her desire. When I am a good student, I find out something about how to hang on with my own teeth to desire, how to throw my body into the fray and to deliver whatever passion is needed to sustain a simple continuity from the arising of desire to its satisfaction.

As Rachel stiffens with protest and the options for my response flash before my mind's eye, her behavior occasions my seeing into a developmental history of desire—how such moments of a young child's desire in the presence of another can go awry. This other person we call "mother," not because it is mothers who are most prone to error, but because, first, in our culture we have left most of the work of child rearing to mothers, a novel and recent cultural arrangement that appears not to be that conducive of sanity in either child or mother. Second, our developmental theory takes analogies between adult thought/behavior and fantasies about early mother–child relations as a causal, factual relation. Thus all pathology is returned to the mother. That the culture has by and large abandoned children—to a single person—and neglected children, segregated and abused children is not seen in such theorizing. One focuses instead on the primary person left to do most of the hard work of caring for the child—the mother. So by "mother" let us read instead "the harboring one" or the "mothering one"—be that father, older brother, daycare teacher, mother, grandmother, siblings, neighbors—the one who is attempting to mother the child at any particular time.

All mothering ones want and need the child at times to want to do what the mothering one wants to do—to provide no resistance to following his/her own desire. Some mothering ones need this more than others because they require a sense of being and remaining in control. At the root of this is the person's incapacity to be nourished by the child's being present to his own desire. The mother can achieve the child's conformity to her desire through overt displays of power and control and/or subtly—or not so subtly—withdrawing her attention and affection from the child until the child mirrors her intentions. Sometimes the mother's affection is not restored just by the child's conformity of behavior, but the child must also yield up a convincing affect, pretending to self and other that his desire is happily the same as mother's. The overt subjugation of the child's desire can be rationalized by extolling the virtues of manners, orderliness, of not spoiling children, of "good" behavior (i.e., conforming, non-independent).

If the adult is alienated from her own desire, if she has accepted

the fulfilling of social form as a substitute, then she will be unable
to value a child's spontaneous desire. Fulfilling desire can make
you late, get you dirty, make you too noisy or too quiet. It can add
to or diminish your activity level. You might not fit in.

The mothering one can also achieve her ends by systematically
misreading the child's desire, causing it to look like her own. At the
beach, she says, "You don't really want to go back into the water
now. It is so cold." The truthful words are not uttered: "I'm bored.
I'd prefer to go, but it looks like you'd have fun swimming some
more."

All of these efforts at conforming the child's desire to the adult's
continuously interrupt the child's spontaneous activity. Once this
is done enough, the child becomes disoriented, out of touch with
desire. Protective of her own vulnerability in this situation, desire
shrinks back, becomes private, silent. To defend herself from
frustration, negation, feelings of helplessness, impotence, and
rage, the child learns to become unaware of her own desires. The
child may simply be confused and not know what she wants, or
she may actually adopt the adult's desires as her own, to ensure her
more wholehearted acceptance and valuing by the narcissistic
adult. Docility and malleability again come to the fore, once again
evoking the "love" and affirmation of the mothering one.

It is interesting and understandable that young children recognize that such a child is little fun, is a "goody goody." He rarely in-
itiates play as he is so used to taking his cues from others. His
range of affect and behavior is narrow, his actions tentative,
waiting for approval. He is too concerned with pleasing to be open
to abandon or the joy of self-assertion. His eyes often cast down
when he is spoken to. They lack sparkle. Once he is older, however, his receptivity may be as valued by friends as it once was by
family. He is a "natural" listener, speaks more cautiously, opens up
rather tentatively. He allows for others to a fault.

The young child whose desire has been continuously interrupted
becomes unable to be alongside that place in herself from which
desire arises. The child becomes depressed—which really means
cut off from that source of energy within that unfolds as one enter-
tains desire and acts to fulfill it. The child may experience an un-
ending boredom. Though she is surrounded by a vastly interesting
world, the impulse to partake has been silenced. When there is not
a total silence, when some desire breaks through, there is often

then a negative judgment, internalized from the adult, that retires the desire with self-condemnation and attempts to bring one's feeling and behavior more in line with the expected and the approved.

To many an adult the advent of desires in the young child announces a profound sense of threat. The relative docility and malleability of the very small baby which confirm the adult and often allow the baby to be adapted to the adult's way of being—all this recedes. In its place is often a most vocal little person who is thoroughly open to giving his heart, body, and soul to execute his desires over against the parents'. Indeed, the toddler is quite willing to engage in activities that are defined as forbidden simply to exercise his desire over against the other's.

One mother ignores all of her child's protests and cries. Her doctor explains that all young children will cry and carry on a certain number of hours each day anyway. A father takes his children to the beach and tethers them to a stake in the ground so that they will be "safe," i.e., so that he will not have to be a part of their wild, excited exploratory behavior. He will read the Sunday papers. Another parent describes her two-and-a-half-year-old as spoiled for not wanting to play alone while she cleans house and talks on the phone. Another one hits her three- and four-year-old boys at a shopping mall, screaming that they are acting like animals because they want to use the stores as a playground, to run and jump. These examples may sound extreme, but only because their ignoring, tethering, and deprecation of desire are so fully and literally enacted. We have a thousand ways of more subtly discouraging and tethering desire. That all of these situations arise from the simple clash of desires is easy to see. That each child receives a message about her desires from the interaction is also clear.

These early clashes of desire and their negotiation are amongst the earliest struggles between parent and child and are repeated daily over years. They weave a great deal of the psychic atmosphere between child and parent, and more gradually they weave as well the internal psychic atmosphere with respect to desire that the child carries forth from childhood into adulthood.

5/23/86

It is 5 A.M. I haven't been able to sleep. My mind has tossed up its worries to me in a most relentless fashion. I realized during the day that depression had set in, that I had lost a sense of wanting to do anything. Rachel, now one and a half, has been sick for three weeks. Each day she demanded that I hold her, not leave her for even a moment. At the time it was simply necessary. When she would try to venture out, her energy could not sustain her. She would fall on the floor, calling for rescue and the safety of my arms.

I disengaged from the rest of my world, cancelled patients, friends, writing, walks. I sat with her watching *Dumbo* and *The Black Stallion*, over and over. I lay with her while she took her fitful naps. Sang to her, read to her—all in my arms.

As of yesterday she is finally well. For both of us this is a difficult transition. She has forgotten about most of her toys. She clings to me defensively, uncertain of what to do otherwise—though clearly she is in possession of her energy. After wandering with me aimlessly about the house in the morning, she happened upon the right idea. She motioned wildly to the radio, as though remembering the magic of dance. Music on, she began to move by herself, or, rather, the music could now move her. She began to giggle and dance wildly, arms askew in abandon. We both laughed, so happy to see desire enliven her again.

Then, later, I heard a banging on the back door. I found her legs badgering the door, trying to get it to yield to her desire to go outside. I went to get her sweater, obviously too frustrating a move. She started screaming and then weeping furiously to be cut off from the one thing she knew would work for her, the one thing she could do at the moment that would allow her a state of simple joy.

I understand and respect her desperation. It can be extremely hard to move back into a relationship with one's desire after being estranged from it. A nexus of situations—her illness, adoption difficulties with our next child, a patient in real trouble, concern over a friend's illness—has drawn me away from myself. Yesterday some open time emerged for the first time in a month, and I did not know what I wanted to do. I lay down. I walked. I did errands, returned phone calls, worried. All this was filling the space but provided no movement, joy, release, or connectedness. I felt rather dead inside, except for a small ache deep in.

Today I get out of bed at 5 A.M. to give myself the chance of coming upon myself before Rachel wakes up, before patients arrive, before my son's birthday party. Some hope arises as I lie on the couch and feel the day begin to unfurl itself. The mist over the pond is very thick. Birdsong pierces the dullness of the fog, as does a pink dogwood tree down the hill, its blossoms bringing the light first to this grey early morning. I know I will be very tired tonight, but tiredness is not what worries me anymore.

As I lie here quietly on the couch, the house begins to disturb me. Its formerly sheltering holding transmutes into a sense of its isolating me from the early morning. It keeps the moist air and chill from my skin. It muffles the sounds of birds calling to one another. I suddenly feel as though if I could arise and walk in the dawn that I might evade not only the barrier of the house's walls but a wall within myself as well, something separating me off. I go to find my shoes.

11/10/86

It looks as though Rachel and I are getting nowhere today. She refuses to let me put on her diaper, then her dress, next her shoes. Anxious to get the dressing over with, I wrestle her to the ground, practically sitting on her as I force her tiny shoes over her lopsided socks and protesting toes. A thin sweat appears all over me this cold November morning. I have things I must do today. Errands to run, food to get. I want to feel like I'm getting something accomplished today, that I'm in control of the chaos about me. Rachel has other ideas.

I must have served the wrong cereal. The dog is eating it up off the floor. The pots and pans are pulled out of the cupboards, along with the spoons and spatulas. This percussion band of Rachel's is making it impossible to walk in our small kitchen. With a wild laugh Rachel scampers away as I approach her sternly with a hairbrush. Now she is hiding under the armchair. She has turned into a fierce lion, threatening to scratch the lady with the brush. I wish I had clipped her nails yesterday when I thought about it. I continue my approach, she darts under the table, and the lamp on top rocks but does not crash to the floor. She's got me now. It's either war or surrender.

I drop down on the floor, and with this surrender finally it all seems funny to me. I start to laugh, and she follows suit. I drop the brush. She invites me to be a mother lion and to come into the den of the coffee table with her. She happily knocks off her shoes with the edge of the couch, no small feat for someone still under two. She practices being fierce with her paws, but no longer toward me. The mother lion is proud of this cub's ferociousness. Then she surprises me. She picks up the hairbrush and indicates that I, the mommy lion, should comb her mane. As I do, my young cub nuzzles her cheek on my neck and allows me to restore her curly confused mane to a more velvety state.

Do you think it is silly that I feel joy as I comb her mane, joy at this small moment when her desire and mine effortlessly crisscross? In love it is imaged as mutual orgasm; in friendship it is effortless conversation that satisfies both partners as it winds into hours. Here, mother and child, each of our desires has transformed the other's; both are satisfied in this new moment, not anticipated before, where playing in the image together, desire and satisfaction are one.

As if this were not enough, she lifts her paw for the tattered sneaker. The ageless koan echoes in the living room, jubilant at being affirmed once more: FIRST BEING, THEN DOING. FIRST BEING, THEN DOING.

1/6/87

Rachel, almost two, has heartily begun to need me to help her unfold her images. She beckons me over to her tiny red chairs, points to where I should sit and where I should place her younger sister so that a train full of bunnies can take off for Boston. This train must make a great many stops in our living room, for Ani and I have been so beckoned at least ten times a day for the past several weeks. If I am busy doing something else—like feeding the dog—when Rachel is compiling her train and so ask her to wait, she appears momentarily undone, grows more insistent, and may even cry from frustration. She has had a spontaneous image which she cannot yet fulfill and thereby enjoy by herself. She needs my presence, my physical and wholehearted participation, to help her bring her desire into reality. Once on the train we are all happy and content.

The repetitive nature of some make-believe can at times strain the mother's patience. Over and over again she is asked to interrupt whatever flow of activity she is involved in to help the child birth the imaginal scene. But when she does, the young child appears to gain confidence in the unfolding of a spontaneous image. She learns the pathway from image and desire to creation and delight. It is a path that once well-worn will require less mediation by the outer mother and more by the inner.

D. W. Winnicott describes an "ordinary mother"—let us read "ordinary mothering"—who is devoted to her baby.[1] This mother does not feel that *she* must constantly enliven her baby. She knows that there is a spark of life in her child which will develop, which is not due to her, which is not under her control, which she need not even "understand." She need only provide a right atmosphere for it to flourish. The child does not depend on the mother for growth and development; he is a "going concern" of his own. This ordinary mother allows her infant "to lie back and float," to be removed from the necessity of being a reactor to mother's liveliness, mother's initiative and desires. It is in this lying back and floating that the baby can experience his own liveliness, his own desire to live.

The ordinary mother learns through her love and devotion the geography of the baby's desire. She knows that now he wants to suck, and now to snuggle, now to be comforted. This calibration of her being to his being does not mean that disillusionment is foreign to the baby, but rather that it is meted out in small enough doses so as not to destroy the baby's perception of the world as a place where one can get one's needs met in an atmosphere of caring.

The mother's attitude toward the baby's feelings communicates strongly how she feels about the free arising of her child in his differentness from her and, at times, his neediness over against her own needs and desires. The ordinary devoted mother Winnicott describes intuitively sorts through and selectively responds to the baby's feelings. Rage is not rejected as destructive to baby or mother; sadness is not coaxed away by tickling and bobbing on knees. The mother trusts in a natural recovery from sadness and anger. She does not worry that the child will lie submerged, helpless in a feeling unless she intervenes.

This "ordinary mothering" evaporates when rage, sadness, and depression are feared. Indeed, in therapy when the therapist shies away from the intense transference feelings, she promulgates again a critical lack of ordinary mothering. Like the parent, she infers by not focusing on the feeling that what arises spontaneously cannot be trusted, perhaps not survived, that it has little value and should be subordinated to the supposedly rational. Why is it so important as parent, as therapist, not to give these messages? Feeling, as imagining, is a way of coming upon the self. When one reaches the depth of a feeling, one has come upon something which can never be taken away. It is as though there is some truth there, some real piece of oneself. And though it may not be the whole truth or a completed reality, it is substantial. When one holds oneself or is held back by another from the depth of a feeling, diffuse anxiety often substitutes for direct feeling, preventing the communion with oneself. Confusion, fear, lack of connectedness, vagueness, fogginess ensue. The therapist again and again asks "what are you feeling?" not because it takes up the hour, but because she wishes to keep open a space in which feelings can emerge, develop, recede.

Winnicott points out that this movement into, through, and out of a feeling is so treasured as a complete experience that "sometimes you will find your child being naughty to us to feel guilty and cry, and then feel forgiven, so eager is he to recapture what he has experienced in true recovery from sadness."[2] Though the child may try to replicate this spontaneous recovery from a feeling, what is so special and deeply faith-building is the very spontaneity and autonomy of these recoveries. This we all have experienced through our own depressions, losses, and rages.

The mother's attunement to her child allows his own initiative to emerge and be fostered. Winnicott describes following a baby play with a spoon, attentive to the beginning, middle, and end of the baby's game, not terminating it for lack of time before the child feels finished and his impulse has moved on. A ten-month-old baby boy sits on his mother's knee while she talks with Dr. Winnicott. Winnicott places a spoon halfway between himself and the mother and watches the baby reach for it and then be overcome with reserve.

It is as if he thought, "I had better think this thing out: I wonder what feelings mother will have on this subject. I had better hold back until I know." So he will turn away from the spoon as if nothing were further from his thoughts. In a few moments, however, he will return to his interest in it, and he will very tentatively put a finger on the spoon. He may perhaps grasp it, and look at mother to see what he can get from her eyes. . . .

He gradually finds from his mother's eyes that this new thing he is doing is not disapproved of, and so he catches hold of the spoon more firmly and begins to make it on his own. He is still very tense, however, because he is not certain what will happen if he does with this thing what he wants to do so badly. He does not even know for sure what it is he wants to do.

We guess that in the course of a little while he will discover what he wants to do with it, because his mouth begins to get excited. He is still very quiet and thoughtful, but saliva begins to flow from his mouth. His tongue looks sloppy. His mouth begins to want the spoon. His gums begin to want to enjoy biting on it. It is not very long before he has put it in his mouth. Then he has feelings about it in the ordinary aggressive way that belongs to lions and tigers, and babies, when they get hold of something good. He makes as if to eat it.

We can now say that the baby has taken this thing and made it his own. He has lost all the stillness that belongs to concentration, and wondering, and doubt. Instead he is confident and very much enriched by the new acquisition. I would say that in imagination he has eaten it. Just as the food goes in and is digested and becomes part of him, so this which has been made his own in an imaginative way is now part of himself and can be used. How will it be used? . . . He will put it to mother's mouth to feed her, and he will want her to play at eating it. Mind you, he does not want her to bite it really, and he would be rather frightened if she actually let it go into her mouth. It's a game; it is an exercise of the imagination. He is playing and he invites play. What else will he do? He will feed me, and he may want me to play at eating it too. He may make a gesture towards the mouth of someone on the other side of the room. Let everybody share this good thing. He has had it; why shouldn't everyone have it? He has something he can be generous with. Now he puts it inside his mother's blouse where her breast is, and then rediscovers it and takes it out again. Now he shoves it under the blotting pad and enjoys the game of losing and finding it again, or he notices a bowl on the table and starts scooping imaginary food out of the bowl, imaginatively eating his broth. . . .

Now the baby has dropped the spoon. I suppose his interest began to get transferred onto something else. I will pick it up and he can take it again. Yes, he seems to want it, and he takes up the game again, using the spoon as before, as an extra bit of himself. Oh, he's dropped it again! Evidently it was not quite by chance that he dropped it. Perhaps he likes the sound of the spoon as it falls on the floor. We will see. I will hand it to him again. Now he just takes it and drops it quite deliberately; dropping it is what he wants to do. Once again I give it back to him, and he practically throws it away. He is now reaching out for other interests, the spoon is finished with; we have come to the end of the show.

We have watched the baby develop an interest in something, and make it part of himself, and we have watched him use it, and then finish with it. . . .

What have we learned watching this little baby boy?

For one thing we have witnessed a completed experience. Because of the controlled circumstances there could be a beginning, a middle, and an end to what happened; there was a total happening. *This is good for the baby.* When you are in a hurry, or are harassed, you cannot allow for *total happenings,* and your baby is poorer. . . .

Do you see how the middle of things can be enjoyed (or if bad, tolerated) only if there is a strong sense of start and finish?

By allowing your baby time for total experiences, and by taking part in them, you gradually lay a foundation for the child's ability eventually to enjoy all sorts of experiences without jumpiness.[3]

Though the object of our desire shifts from spoons to other things as our life goes on, is not the process of patiently allowing our movement toward, through, and away from the object of our desire the same? And is not this allowing for a total happening, a completed experience, at one and the same time an advent into being, into presence? In this being present the distinction between inner and outer erodes, because the desire that arises inwardly allows us to cross over into the world of things and others with a smooth motion.

It looks like a simple sequence of moments, the boy with the spoon. But what if no spoon had been provided? What if the mother had given an inhibiting look in her eyes? What if the adults imposed their own ideas about what to do with the spoon before the baby himself could arrive at his desire? What if mother had so wanted to talk with Dr. Winnicott that her desire to have the baby disappear silenced or agitated him? What if the mother disliked the baby's drooling and sloppy tongue or was embarrassed by them and interrupted the play? What if she or Dr. Winnicott ignored the boy's effort to share his spoon games or failed somehow to see and appreciate and join in with his joyful owning and sharing of the spoon? What if mother's timidity disallowed the losing and recovering of the spoon down her dress? What if the adults wanted him to stop this game and so prematurely interpreted dropping the spoon as an ending rather than a new version of recovery? Or what if they wanted him to persist in this engrossing game even when he was finished and was ready for the next happening?

No one of these miscalibrations is disastrous, thank goodness, for there are so many ways to go wrong. But what should be clear is how there will arise in any dyad certain repetitive patterns of allowing and disallowing desire, their characteristics dependent on who the partners are. These patterns become internalized over time, shaping the way each of us moves in relation to the free arising of desires, images, and feelings.

When I go to my writing desk, I too place before myself a spoon of some sort, something of possible interest, or there is something there placed by someone else. Perhaps my being does not gravitate toward it but tosses up some other thing. Do I condemn myself for not having the "right" interest this sunny morning? Do I call myself names: self-absorbed, lazy, lacking in discipline? Do I threaten that nothing will come of anything because I am not attending to what I am supposed to? Or do I wait patiently and with interest to what has caught my eye and energy? Do I have faith that this attending and respecting will lay the ground for some good happening to occur, particularly for the possibility of being present to my own aliveness and allowing work or whatever to flow from this place?

Perhaps the spoon placed before me, after some hesitation, does become interesting. Do I have a critical commentary going on about not getting into it fast enough or immersing myself too fast and too thoroughly in my relation with it? Can I allow for the mess of mouthing it? Am I critical of myself when I drop it for a moment—to answer the phone, get a cup of tea—as though thinking that I have finished with it prematurely? Or do I allow for dropping and rejoining, forgetting and rediscovering to happen several times this morning if it needs to? And when I share it with myself—and then with others—how do I and they greet it: ignoring it, overtaking it, making it the ego's or theirs? Or does this bridge to others and back to myself happen smoothly, not alienating me from what I have been doing and yet still making the time richer through the sharing? In a short morning of work, are there not just as many ways to go wrong internally as there were for the little boy playing with the spoon in the presence of his mother and Dr. Winnicott?

For those who gain adulthood without having had ample freedom to experience the arising, the doing, and the fulfillment of desire, this "ordinary mothering" must be learned—be it through psychotherapy, meditation, walking, dancing, abiding with oneself. Otherwise, the "mothering" which one has suffered—be it interruptive, distorting, maligning, or negating of desire—will be repeated internally.

Winnicott describes a psychic atmosphere provided by some actual mothers, but his description also fits an internal atmosphere necessary for the lifting of depression. This "ordinary mothering" allows extraordinary, seemingly simple moments to arise and fall away—the kinds of moments that allow us to be glad we are alive, even amidst adversity.

3/15/88

Today the snow finally melted from under the swings. The surface of ice on the lake by our house gave way to the swaying water beneath it. Finally the whole lake is moving again. My daughters and I search foolheartedly for crocus and tulips, but we do not mind being foolish. They will shoot their stems into this cold air soon. It might well have been today.

I pass by my husband's rosebushes. One is ungainly, tall, withered, and brown. I think perhaps it should have been cut back in the fall or pruned now. It is taller than all the rest, but it no longer looks promising. I remember at our last home that I, like my husband now, could not believe that I was supposed to cut back the rose stems so close to the ground. It seemed safest to let them keep climbing and growing in their own way. But after five years of such little faith on my part, they bloomed weakly and were not happy, but tangled, thin, bony.

Some Buddhists say not to encourage virtue directly but to cut back on error—impatience, anger, greed, wrong speech, holding grudges. Then when space is freed from these negatives, spaciousness is possible and virtue has room.

It has been hard to keep pruning my life. One shoot takes off in one direction, off-balancing the rest, casting much of my life in its shadow. I try to prune but do not do it radically enough, anxious that no new growth will appear and that I will be left with bare stems that will themselves slowly wither. I give up one piece of work and cling to the next. Each day I must learn more about pruning, and I must tend to it. Or else I get lost once again in the overgrowth, the tangle, the struggle of one against another, each choking the other out. I grow tall, strained, unable to support what blossoms there are with my thin stems. I fall over. The blossoms thin, their faces next to the moist earth, rotting, decomposing, until there is no sight of them. Shoots, then small, unfurling leaves appear.

For me what needs to be pruned again and again is what I do out of fear of emptiness, rather than out of desire for the thing in itself. Sometimes I see this fear when I realize I have not let a friendship change from a former intensity to what it needs to be now—more space and distance surrounding it. Sometimes I start a work project with good intention and desire, but once into it realize my judgment was wrong and that staying invested in it serves only my self-image. Sometimes I glimpse this fear when I reach for a glass of wine rather than sit in the stillness. Over and over again I feel it intensely when I have left things unpruned for a while, and a sense of spaciousness seems strangled out by a welter of activity that is not thriving, activity that can only draw on my ego's energy because it is no longer connected to the heart's desire.

In times that go well, it seems my pruning shears are in my back pocket. Every now and then I clip the faded blossoms as I stroll. I cut back stems and branches with sureness and with faith that this enforced rest will give a possibility for new beginning. I don't let the garden get too crowded, but neither do I enforce a spindliness.

Now with little people to love and struggle with, pruning seems too pale a word almost. I reach down and yank out whole plants, throwing them over my shoulder. Not just spindly roses but flowering trees, lush bamboos. All this to make some room. The pre-motherhood tending of bonsai—requiring just the right light, moisture, solitude—has given way utterly to the muck and mud of community gardening. Rachel and Ani are throwing in seeds more quickly that I can dig holes. Things are coming up everywhere, and I have no idea what they are. It is a different way to garden. Rachel picks the strawberries by pulling the plant from the ground. Ani waters the bricks by stepping on the flowers.

There is a male fantasy in developmental psychology that goes this way: the mother's maternal preoccupation makes her baby's desires her own. This taking on of the child's agenda is imagined as an effortless process, aided by maternal hormones and female proclivities toward caretaking. It is not always like this in our culture. Though raised to be nurturant, women are also taught to retreat to their own subjectivities, to take care of themselves in solitude, to identify themselves as individuals, and to experience their own desire over against the other's.

Coming to be with one's first child bulldozes these notions, as psychic survival requires finding joy in the other's satisfaction, in finding a way to surrender what cannot be accomplished during the child's early years, in wiping away large portions of one's identity that require separateness and solitude to maintain. None of this comes "naturally," easily. Each refigures our understanding of desire away from a personalistic, individualistic, privatistic model: my desire, internal, private; my desire to have and to do; my desire experienced as need, as right. In its stead, the arising of desire comes to be experienced as grace, its satisfaction seeming not as important as its advent. The mother's psychic reality becomes gradually restructured so that satisfying the child's desire is often experienced as sweeter than satisfying any of her own. Thus the child's desire has really become the mother's in this baffling psychic melange called mother and child. But this has not occurred naturally, suddenly, always, or for all time.

3/20/88

It is 5 P.M. The sink is filled with dirty dishes, the laundry baskets with muddy overalls and damp socks the size of my thumbs. There are five phone calls to return, one of them urgent. On the dining table lies three days of unopened mail. Yesterday I had an idea that I've not yet written down and which now seems dull and dim. I've been up since 5 A.M., and Rachel hasn't taken a nap. Dinner is unbought and unmade. My mind occasionally stumbles on the fact that I have to give a lecture tomorrow and the further fact that momentarily I can't remember what it is on, much less what it is about, sends shortlived streaks of panic through my limbs.

My daughter Ani, now just two, is placing a mother, father, and baby on the back of a black stallion. She indicates that they are us—her mother, father, and she—and wants me to sit on the floor beside her to enjoy this scene.

I take my pruning shears from my back pocket and snip these undone things away. I fall to the floor and pick up the baby who has fallen from the horse.

We are simply here together now. A spaciousness begins to wrap around us. The horse wants to run across the table, and so we help by holding our friends, ourselves, on his back. We are laughing, having such a great ride, being jostled, falling off every once in a while with a wild whoot.

---

1. D. W. Winnicott, *The Child, the Family, and the Outside World* (Middlesex, England: Penguin, 1964), p. 27.

2. Ibid., p. 67.

3. Ibid., pp. 75–78.

The Step-Mother in Fairytales
Bereavement and the Feminine Shadow
Jackie Schectman

I.

EVEN THE MOST casual familiarity with fairytales would deny child abuse as a new phenomenon. Mistreated children have been with us always. Cinderella suffers terribly at home; Hansel and Gretel are abandoned by their parents in the woods; Snow White barely escapes with her life. When we read these tales, just as when we hear of child abuse on the evening news, our connection to the child is visceral, immediate. While it's easy enough to identify with abused children, one finds it considerably more difficult to identify with the abuser.

We want to think of abusive parents as strangers, as people far removed from our circle of intimacy. We put them in special categories of being: they are sick, inhuman; they are possessed, members of satanic cults; they are criminals or to be pitied, having surely been abused themselves. They are not like us.

Fairytales, while speaking to the collective aspects of child abuse, offer a collective means of denying the abuser in ourselves. In these tales we seldom see *real* parents visiting mayhem on their children, but rather their shadowy counterparts. Cannibalistic giants and ogres stand in for bad fathers, and, more frequently, the Wicked Step-Mother (a redundant term) carries the role of the dark, envious, vengeful mother. Natural parents, the tales seem to say, would not treat their children so.

There is evidence that the Brothers Grimm changed "Mother" to

"Step-Mother" in most of their child abuse tales by killing off the good mother to make way for the bad.[1] Their wish was to make the stories more palatable for children, but they did more than protect the image of Good Motherhood. The altered tales are in keeping with stories of dark Step-Mothers told around the world, and there would seem to be some purpose in this good/bad mother split. Bruno Bettelheim sees the Mother/Step-Mother dichotomy as a device which allows for a gradual integration of the dark forces of the unconscious.[2] Until a child (of whatever age) has enough ego strength to carry his/her own ambivalence, he can love the good and nurturing mother while thinking of the scolding and withholding one as a hateful stranger. The tales allow him to take the negative mother into consciousness as a developing tolerance for her permits. Moreover, the image of the Step-Mother as an intruder in the happy home is in keeping with the felt experience of mothers pushed to the limits of their patience. When the dark one enters, we hear:

> *"I don't know what happened; it was some wild banshee screaming at those kids!"*

> *"I was beside myself. I wanted to kill them!"*

> *"I thought, 'That's not my child.'"*

Children surely recognize Step-Mother's presence in the home. A woman recalls rifling through her parents' papers as a child, certain she'd discover her "true" origins. The hateful woman that she knew as Mom could not *really* be her relative by blood!

Whether we view the Step-Mother from the perspective of the parent or the child, it seems necessary to keep her at a distance, to hold her at psychological arms length until we feel strong enough to take her on or to take her in. The fairytales in which she plays a major role offer us the opportunity to do both. If we read the stories from her perspective, we can build an empathic connection to her and allow her a place at the table. When we begin to understand the meaning and purpose she serves in the tales and in our lives, we need not be so fearful of her witch-like power. She will have been invited into consciousness.

The *Step-* in Step-Mother derives from the Middle English "steif," meaning bereaved, and was originally applied to orphaned children. A Step-Mother, then, is the mother of a bereaved child. Loss and grief are her milieu, her raison d'être. In fairytales she arrives in the midst of grieving; she is summoned by loss. Often, through her dark machinations, evil ultimately turns against itself; grief is resolved. She is the force which moves the bereaved child beyond tears and into action on his own behalf. In meeting his/her own needs, the fairytale child defeats the Step-Mother, writes her out of the script. Bereavement gone, there is no longer a place for her; she meets her terrible end.

There is no question, however, that she has served to move the story toward its conclusion. As the agent of change, she has a major role in the psychology of bereavement. If she is not recognized, if she remains in her dark, unconscious position of power, she has much to do with the bereavement of psyche. Her scolding presence mocks the one who dares to dream, to imagine.

A clarifying note may be in order here. When I refer to The Good Mother, to The Step-Mother, to Bereavement, I refer to impersonal, archetypal forces, psychological states of being which belong to no one and to everyone. The Good Mother/Step-Mother in imagination may wear the clothing of personal experience, may affect us in profoundly personal ways, but she is not to be confused with the personal mother (nor with the step-mother—this is not about those brave souls who try to raise other people's children). When bereavement enters the psychological field, it is not my bereavement, nor yours; it simply *is*, and we are all caught in its power. Thus, when Step-Mother makes her entrance, she may do so through projection—I (you) see you (me) as abusive and neglectful; through introjection—I (we) hear her as a scolding, belittling inner voice; or through acting out—caught in her, I (we) act in abusive, unconscionable ways. (The human psyche and human relationships being what they are, it is likely that all of this is going on at once.) However she manifests herself, the Step-Mother lives in imagination, interiorly and in the air between us, to be recognized and suffered through and acknowledged as the dark power that she is.

My personal interest in the archetypal Step-Mother began around a double bereavement: I was losing my youth, and I was about to lose my younger child. In the summer of my fortieth year I moved into a small Boston apartment with my seventeen-year-old daughter. She would be leaving for college in the fall, but in the interim we were together, in very close quarters. While all was well on the surface—I'd planned for this moment for many years—my dreams were full of rage, full of envy of my daughter's beauty and vitality. In one such dream she'd taken all of my bright, silky clothes and put them on a high closet shelf, just out of my reach; I was left standing in faded polyester, screaming at my mirror. My analyst observed: "Now you know about Snow White's Mother," and so I did. I felt immediate empathy for the terrible Step-Mother/Queen and considerable comfort in recognizing her archetypal presence in my dreams. The work with her allowed me to let go of my daughter (slowly) while maintaining a dialogue with my truth-telling mirror.

On a professional level, I've come to know the Step-Mother all too well in my countertransferential response to the children in my practice. To the degree that these children have experienced abuse, neglect, and abandonment in their lives, they demand the presence of the Step-Mother in the playroom. She is an irreducible part of their bereavement, and they will work and work at my limits until they have brought her into the hour. The great challenge of the work then is in allowing her entrée and in keeping her in consciousness long enough to address her presence, often with the telling and retelling of her tales. She must not, of course, be allowed to act on her murderous desires. This challenge needs to be met with each new hour, but treated with due respect the Step-Mother can serve as she does in fairytales: she is a force against which the child can test his growing strength and maturity.

My approach here reflects my work with families and young children in that I tend to read fairytales as bridges between inner and outer life, as stories of the struggle to find and define one's place in the world. For the child, that world begins with family, and fairytales can serve as metaphors for family life. Thus, my reading of a tale is likely to focus, first, on its implications for relationship, for family: what has happened to kill off the Good Mother, to bring the Step-Mother to the tale? Where is this family's loss? How does the Step-Mother's presence affect those around her; what is this family like seen through her eyes? This treatment does not preclude reading the tale as subjective inner drama but adds the dimension of outer life I've found so very helpful in my work.

To re-view Step-Mother tales from the Step-Mother's perspective is to turn the stories upside down, shaking loose new meaning as we go. "Snow White," then, is not just a romance of a young girl's growing into womanhood but a story of a woman's aging and decline, of her bitter battle against nature. It speaks to the rage, envy, and frustration that separate us from our youth. "Hansel and Gretel," more than a survivor's tale, serves as a primer on "bad" mothering, on the seductions and betrayals necessary in raising a child. In our depletion, at those times when we have nothing left to give, we may try to lose our children in the woods and hope with all our hearts they'll not return; or, perhaps to defend against this cold, rejecting one, we keep our children close within our milk-and-cookies house, only to devour them in time.

In the less familiar tale below, the Witch/Step-Mother/Queen, brought to the story by the Good Queen's death, carries grief in all its awful power to transform.[3] She is the essence of bereavement. Her dark enchantments serve to reunite her shattered family, and she remains, transformed herself into a loathsome toad, to croak the kingdom into consciousness.

I came to know this Northumbrian tale, "The Laidly Worm of Spindleston Heugh," in Winona Hubrecht's Boston seminar on fairytales. I'd volunteered to amplify the image of the story's evil queen and began, then, to understand the "Step-Mother" in the context of bereavement. She is a product of and a mover in the process of initiatory grief. John Bowlby's schema of the stages of bereavement proved most helpful in reading the tale, but the tale itself is a treasure of rich imagery.[4] The evil Queen of Bamborough Keep is a Step-Mother one can love to hate.

II.

Webster's defines *bereavement* as a state of deprivation; as loss, particularly through death, of a friend or relative.[5] To bereave is to strip, to divest, to dispossess. To be bereft is to be left sad and alone. The term implies destitution, affliction; mourning *and* melancholia. It speaks to grief, objectively and subjectively experienced.

Step-Mother tales, I believe, are essentially stories of loss and of working through loss. They speak to the experience of deprivation and to the dark aspects of the psyche constellated by deep grief:

rage, envy, despair, the desire for revenge and for the undoing of harsh reality. In the literature of bereavement, we find a context for understanding the Dark Mother and a structure for reading Step-Mother tales as unfolding stories of grief.

In his definitive work on *Attachment and Loss*, Bowlby outlines four phases of mourning:

> 1. Numbing that may be interrupted by outbursts of extremely intense distress and/or anger
> 2. Yearning and searching for the lost figure; anger
> 3. Disorganization and despair
> 4. Reorganization and reorientation to reality

In the language of fairytales, we might recite the phases of bereavement thus: (1) The kingdom suffers a terrible loss, and the Good Queen dies of grief. (2) A new Queen is sought and found, but she is evil, an enchantress. (3) The Witch/Step-Mother/Queen, caught up in envy and in rage, wreaks havoc in the kingdom and upon her family. (4) Her step-children rally round, perform heroic deeds, and depotentiate the Witch. The Kingdom is returned to new levels of harmony.

We may now look at Bowlby's anatomy of loss and at "The Laidly Worm" as the tale unfolds.

Phase 1—Numbing and the Death of the Good Mother

In the initial phase of grief the bereaved one is stunned, unable to take in the reality of loss. Life goes on as usual but as if in a dream. Consciousness is lost, shut away, protecting itself. In the language of fairytales, this numbing is the death of the Good Queen, of the (Natural) Mother. The bereaved one is so far removed from her own feelings that she is available to no one, dead to the world.

Elizabeth Kubler-Ross speaks to the confusion of young children in the face of this initial, emotionally muffled response.[6] She quotes a young woman recalling the death of her brother some years before:

> I had gone to school, and when I came home for lunch, I asked my mother how Danny was. She told me he was fine. Fine to me meant he would get well. I asked her when he would be

coming home, and she told me that Danny had died.... I
started telling myself that I shouldn't cry—that I was a big girl
and big girls don't cry.

The day of the funeral [the boy's body had been viewed at
home] my mother sent me to a neighbor's house. When I came
home Danny was gone. No one had told me he would be gone
when I came back.... It seemed as if everyone was having a
party, and I couldn't figure out why everyone seemed so happy
when my baby brother was dead.

In losing consciousness in the face of terrible reality, a woman
can seem removed from all around her. Poet Stan Rice, having lost
his child to leukemia, struggles against the loss of his wife to her
grief:

Singing Death

Illustrious one, in whom death is the vagrom wound
& who wanders on the wet grass singing, sing no more
to me. I have heard your voice plenty
          & I hunger for health.
Yes, though it is beautiful & it seduces, Hush. Come no more
glaze eyed to my arms asking for pity then push me aside
when the urge strikes to start singing. Transfixed
& then unhinged, crazed with the wish to die
          & then with the fear
the wish might be granted. I have heard your
song and it shall not drag me down with it
          on the wet grasses.[7]

Literal death is far from the only cause for bereavement. Other
feelings of loss may well "kill" the loving and nurturing mother.
Each passage through a life stage (hers, her child's), each initiation
with its implications of death-and-rebirth may evoke mother's
mourning and her sense of her own death.

"The Laidly Worm" speaks eloquently to the grief of a mother
witnessing her son's journey into manhood. The story begins with
a happy quaternity: King and Queen, Prince and Princess live

peacefully in Bamborough Castle. Then, as young princes must, "Childe Wynd went forth to seek his fortune. . . ."

An illustration in another version of this tale shows a stiff-backed Queen, standing in profile, watching a small ship sail toward the horizon. One can imagine the sadness in the moment, feel the wrenching loss, as the hero's journey is experienced from Mother's perspective. For Childe Wynd it is the beginning of his life as a man. For the Queen, it is the end of a part of her life: "soon after he had gone, the queen his mother died."

In primitive tribes, women keen and wail as their sons leave the mothers' lodge to march off to their initiation rites. My son's Bar Mitzva, a presumably more civilized movement into manhood, nonetheless left me with some vividly painful feelings of loss. We'd kept equally busy in the months of preparation. He'd studied and chanted and prepared his reading from the Torah; I'd baked and cooked and filled the freezer with party foods. We would, I thought, share in the triumph of the moment, each in his/her own way. I'd not truly understood the nature of the rite, but on the Friday evening before the big day some understanding must have reached my son. Surrounded by friends and relatives, he began to cry. Before I could reach him in the crowd his father, grandfather, and cousin gathered around him and comforted him with Bar Mitzva stories out of their own memories. He soon began to laugh—I watched this from a distance—and I experienced a terrible sense of obsolescence. He was in a place where I could no longer reach him; only the words of men had meaning for him at that moment. The ceremonies of the next day, in which he was officially welcomed into the world of the Fathers, seemed anticlimactic.

Mother—that is, that part of a woman (or a man) which is wholly and nothing but Mother—senses her impending loss and subsequent small death with each step in her child's development. She may not let go easily, and her fear of bereavement, at its greatest intensity, can have pathological consequences:

> F., whose four-year-old daughter was referred for acute separation anxiety, mourned each of her child's birthdays and developmental milestones as the loss of her "baby" and as the loss of her own purpose in life. Far from being celebrational at

such moments, she became depressed and withdrawn, thus sending the girl messages at odds with the child's natural desire for mastery. Not surprisingly, the girl was developmentally delayed in a number of areas, but she was intuitively aware of the nature of her difficulties. Her first sandtray had a mother frantically digging through the sand in search of her lost babies. Her favorite story became that of Persephone and Demeter; she perceived her own struggle for autonomy as a separation from her mother's grief. She sometimes used her hour to prepare elaborate birthday parties for Persephone.

Movement toward autonomy is often understood, in the psyche, as a betrayal of Mother, an act that may lead toward her death:

T. at twenty-five lived in her parents' home, as did her two adult brothers. None had found a satisfying means of making a living. As T. approached the possibility of a good position in another city, she dreamt that her father had been unfaithful to her mother; he had betrayed her. In moving out into the world, in using her internalized Father, T. was breaking faith with that inner Mother who needed to keep her children in the nest.

After four years of paralyzing indecision E. had decided to marry, but her fear was palpable, particularly after a visit to her parents in her country childhood home. She'd be giving up much that was dear and familiar to her. Having reaffirmed her decision upon returning to the city, she dreamt: "A woman, probably my mother, has died. I can see her upper body, her breasts, disintegrating."

The Queen in our story suffers from a killing loss. On a subjective level, I know of no more apt a definition of depression than the departure of one's own youthful spirit. When Childe Wynd sets sail, he takes all that is hopeful and exuberant with him, leaving darkness and despair in his place. At this point, that which is kind and nurturing within us dies, to be replaced by a scolding, mocking Step-Mother voice always ready to remind us of our worthlessness. We are consumed by mourning for all we have lost; the future has left us behind. The dreams of a depressed woman reflected the loss of her youthful exuberance:

> G. at thirty-eight came into therapy full of despair. She found herself constantly raging at her two small sons; she was unable to find any joy in her work, unable to relate to her husband without a feeling of revulsion. Her dreams were fleeting, but those she could remember concerned a high school sweetheart, a wonderful young man who'd brightened her adolescence. In one such dream she felt that she'd lost him forever. She could feel herself sobbing in her sleep.

Whatever the form of bereavement, whatever its cause, the death of the Good Mother prepares the way for the Step-Mother, for the second stage of mourning characterized by rage, blame, and a search for the lost object.

Phase 2—Searching, Anger: Enter the Step-Mother

"The Laidly Worm" continues: "The king mourned her [the queen] long and faithfully, but one day while he was hunting he came across a lady of great beauty. . . ."

Hunting may be the operative word here, as the search for the lost object consumes the energy of the mourner. Recently bereaved widows and widowers report scanning crowds for the face of the lost spouse; they find themselves approaching seemingly familiar figures on the street. Movements are heard in the house late at night: a doorknob turning, footsteps in the hall. Shadows, spellbinding phantoms of the past, move in empty rooms. Far from providing comfort, these elusive images disturb sleep, exacerbate emptiness. The failed search constellates a raging fury, a fury that has the dead, abandoning partner as its true object but is likely to be displaced to family and friends, to those attempting to provide comfort, to anyone not suffering the same fate. "Loss of a loved person gives rise not only to a cry for help but sometimes also to a rejection of those who respond . . . not only to an intense desire for reunion but to anger at his departure. . . . "[8]

Where the loving mother had been, the Step-Mother enters in all her witchy darkness. She may first be experienced in projection:

H. had been in analysis for three years when her analyst
became terminally ill. The nature of the analyst's illness had
been taken up to some extent, but H. was by no means
prepared for the precipitous death when it came. She blamed
herself for having focused on the "trivialities" of her life in the
months preceding the death, for not properly having said
goodbye, for not having been a good enough patient to keep
her analyst alive. She came to me for therapy immediately after
the death but was terribly dissatisfied with me: I said things
her analyst would never have said; I was poorly trained; I was
neither old enough, large enough, nor sufficiently detached; I
was not the sort of person one could really trust. Moreover,
her departed analyst, in a dream, had warned her against me.
After six hours, having exhausted every possible reproach in
describing me (while asking to see me three hours a week), she
was finally clear on my greatest deficiency: I was not the dead
analyst, nor could I ever be. With this, her anger abated, and
our work began.

The Step-Mother's rage is felt most acutely by those closest to her:

P. remembers his mother after his parents' divorce: she worked
all day and he never knew what to expect when she came home
at night. She would either be enraged, ready to pounce on P.
and his siblings at the smallest irritation, or she'd withdraw to
her room and cry, refusing to speak to them at all. They learned
to tiptoe around her. P. felt frightened, angry, and often
guilty, as if he should have been helping her in some undefined
way.

The healthiest members of a family may generate the most
anger; they are blamed for their well-being. In "The Laidly
Worm," Margaret, the King's dutiful daughter, greets her Step-
Mother with the keys to the castle:

One of the king's knights who had escorted the new queen,
cried out in admiration: "Surely this Northern princess is the
loveliest of her kind." At that the new queen flushed up and
cried out: "At least your courtesy might have excepted
me". . . .

Phase 3—Disorganization and Despair

Bowlby writes of the effects of parental despair on family members:

> There can be little doubt that much of the disturbance reported
> in the surviving children is a result more of the behavior of the
> parents toward them than of any direct effect the death may
> have on the children themselves. Breakup of the marriage,
> mother's depression, explanations that God had taken the
> child who died can lead readily to anxiety . . . and to angry
> behavior.[9]

In our story, the Step-Mother immediately repairs to her dungeon
to cast a spell on Margaret. The girl goes to sleep a princess and
wakes up a Laidly Worm—an ugly, ravenous Dragon.

> The Laidly Worm crawled and crept . . . till it reached the
> Heugh or rock of the Spindleston round which it coiled itself,
> and lay there basking with its terrible snout in the air.
>
> Soon the country round about had reason to know of the
> Laidly Worm of Spindleston Heugh. For hunger drove the
> monster out from its cave and it used to devour everything it
> could come across.

C. G. Jung, and Frances Wickes after him, spoke of this "spell"
as the legacy of the parental unconscious:

> Children are so deeply involved in the psychological attitude of
> their parents that it is no wonder that most of the nervous
> disturbances of childhood can be traced back to a disturbed
> psychic atmosphere in the home . . . the things which have the
> most powerful effect upon children do not come from the
> conscious state of the parents but from their unconscious
> background. . . . How are we to protect our children from
> ourselves. . . ?[10]

Jung, however, did not see the child's psyche as a tabula rasa but
full of the collective wisdom of the ages, very close to unmediated
archetypal power.[11] It is in the child's grandiosity, in his identifica-

tion with this power, that the projection of the Dragon finds its
hook. A child sees change in his environment, particularly emotional change in a caretaker, as a cataclysmic event for which he is
somehow responsible: if he'd been a more obedient child, had had
fewer angry thoughts, had better anticipated his parents' desires,
father (mother) would not have left (died, withdrawn affection);
mother (father) would not be so unhappy, so angry, so distant.
The child, in compensation for his actual powerlessness in the
situation, imagines himself a Dragon, as powerful enough to tear
apart his home, as powerful enough to undo what has been done:

> A., the eight-year-old son of a firefighter, "made up" this story
> shortly after his parents' divorce: "Once upon a time there was
> a fireman who decided to leave the firehouse because the kids
> in the neighborhood set too many fires and pulled too many
> false alarms. When they heard he was leaving the kids went to
> the fireman and promised never to do these things again. The
> fireman thought about it and decided to stay at the firehouse."
> The boy clung to this fantasy until his father remarried some
> months later.

In an effort to regain the Good Mother, good behavior failing,
the smiling princess may indeed become a Dragon:

> M., in her despair around her husband's mistreatment of her,
> found herself unable to manage both her job and her family;
> needing to work, she sent her daughters off to live with their
> grandmother. The older girl initially felt some relief—she was
> out of the war zone—but soon began to act out in school and
> in the neighborhood. Her teacher warned her that her mother
> would be called if her behavior did not improve; predictably,
> the disruptions continued until mother was summoned into
> school. The girl tried to look serious and contrite at this
> meeting but was clearly elated at her accomplishment. She had
> her mother back, if only for an hour.

> O.'s parents had parted amicably, with an agreement for joint
> custody. A great deal of energy went into keeping the peace,
> but the intuitive child sensed her mother's unhappiness, her
> unspoken rage turned inward in barely contained depression.

She also felt her father's growing distance from the family. Ex-
pressions of anger were so poorly tolerated in both households
that the child was left to breathe her fire around the country-
side: she bullied her classmates, tormented her teachers,
and was deliberately rude to neighbors. Both parents received
reports and were forced to deal with one another in dealing
with her.

Kubler-Ross describes the brother of a cancer victim who found himself virtually ignored by his grieving, angry parents:

Billy started to injure himself weekly, but no one paid attention to him. . . . When he asked for a sandwich for lunch, his mother snapped at him, "Can't you see I'm busy? Fix it your-self." Billy started to wet his bed, and got a spanking for it. Later, a few months before his brother died, a teacher noticed that Billy was very cruel to a handicapped child who attended school in a wheelchair.[12]

Billy later told Kubler-Ross, "Do you know I have asthma? But I guess that's not enough."

The Dragon Spell, burdensome as it is for the child, may have its purpose in bringing light into the darkness, for once the Dragon is out and about in the countryside the problems in the castle cannot be ignored. Where a woman may hesitate to ask for help for herself, for her raging Step-Mother within, she may well seek help for her fire-breathing child. It is an axiom of family therapy that the "identified patient" speaks the family's truth. It is no less true that the disturbed child in treatment often brings a measure of healing to the family. The Dragon, in all its loathsome neediness, is most intimately connected to the Step-Mother and best able, perhaps, to feel into her pain, to reconnect with her through their mutual experience of shadow:

A seven-year-old daughter of an alcoholic mother raged and
raged at her fate: she and her brother lived with their father
while mother, living apart from them and drinking heavily,
often missed their scheduled visits. In the girl's first sandtray
a shark moved underwater, devouring small creatures hiding
in the corners of the tray. Mid-play, the child stopped and

dripped red paint on the shark. "I think it's wounded," she told
me.

The countryfolk in our story are now acutely aware of the problem; they go to a warlock—one presumably in touch with the dark
powers at play—for help and advice. He tells them:

> "Put aside for her seven kine, and each day as the sun goes
> down, carry every drop of milk they yield to the stone trough
> at the foot of the Heugh, and the Laidly Worm will trouble the
> country no longer."

There would appear to be a message here concerning work
with the fire-breathing patients who are a part of every practice. However they've acquired their Dragon skins, they are very
hungry. If we can reliably provide enough milk—attention, interpretation, empathy (and remember that it is placid cows' milk that
is needed, something more removed, less personal, than mothering)—we may satisfy the Dragon hunger for a time. But for all of
that, the Dragon will remain within its loathsome shell.

> *N., in her depression and rigidity, made every hour a struggle*
> *that left me completely drained. She presented dreams without*
> *affect or associations, then sat in stony silence, often refusing*
> *eye contact throughout the hour. She reminded me with some*
> *frequency that nothing had changed in her life except for*
> *those things which had deteriorated, and she seemed so en-*
> *raged that I wondered why she returned each week, except to*
> *pass her sense of helplessness along to me. When we began to*
> *plan around my vacation she confessed, in great anger, that*
> *the hour was all that kept her going through the week; she*
> *was furious, and ashamed, to find herself so needy and de-*
> *pendent.*

The Dragon must be fed and contained, but if there is any hope
of transformation, of freeing the Dragon from the Step-Mother's
spell, it must come from somewhere beyond technique, beyond the
egos of analyst and patient, from "over the seas." The warlock tells
the countryfolk:

"But if ye would that she be borrowed to her natural shape,
and that she who bespelled her be rightly punished, send over
the seas for her brother, Childe Wynd."

The bereavement in this tale began with the departure of Childe
Wynd; resolution of that bereavement depends on his return, on
the spiritual renewal he represents, on the potential for wholeness
he brings. When he arrives in heroic splendor in a witch-proof
ship, an army of loyal men at his side, the Step-Mother correctly
perceives a threat to her grief-borne existence. C. S. Lewis, in his
memoir *A Grief Observed,* welcomes his own returning good
spirits with considerable ambivalence:

> There's no denying that in some sense I "feel better", and with
> that comes a sort of shame, and a feeling that one is under a
> sort of obligation to cherish and foment and prolong one's
> unhappiness.... every stile or clump of trees summoned me
> into a past kind of happiness, my pre-H. happiness. But the in-
> vitation seemed to me horrible ... H. would die in me a sec-
> ond time; a worse bereavement than the first.[13]

The Step-Mother, in her fear, casts yet another spell, this one
setting brother and sister against one another. The Dragon, caught
in this dark power, fights to keep her brother's ship from the land.
In an illustration, the Dragon and the rescue ship struggle in the
harbor, locked in entangled animosity. They can neither separate
nor embrace.

> *P. presented the following dream, with the association that his
> mother was in fact a nurse: "I am working in a hospital, on an
> acute care unit. One of the younger female patients is a par-
> ticular problem. A nurse warns me to be careful around this
> patient—she is dangerous and may try to harm anyone who
> comes near her. I imagine the patient trying to slash me with a
> razor blade. When I come upon her in the hallway she tries to
> hit me with a mop handle [held out in front of her, perpen-
> dicular to her body]. I disarm her and restrain her in my arms."
> In working on this dream, P. recognized the girl as his younger
> sister, with whom he'd fought viciously during his adolescence.*

> *Remembering this, P. was flooded with remorse. His sister had*
> *done little to provoke his attacks, and she was too fearful of*
> *their mother to appeal to her for protection.*

It requires very little witchcraft to turn a brother and sister against one another in a spate of sibling rivalry. Any inequity will do, and no parent is capable of perfect equity in dealing with children. (Cf. Mara Sidoli, "The Myth of Cain and Abel," for observations of sibling rivalry in early infancy.)[14] The spell that has been cast in this tale, however, seems to be less about competition for the breast than about unconscious projection of parental fear and rage into the brother/sister relationship. They fight one another at Step-Mother's bidding, thus keeping her safely empowered. Brother/sister eros, the intense empathy and intimacy it engenders, is the greatest threat to her existence; their battles keep her darkness alive.

> *C.'s childhood was defined by dire warnings and cautionary*
> *tales, issued on every occasion by her unhappy mother. At*
> *thirty-five, she has so incorporated and amplified this dark*
> *voice that it is overpowering; she finds herself alone and ter-*
> *ribly isolated, fending off any opportunity for intimacy. Her*
> *closest male friend has similar difficulties, and their relation-*
> *ship is a standoff. She presented the following dream: "I was*
> *leading R. up a staircase; we were close. I told him he was just*
> *like family, and he embraced me. When I whispered that I loved*
> *him he became angry and withdrew; I called after him, saying*
> *that I loved him like a sister. Later—R. leaves when his mother*
> *phones—his mother and mine are sitting in the dining room,*
> *complaining to one another about their lives. I sit with my eyes*
> *closed, my hands raised in prayer."*

In a number of fairytales, Step-Mothers face defeat at the hands of loving brothers and sisters. "Hansel and Gretel," "Brother and Sister," and "The Six Swans" come immediately to mind, but the imagery of "Fundevogel" best conveys the healing nature of the brother–sister bond. In this story a pair of foster children—father brings a foundling home as companion for his orphaned daughter—are united by their mutual bereavement; they pledge one another their undying love. In their flight from the cook/step-mother/witch he becomes a rose-bush, she a rose upon the bush; he a church, she a lamp inside the church; he a pond, she a duck swimming in the pond. They outwit the witch, together, in a way neither could do alone.

Brother–Sister relationships always carry the potential for intense intimacy. Who is closer, yet more mysterious, than one's opposite in the family? When the Good Mother has given way to her dark counterpart, when father is absent or abusive, child-eros unreceived and unreturned by parents flows most naturally to that intimate other. The bond that develops between brother and sister can be a saving grace, a bridge between infantile and adult libido, a healing container for wounded eros. This bond may live in the psyche in the imaginal relation to anima/animus figures; it may be experienced with a natural brother/sister or discovered in one "found" in outer life. In any case, the existence of such a mutually loving and protective relationship may be the greatest proof against the ravages and machinations of the Step-Mother. The wholeness implicit in the incest bond is the antithesis of bereavement.

The Step-Mother's darkest spells, intended to split and separate brother and sister, may have the paradoxical effect of deepening their relationship. The witchcraft that keeps Childe Wynd from entering the harbor, from phallically acting out the love-bond with his sister, does not deter him. It only stirs his creativity.

> The incest prohibition acts as an obstacle and makes the creative fantasy inventive. . . . In this way the libido becomes imperceptibly spiritualized. The power which "always desires evil" thus creates spiritual life.[15]

Phase 4—Reorganization: The Defeat of the Step-Mother

In the last phase of mourning, the bereaved often feel a renewed sense of spiritual communion with the dead; loved ones lost in the flesh become loving inner companions. Paradoxically, this communion facilitates movement back into life in all its possibilities. C. S. Lewis, at the end of *A Grief Observed,* describes such a freeing encounter, wonderful in its mundanity:

It was quite incredibly unemotional. Just the impression of her *mind* momentarily facing my own. Not at all like a rapturous re-union of lovers. Much more like getting a telephone call or a wire from her about some practical arrangement. Not that there was any "message"—just intelligence and attention. . . . I had never in any mood imagined the dead as being so— well, so business-like. Yet there was an extreme and cheerful intimacy. . . .[16]

In James Agee's *A Death in the Family,* the widow senses her husband's presence and finds, in that presence, some strength to go on:

"Be with us all you can," she whispered. "This is goodbye." And again she went to her knees. Good-bye, she said again, within herself; "God help me to *realize* it."

"Soon, Jay. Soon, dear," she whispered; but she knew it would not be soon. She knew that a long life lay ahead of her. . . . She felt at once a calm and annihilating emptiness, and a cold and overwhelming fullness.

[Later, as she recalls the mutuality of their "meeting"]: "I'm so grateful I could assure him. It's so good he can rest at last. . . ." And her heart was restored from its desolation, into warmth and love and almost into wholeness.[17]

In our story, Childe Wynd has been denied entry, his healing presence held at bay until he is forced into inventiveness. Straight-on heroics will not do here; he must retreat, make a lateral move, and approach the Dragon from an unexpected, unorthodox direction. I am reminded of the left-handed greeting of King and Queen in the "Rosarium Philosophorum":

The gesture points to a closely guarded secret, to the "left-hand path," as the Indian Tantrists call their Shiva and Shakti worship. The left-hand (sinister) side is the dark, the unconscious side. The left is inauspicious and awkward: also, it is the side of the heart, from which comes not only love but all the evil thoughts connected with it, the moral contradictions in human nature that are expressed most clearly in our affective life.[18]

Childe Wynd, risking all the dark confusion of the approach from the heart, confronts his sister in her most frightening aspect. Despite all that he has been told, he cannot believe that this loathsome Dragon is the Princess Margaret; had she not kept him from the harbor, opposed him in a way his true sister would never have done? He draws his sword, prepared to slay the Dragon, to kill soul, just as she had resisted spirit.[15] At this critical moment, Margaret speaks from the depths of her Dragon-prison:

> "O, quit your sword, unbend your bow,
> And give me kisses three;
> For though I am a poisonous worm,
> No harm I'll do to thee."

Margaret, in naming the complex in which she is caught—perhaps she sees herself reflected in her brother's frightened eyes—finds her own voice within it. She is able to make herself heard above the Dragon-sound of antagonism and to speak for eros. Thus, when she asks her brother to embrace the beast, as she has done herself, her voice rings with the authenticity born of recognition and responsibility.

Upon hearing his sister's voice, Childe Wynd lays down his sword and listens. She speaks again:

> "O, quit your sword, unbend your bow,
> And give me kisses three;
> If I'm not won ere set of sun,
> Won never shall I be."

This is the moment of enantiodromia, of the eleventh-hour desperation that constellates its opposite. Margaret's life, the shape of her being, is at stake here; it is now or never. Her voice is so clear and strong in this moment that her brother can no longer deny her. Her consciousness of her own beastliness moves him through his fear and loathing, and he kisses the Dragon in all its ugliness. Like the kisses in "Snow White" and "Sleeping Beauty," these are kisses of redemption and rebirth. Childe Wynd serves as midwife:

With a hiss and a roar the Laidly Worm reared back and before
Childe Wynd stood his sister Margaret. He wrapped his cloak
about her, and then went up to the castle with her.

Brother and sister, together, have broken the Step-Mother's dark
spell; when this occurs in psyche the very air in the room seems to
change:

> *After a week's hiatus, T., who generally presented as rigid and
> constricted, looked very different. She'd had some sun, but the
> difference was more in her relaxed body posture, the smile that
> played around her mouth, the warmth in her eyes. Nothing
> had improved in her outer life—quite the contrary—but
> something had surely changed. Toward the end of the hour,
> she tentatively offered a dream: "I'm about to have incest with
> my brother. . . ."*

III. Conclusion: An Unfinished Story

Childe Wynd enfolds Margaret in his cloak, and they return
together to the castle to confront the wicked Queen. Surprisingly,
they make no move to kill her but with the touch of a rowan twig
return her to what must be her true shape: she becomes a loathly
toad, hopping and croaking about the castle grounds, a small,
merely annoying version of the Dragon she'd cast upon Margaret.[20] The King is now free to rule his kingdom, son and daughter
by his side, but what are we to make of a quaternity that includes a
toad?
  In alchemical texts, the toad is paired with the soaring eagle,
"which flies up to the clouds and receives the rays of the sun in his
eyes":

> The toad is the opposite of air, it is the contrary element,
> namely earth, whereon alone it moves in slow steps, and does
> not trust itself to another element. Its head is very heavy and
> gazes at the earth. For this reason it denotes the philosophic
> earth, which cannot fly, as it is firm and solid. Upon it as a
> foundation the golden house is to be built. Were it not for the

earth in our work the air would fly away, neither would the
fire have its nourishment, nor the water its vessel.[21]

With her heavy-headed, earthbound vision, the toad has a necessary place in this royal family. The Step-Mother's croaking voice,
unpleasant as it may be, must continue to be heard in the castle
grounds. She brings her dark weight to the airiness about her: to a
king prone to enchantment by beautiful women, to a young, heroic
prince, to a maidenly princess born afresh after a terrible ordeal.

Brother and sister are together now, but their union, healing as it
has been, is not meant to last in this form forever. Childe Wynd,
still a prince after all, must continue his interrupted journey;
Margaret must shed her brother's cloak and find one of her own.
Each must seek a stranger to bring new life into the kingdom. The
croaking toad, I suspect, will remind them of that.

She speaks for the dark necessities of nature, for leaving what is
safe and familiar and taking one's chances in the world. While the
Good Mother protects and enfolds, the Step-Mother rejects her
young, pushes them kicking and screaming into the cold. The
toad's continuing presence in the castle is to remind all of unfinished business.

Just so, the business of bereavement is never quite done.
Memorial services, Memorial Days, candles for the dead keep us
connected to our loss, to those dark, still wounded places in the
soul. It is in the realm of Death that psyche seeks beauty. We are
not meant to forget:

> The sorrow for the dead is the only sorrow from which we
> refuse to be divorced. Every other wound we seek to heal,
> every other affliction to forget; but this wound we consider it a
> duty to keep open; this affliction we cherish and brood over in
> solitude.[22]

The Step-Mother serves Psyche by not letting us forget our
losses; she insists upon her darkness. She may enter, in her
loathsome way, as depression, as somatic pain, as a nightmare
whose darkness lingers through our waking hours. As toad, with
her heavy, earthward gaze, she maintains the necessary perspective
of death.

1. Cf. M. Tatar, *The Hard Facts of the Grimms' Fairy Tales* (Princeton: Princeton University Press, 1987), p. 143. Two exceptions that come to mind are "The Raven" (#93) and "The Seven Ravens" (#25). In these tales, natural, impatient, and ultimately regretful parents wish their children into birds who fly away.

2. B. Bettelheim, *The Uses of Enchantment: The Meaning and Importance of Fairy Tales* (New York: Vintage Books, 1977), pp. 66–69.

3. The text used here (the full text follows this essay) is taken from *English Fairy Tales,* collected by Joseph Jacobs (New York: Schocken Books), no copyright. The illustrations I refer to accompany the retelling of the tale by D. Weisner and K. Kahng (*The Loathsome Dragon* [New York: C. P. Putnam's Sons, 1987]).

4. J. Bowlby, *Attachment and Loss,* vol. 3, *Loss* (New York: Basic Books, Inc., 1980), p. 85.

5. *Webster's New Twentieth Century Dictionary,* 2d ed.

6. E. Kubler-Ross, *On Children and Death* (New York: Macmillan Publishing Co., 1983), p. 78.

7. S. Rice, *Some Lamb* (Berkeley: Serendipity Books, 1975), p. 52.

8. Bowlby, p. 31.

9. Ibid., p. 121.

10. C. G. Jung, *CW* 17, §§ 80–85.

11. Ibid., §§ 94–95.

12. Kubler-Ross, p. 4.

13. C. S. Lewis, *A Grief Observed,* quoted in M. J. Moffat, *In the Midst of Winter: Selections from the Literature of Mourning* (New York: Random House, 1982), p. 65.

14. This is chapter 4 in Mara Sidoli, *The Unfolding Self* (Boston: Sigo Press, 1989).

15. C. G. Jung, *CW* 5, § 332.

16. Lewis, in Moffat, pp. 118–19.

17. J. Agee, in Moffat, pp. 213–18.

18. C. G. Jung, *CW* 16, § 410.

19. J. Hillman sees soul-danger in the Heroic Ego's logos-driven swordsmanship: " ... efforts to integrate, 'to bring these contents to light,' become a depotentiating of personifications and of their imaginal power, a drying up of the waters, and a slaying of the angel (seen to be a dangerous fairy demon by the ego), whose real purpose is to individualize itself. .... The feminine image that the hero meets is his guardian angel, not his enemy, and it is her individualization ... that matters to the soul." J. Hillman, *Anima* (Dallas: Spring Publications, 1985), p. 117.

20. C. G. Jung, *CW* 14, § 25.

21. Ibid., §2.
22. W. Irving, in Moffat, p. 270.

The Laidly Worm of Spindleston Heugh

In Bamborough Castle once lived a king who had a fair wife and two children, a son named Childe Wynd and a daughter named Margaret. Childe Wynd went forth to seek his fortune, and soon after he had gone the queen his mother died. The king mourned her long and faithfully, but one day while he was hunting he came across a lady of great beauty, and fell so much in love with her that he determined to marry her. So he sent word home that he was going to bring a new queen to Bamborough Castle.

Princess Margaret was not very glad to hear of her mother's place being taken, but she did not repine, but did her father's bidding, and at the appointed day came down to the castle gate with the keys all ready to hand over to her stepmother. Soon the procession drew near, and the new queen came towards Princess Margaret, who bowed low and handed her the keys of the castle. She stood there with blushing cheeks and eyes on ground, and said: "O welcome, father dear, to your halls and bowers, and welcome to you, my new mother, for all that's here is yours," and again she offered the keys. One of the king's knights who had escorted the new queen cried out in admiration: "Surely this Northern princess is the loveliest of her kind." At that the new queen flushed up and cried out: "At least your courtesy might have excepted me," and then she muttered below her breath: "I'll soon put an end to her beauty."

That same night the queen, who was a noted witch, stole down to a lonely dungeon wherein she did her magic and with spells three times three, and with passes nine times nine she cast Princess Margaret under her spell. And this was her spell:

> I weird ye to be a Laidly Worm,
> And borrowed shall ye never be,
> Until Childe Wynd, the King's own son,
> Come to the Heugh and thrice kiss thee;
> Until the world comes to an end,
> Borrowed shall ye never be.

So Lady Margaret went to bed a beauteous maiden, and rose up a Laidly

Worm. And when her maidens came in to dress her in the morning they found coiled up on the bed a dreadful dragon, which uncoiled itself and came towards them. But they ran away shrieking, and the Laidly Worm crawled and crept, and crept and crawled till it reached the Heugh or rock of the Spindleston round which it coiled itself, and lay there basking with its terrible snout in the air.

Soon the country round about had reason to know of the Laidly Worm of Spindleston Heugh. For hunger drove the monster out from its cave and it used to devour everything it could come across. So at last they went to a mighty warlock and asked him what they should do. Then he consulted his works and his familiar, and told them: "The Laidly Worm is really the Princess Margaret and it is hunger that drives her forth to do such deeds. Put aside for her seven kine, and each day as the sun goes down, carry every drop of milk they yield to the stone trough at the foot of the Heugh, and the Laidly Worm will trouble the country no longer. But if ye would that she be borrowed to her natural shape, and that she who bespelled her be rightly punished, send over the seas for her brother, Childe Wynd."

All was done as the warlock advised, the Laidly Worm lived on the milk of the seven kine, and the country was troubled no longer. But when Childe Wynd heard the news, he swore a mighty oath to rescue his sister and revenge her on her cruel stepmother. And three-and-thirty of his men took the oath with him. Then they set to work and built a long ship, and its keel they made of the rowan tree. And when all was ready, they out with their oars and pulled sheer for Bamborough Keep.

But as they got near the keep, the stepmother felt by her magic power that something was being wrought against her, so she summoned her familiar imps and said: "Childe Wynd is coming over the seas; he must never land. Raise storms, or bore the hull, but nohow must he touch the shore." Then the imps went forth to meet Childe Wynd's ship, but when they got near, they found they had no power over the ship, for its keel was made of the rowan tree. So back they came to the queen witch who knew not what to do. She ordered her men-at-arms to resist Childe Wynd if he should land near them, and by her spells she caused the Laidly Worm to wait by the entrance of the harbour.

As the ship came near, the Worm unfolded its coils, and, dipping into the sea, caught hold of the ship of Childe Wynd, and banged it off the shore. Three times Childe Wynd urged his men on to row bravely and strong, but each time the Laidly Worm kept it off the shore. Then Childe

Wynd ordered the ship to be put about, and the witch-queen thought he had given up the attempt. But instead of that, he only rounded the next point and landed safe and sound in Buddle Creek, and then, with sword drawn and bow bent, rushed up followed by his men, to fight the terrible Worm that had kept him from landing.

But the moment Childe Wynd had landed, the witch-queen's power over the Laidly Worm had gone, and she went back to her bower all alone, not an imp, nor a man-at-arms to help her, for she knew her hour was come. So when Childe Wynd came rushing up to the Laidly Worm it made no attempt to stop him or hurt him, but just as he was going to raise his sword to slay it, the voice of his own sister Margaret came from its jaws saying:

> "O, quit your sword, unbend your bow,
> And give me kisses three;
> For though I am a poisonous worm
> No harm I'll do to thee."

Childe Wynd stayed his hand, but he did not know what to think if some witchery were not in it. Then said the Laidly Worm again:

> "O, quit your sword, unbend your bow,
> And give me kisses three;
> If I'm not won ere set of sun,
> Won never shall I be."

Then Childe Wynd went up to the Laidly Worm and kissed it once; but no change came over it. Then Childe Wynd kissed it once more; but yet no change came over it. For a third time he kissed the loathsome thing, and with a hiss and a roar the Laidly Worm reared back and before Childe Wynd stood his sister Margaret. He wrapped his cloak about her, and then went up to the castle with her. When he reached the keep, he went off to the witch-queen's bower, and when he saw her, he touched her with a twig of a rowan tree. No sooner had he touched her than she shrivelled up and shrivelled up, till she became a huge ugly toad, with bold staring eyes and a horrible hiss. She croaked and she hissed, and then hopped away down the castle steps, and Childe Wynd took his father's place as king, and they all lived happily afterwards.

But to this day a loathsome toad is seen at times haunting the neighbourhood of Bamborough Keep, and the wicked witch-queen is that Laidly Toad.

A Child Bride
Ursula K. Le Guin

DID HE TAKE me away from her or did she make me leave him? I
don't know if what came first was the light. I don't know where
my home was. I remember the dark car. Long, and large, and so
fast that the road broke like a wave. There was the smell of the car
and the smell of the sod, a cleft, an opening. The road went down,
I know. What flowers smell like sometimes I remember. In the
name of the hyacinth I find the colors purple, pink, red, and the
color of pomegranate. But there is a forbidden color. If I say its
name the punishment will come upon me, the breaking, the terrible
calling, if I say the name of milk the earth will ache. The earth will
ache and reach for me again, brown arms, long arms groping and
grasping, seeking, choking. If I was there, under his roof, was it
wrong that I was there? Was I not wanted there? I was chosen,
I was queen. The arms reached out but they couldn't catch me. I
didn't look up as we drove by the black rivers. The car went so fast
by the rivers! But we would stop for me to name the rivers:
Memory that carries remembering away, and Anger that runs so
gently smoothing the pebbles round, and Terror that we swam in
fearlessly. And then the waterfalls! I gave them no names. They
are still falling down and down from deep to deeper dark till the
last glimmering is lost and only the long voice of water comes back
from below saying what we cannot say. Sound is a slower traveler
than light, and so more sure. It was the calling that came to me
from the high places, never the light. How could the light come
here within? This is no place for light. It's too heavy here. But in

the calling came the hyacinth, the colors that come before the
light. O Mother! Mother! Mother! Who called? Who called her?
me?

He's rich, Mother. He lives there in the basement of the old
house with old things, dried things, roots and coins and chests and
shadows and closets. He lives down in the cellar, but he's rich. He
could buy anything.

No, he didn't hurt me only once. When I was frightened when
he came when I was there alone. He took me away then he made
me go down inside. We went inside where I have never been and I
was there then. Yes, when my mother's working I always stay
alone. I stay in the house and garden, where else is there to go?
No, I don't know my daddy. Yes, no, I don't know. I don't know
what it means. He made me come with him in the car. I went with
him. Yes he touched me there. Yes he did that. Yes he did that. Yes
we did that. Yes I said no I didn't say. He said I was his wife. He
said everything he had was mine. Can I see my mother now?

Yes he gave me jewelry. I took it yes. I wore it yes. It was
beautiful, the stones, amethyst, rose amethyst, ruby. He gave me
the crown of hyacinth, of pomegranate stone. He gave me the ring
of gold I wear. We never left the basement no. He said it was
dangerous outside. He said there was a war. He said there were
enemies. He never hurt me only at the start. He needed me. We did
that yes I am his wife. With him I rule that place. With him I judge
you all. To whom do you think you come?

She came to me and came back to me, the musician's wife, my
friend. I knew she would come back. She came back crying. I
knew she would. I was waiting for her by the road, and cried with
her when she came back alone, but not for long. Here tears dry
away. Here in the dark no mourning is. A few tears, like pomegranate seeds, five or six little half-transparent seeds that look
like uncut rubies, that's enough, enough to eat, enough.

O Mother don't cry, I was only playing hide and seek! I only
hid! I was joking, Mother, I didn't mean to stay so long. I didn't
know it was so late. I didn't notice it was dark. We were playing
kings and queens and hide and seek and I didn't know, I didn't
know, I didn't know. Do I live there? Is this my home? This is outside the earth and I have lived inside. This is inside the earth and I
have lived outside. This is dark and I come from the light, from the

dark into this light. He loves me well. He waits for me. Why is
your love winter, Mother? Why are his hands so cold?

What does my mother do? She keeps the house.

There is no river long enough to wear her anger down. She will
never forget and will always be afraid. You have made an enemy
indeed, my lord.

Mother, be comforted. Don't cry and make me cry. Come
winter I'll come back and spring is my return. I'll bring the hya-
cinths. You depend on me, you know, I'm not a child now. But if I
am your daughter how can I be his wife? How can I be your wife
when I am her daughter? What do you want of me, who sleep in
my arms? These are her arms around me rocking me, rocking me. I
wear the ring of gold he gave me as I walk in the garden she grew
for me, the red flowers, the purple flowers, the pomegranate trees
with roots of white and brown that reach down deep. To be
sought forever, but shall I be found and never seek myself and
never find? To be one body root and flower, to break the sod, to
drive the dark car home, to turn, return, where is my home? Shall I
bear no daughter?

The Great Mother, Her Son, Her Hero, and the Puer
James Hillman

> Perhaps it would not be too much to say that the most crucial problems of the individual and of society turn upon the way the psyche functions in regard to spirit and matter.
>
> C. G. Jung

> Great Mother Nature has proved most potent . . . down to the present day. It is "she" who does nothing by leaps, abhors a vacuum, is *die gute Mutter,* is red in tooth and claw, "never did betray the heart that loved her," eliminates the unfit, surges to ever higher and higher forms of life, decrees, purposes, warns, punishes and consoles. . . . Of all the pantheon Great Mother Nature has . . . been the hardest to kill.
>
> C. S. Lewis

I.

WE ARE TRYING to present the puer within a structure which recognizes it primarily as a spiritual phenomenon. We would differentiate puer, hero, and son, and, contrary to the classical analytical view, we would suggest that the son who succumbs and the hero who overcomes both take their definition through the relationship with the magna mater, whereas the puer takes its definition from

the senex–puer polarity. The young dominant of rising consciousness that rules the style of the ego personality can be determined by
the puer (and senex) or by the son and hero (and Goddess).

The mythologem of Horus who rises hawk-like above the father
to redeem the father is one example in which aspiration is primarily masculine, belonging within a puer–senex pattern. The Horus
motif is paradigmatic for many such father–son situations, where
the aim is not to overcome or slay the mother but to redeem the
father by surpassing him. The Mother Goddess Isis even encourages the puer ambition and is instrumental to senex–puer reunion.
In this pattern the mother can be relatively secondary, while focus
is upon the puer necessity: redeeming the father. In a young man's
life, maybe in any life, the puer represents the necessity of seeking
the fathering spirit, the capacity to father. The Horus image of flying higher and further connotes a spiritual fathering. And the
movement so flaming with libidinal charge reflects the unbearable
tension within the senex–puer archetype.

Nonetheless, analytical psychology has for the most part taken
for granted that puer and great mother belong together: the puer-
man has, or is, a mother-complex. The puer succumbs to the
mother; the hero fights and overcomes her.[1]

Henderson makes one distinction worth noting—and refuting.
He associates only the negative puer aeternus with the mother-
complex and rightly points to the faulty anima relationship, a main
psychological lacuna of the puer-man. But, because he derives this
anima peculiarity from the mother-complex, his view too begins
and ends with early Jung: puer consciousness is a function of a
mother-bound psychology. Henderson's distinction between a
"positive" and a "negative" puer aeternus is anyway suspect, since
it divides in the morality of mind what is not divided in the reality
of psyche. Positive and negative signs affixed to psychic events offer the illusion that there are positive and negative aspects of an archetype per se and that the plus or minus signs we attribute are
valid descriptions. But the signs are relative, placed there by the
fantasy of the ego, its decisions in terms of its values and realities.
Jung never let us forget that the psyche's opposites contain each
other, so that every virtue can be a vice, or vice a virtue. To declare
a complex negative is to freeze it in hell. What can it do; where can
it go? Not only does the idea of positive and negative puer need re-

thinking, but also the crucial question of the puer in relation with the mother needs fresh examination.

II.

In classical mythology this special entanglement of spirit and maternal world is depicted by the Great Goddess and her young male consort, her son, her lover, her priest. Attis, Adonis, Hippolytus, Phaethon, Tammuz, Endymion, Oedipus are examples of this erotic bind.[2] Each figure in each tale shows its own variation; the Oedipus complex is but one pattern of son and mother which produces those fateful entanglements of spirit with matter which in the twentieth century we have learned to call neurotic. The very desperation of neurosis shows how strong are their mutual needs and that the attempts to untie this primary knot are truly in the ancient sense agonizing and tragic. The primary knot of spirit and matter is personified in the clinging embrace of erotic conjunction of mother and son.

Alchemy—the fullest and most precise background yet worked out for the processes of analytical work—presents a seemingly similar motif: the extraction of spirit from matter and then their reunion. But the tradition of alchemy pairs the puer figures mainly with the senex (as the young and old Mercury, as Christ *puer-et-senex*, as King and King's Son), *not* with the mother!

There are many alchemists and many alchemies. There are dragons, devourings, and dissolutions. The material at the beginning is often female and the child at the end often male. Nevertheless, the Great Goddess (as *materia prima*) is not the primary constellating factor of the puer aeternus of renewal. The divine child who is called *renovatus in novum infantum, peullus regius, filius philosophorum* is a new spirit born of an old spirit. The process is rather male to male to hermaphrodite and only takes place within the female as material and vessel. There seems a subtle and yet crucial difference between the alchemical conception of the movement of the spirit (puer) and this same movement in hero myths and heroic fairytales. There the hero is unthinkable without his opposition to a Great Goddess or Dragon Witch in one form or another.

Spirit seems differently imagined in alchemy, implying a different theory of neurosis and of psychic movement. In the hero myths, the psyche moves mainly by means of the will into an enlargement of rational order. In alchemy, it seems to be an enlargement of imagination, a freeing of fantasy from various imprisoning literalizations. When Jung shifted the main analogy for the individuation process from the hero myth in *Symbols of Transformation* (in German, 1911) to *Psychology and Alchemy* (in German, Eranos lectures 1936 and 1937), one result was also a shift from the rational and voluntary faculties of the soul to its third faculty, the imagination or *memoria*.[3]

There may be many historical and philosophical reasons for alchemy's presentation of the puer without the great mother as main counterpart, not the least of them being the Christian doctrine of a God who is both Father and Son. Besides these influences upon alchemy's formulations of the puer, more significant are the spontaneous fantasies of the psyche as expressed in alchemical formulations about redemption. In alchemy too, the embrace of spirit and matter is a suffering and an evil, or what we now call neurotic. However, the way out of this embrace is different. It is not only in terms of a heroic mother–son battle for which St. George and the Dragon has become the major Western paradigm. In alchemy the dragon is also the creative Mercury and a figuration (or prefiguration) of the puer. Killing the dragon in the hero myth means nothing less than killing the imagination, the very spirit that is the way and the goal. The dragon, let us remember, is not a snake, not an animal at all. It is a fictitious animal, an imaginal instinct, and thus the instinct of imagination or the imagination as a vital, instinctual force. Even the fight with the dragon in Jung's alchemical account of it (CW 12, § 437) differs from St. George's behavior. The alchemical hero is devoured by the dragon, or, we would say, imagination takes over. Then comes the activity of discrimination from within the belly where *nous* separates and makes distinctions within the literalizations of *physis*, the physically concrete fantasies. This process of discrimination is imaged in alchemy as cutting through the belly of the beast from within.

Moreover, the myth of the hero is but one motif of alchemy's hundreds, but one way of proceeding, one operation useful at a specific moment or within one constellation; whereas the myth of the hero in modern psychology has become *the* dominant interpretative background for puer psychology.

In yet another way there is a difference between our usual heroic-ego way of thinking about spirit and matter (puer and mother) and the images of alchemy. There, spirit is not mainly presented within a Darwinian fantasy. The pattern is not usually one of generation, spirit born out of maternal matter. The alchemical techné aims at another kind of relationship between *materia* and *spiritus* where polarities become complementaries, different but equal and joined, as king and queen—and where the close union is *an incest that is a virtue*. Oedipus is altogether irrelevant here, because the entire process is not heroic, not literalized, and not viewed from ego-consciousness.

Usually, too, the generation of the new does not come about through a royal pair producing the divine child, a puer, as a third figure. The generation of the new in alchemy is not directly linear, not a declension or descent. Rather, generation tends to be circular: the new is prefigured from the beginning in the old, and the king is himself both senex and puer. In this sense the alchemical representation of development seems never to depart from the unity of the archetype; development of puer consciousness is not *away* from or *against* matter (mother) but always a mercurial business involved with her; *puer-et-senex* needs matter for its foil, for its stuff, for its physicality that gives to its imagination literal materialᵉ upon which to fantasy.

We might consider alchemy, then, to be a discipline that is not conceived within the mother-complex, because its view of spirit is not conceived as a derivative matter. Its psychology differs from the psychology of science, and so alchemy and science offer different backgrounds to psychology. Because the science-fantasy implies conquering matter, science works within the archetype of the great mother. And when we look at the psyche scientifically, our consciousness tends to become appropriated by the archetypal great mother. The alchemist-fantasy is less bound by the 'laws' of matter and by quantitative considerations. Qualitative change and precision of it are more important. The alchemical way through the material of the mother is the discipline of fantasy, and alchemical psychology is dominated by the puer–senex pair, its tensions and problems, and its relation with anima.

III.

In our lives the mother/son-complex is the personalized formulation (within that family language so fondly constellated by the very
same mother/son archetype) of the matter–spirit relation.
"Mother-complex" is another way of stating that spirit cannot present itself, has no effect or reality, except in regard to matter. It
only knows itself in contradistinction to matter. If the spirit is
heroic, the contradistinction is presented as opposition; if it is
materialistic and worldly, it is in that complex's service. Either way
its first fascination is with the transformation of matter, earth-
shakers, world-movers, city-planners; spiritual acts are materialized in some aspect of concrete reality. The "mother-complex" is
such a widespread neurosis, spirit is so immersed in the body of
matter, delighting there or squirming to shake free, that we can
hardly discover other interpretations of spirit—such as the alchemical one—except within a polarity to matter. Whenever we think
of spirit in these terms, we are "in the mother-complex."

But is there not another spirit—or other spirits—of nature, or of
the seas, or the woods and mountains, of fiery volcanoes or of the
underworld that comes from the lower Gods (Poseidon, Dionysos,
Hades, Hephaistos, Pan) which are male—or hermaphroditic?
And is there not a Hermes and a Zeus Chthonios? Must everything
below, of nature and of darkness, be mother? The spirit can discover itself by means of another spirit, male with male as parallels,
or friends and enemies; so too, the spirit can have as opposite and
partner the soul or the body, neither of which must be the Great
Goddess. Nor are we obliged to think genetically, as if the only
correlate with 'child' is 'mother,' so that the cause and origins of
spirit must be traceable to some material principle somewhere.
Matter is therefore not the only principle with which spirit can be
coupled and thereby define itself. We may question even whether
the spirit can know itself, become conscious, within that mother–
son polarity. The blindness of Oedipus would indicate the contrary. Finally, the need of the puer for a corresponding male
(senex), for the chthonic, and for the soul and body as counterparts—rather than the Great Goddess—offers themes that are yet
to be developed in depth psychology, owing to its domination by
the mother-complex. It is precisely the loss of these other polarities

for the spirit which have caused its sonship, its subdued and frustratedly rebellious spirit that continually casts all phenomena into the same mold and forces us to go on viewing the puer in terms of the mother. If psychology is to free itself for other fantasies for comprehending the psyche's immense range of events, it must first free the puer from the mother, else the spirit of psychology can do nothing better than repeat and confirm what mother has told it to do.

Neurosis cannot be separated from Weltanschauung, which always is an expression of one or another variety of the spirit–matter issue and is thus loaded with the archetypal problematics of the great mother/puer relation. Hence the therapists of neurosis, as Jung pointed out, are and must be also doctors of philosophy.[4] The puer/great mother relation is also a philosophical problem that can be expressed in philosophical language. The puer cannot be a functioning psychological organ without having its ideational effects. If therapists of neurosis are doctors of philosophy, they should be able to see not only the neurotic in all philosophy but as well the philosophical in all neurosis. Metaphysical ideas are hardly independent of their complex roots; so ideas can be foci of sickness, part of an archetypal syndrome. For example, is not the materialism of some natural science a philosophy of matriarchy in which the scientist willy-nilly becomes a priestly or a heroic son? Does not Vedanta and its transcendence of matter reflect a spirit so entangled in the great world mother that it must resort to disciplined exercises to find liberation? In our metaphysics we state our fantasies about the physical and transcendence of it. A metaphysical statement can be taken as a psychological fantasy about the matter–spirit relation. These statements are fantasies whose author is the 'archetypal neurosis' of puer and mother, reflected in philosophy by the terms spirit and matter. The archetypal neurosis is collective, affecting everyone with metaphysical affliction. Working out this affliction is individual, which makes therapy a metaphysical engagement in which ideas and not only feelings and complexes undergo process and change. The appearance of puer-figures, particularly in the dreams of women, brings new impetus and new struggles also in the realm of ideas, indicating transformations of Weltanschauung in regard to all that is included by the term *physis*.

IV.

Now we must inquire more precisely into this archetypal contamination of mother and puer. What occurs when the puer as a fundamental structure of the psyche loses its self-identity, its position within the senex–puer whole, and is subtly replaced by the figure of the mother's son?

When the father is absent, we fall more readily into the arms of the mother. And indeed the father is missing; God is dead. We cannot go backward by propping up senex religion. The missing father is not your or my personal father. He is the absent father of our culture, the viable senex who provides not daily bread but spirit through meaning and order.[5] The missing father is the dead God who offered a focus for spiritual things. Without this focus, we turn to dreams and oracles, rather than to prayer, code, tradition, and ritual. When mother replaces father, magic substitutes for logos, and son-priests contaminate the puer spirit.

Unable to go backward to revive the dead father of tradition, we go downward into the mothers of the collective unconscious, seeking an all-embracing comprehension. We ask for help in getting through the narrow straits without harm; the son wants invulnerability. Grant us protection, foreknowledge; cherish us. Our prayer is to the night for a dream, to a love for understanding, to a little rite or exercise for a moment of wisdom. Above all we want assurance through a vision beforehand that it will all come out all right. Here is the motif of protection again and a protection of a specific sort: invulnerability, foresight, guarantee that all shall be well, no matter what.

Just here we catch one glimpse of a difference between puer and son. Existential guarantees are given by mothers. Loyalty to her gives her loyalty in return. She won't let you down if you remain loyal to her. Mother assures safety and gives life, but mother does not give true spirit that comes from uncertainty, risk, failure —aspects of the puer. The son does not need the father, whereas the puer seeks recognition from the father, a recognition of spirit by spirit that leads to eventual fatherhood in the puer itself. As we cannot get to the father through the mother, so we cannot get to the hot sperm seed of logos through its imitations in moon-magic.

Psychology is not dissolution into psychic magic; psychology is a *logos* of the psyche; it requires spirit. Psychology advances not only through philosophies of the mother: evolution in growth and development, naturalism, materialism, the social adaptation of a feeling-loaded humanism, comparisons with the animal realm, reductions to emotional simplicities like love, sexuality, and aggression. Psychology requires other patterns for advancing its thought and other archetypal carriers, such as the puer which might liberate psychology's speculative fantasy and insist upon psychology's spiritual significance.

Without the father we lose also that capacity which the Church recognized as "discrimination of the spirits": the ability to know a call when we hear one and to discriminate between the voices, an activity so necessary for a precise psychology of the unconscious. But the spirit that has no father has no guide for such niceties. The senex–puer division puts an end to spiritual discrimination; instead we have promiscuity of spirits (astrology, yoga, spiritual philosophies, cybernetics, atomic physics, Jungianism, etc.—all enjoyed currently) and the indiscrimination among them of an all-understanding mother. The mother encourages her son: go ahead, embrace it all. For her, all equals everything. The father's instruction, on the contrary, is: all equals nothing—unless the all be precisely discriminated.

The realm of the Great Goddess is characterized by the passive inertia and compulsive dynamus of nature; the protective, nourishing, generative cycle in animal and plant from seed to death; an affinity for beauty, timelessness, and emotionality; a preference for opacity, obscurity, coagulation, and darkness; a mystique of the blood per se or in kinship ties.[6] All these areas under the domination of the Great Goddess, with but a slight shift of emphasis toward the spiritual, could as well be reflected by the puer. Thus, the puer impulse is *exaggerated* by the mother-complex. A contamination of any two archetypes may reinforce them both, or it may depotentiate one in favor of the other.[7] In the special case of the mother–puer confluence, the mother seems to win out, not only by depotentiating spirit but by exaggerating it. Mother, as giver and nourisher, as natural life itself, supplies the puer with an overdose of energetic supplies, and by reinforcing certain of the puer's basic traits she claims him as her dependent son.

When the mother gets hold of these traits, she draws them in extreme. The puer pensiveness becomes an ineffectual daydream;

death becomes no longer a terror but a welcomed and natural comfort; laming, instead of an opening into human vulnerability, is turned exaggeratedly by mother into a castration, a paralysis, a suicide. The vertical flights so authentic to the Horus root of the puer become instead a contemptuous soaring over a corrupt and shoddy world; the family problem takes on a religious mystique: all the family members, personages in a matriarchal epic. Then, too, eternity, instead of being an aspect of events and the way in which puer consciousness perceives through to archetypal significance, is distorted into a disregard for time, even a denial of all temporal things. Or a materialistic opportunism appears instead of the genuine puer sense of opportunity, its way of proceeding by hunch and luck, its ambition carried by play and Mercury. There is materialism too in a peculiar concretism of metaphysical ideas (they must be put in force, acted out in body and clothes and community), in ethics, in sexuality, money, diet, as the mother's matter, repressed, returns in the literalizations of puer abstractions. The cycle of nature (which in puer consciousness is a field out of which to draw metaphors to make jokes upon, play and experiment with) in son-consciousness becomes a pious nature 'out-there,' a shack in the woods, soiled clothes, Hatha Yoga; and beauty, which for the puer reflects Platonic ideals and is a revelation of the essence of value, narrows instead into the vanities of my own image, my own aesthetic productions and sensitivities.

The close association of mother and son in the psyche is imaged as incest and experienced as ecstasy and guilt. The ecstasy goes in both vertical directions, divine and hellward, but the guilt is not assuaged. The great mother changes the puer's debt to the transcendent—what he owes the Gods for his gifts—into a debt of feeling, a guilt toward her symbols in the round of material life. He overpays society in family, job, civic duties and avoids his destiny. Through her, his relation with material life oscillates between ecstatic springing of its binds or guilty submission to them. In the sexual sphere, psychoanalysts have called this "oscillation," the continual back and forth between lust and guilt, guilt and lust.

The ecstatic aspect in a man carried by the conjoined archetype of mother–son takes him yet further from the father's inhibitions of order and limit. Ecstasy is one of the Goddess's ways of seducing the puer from its senex connection. By overcoming limit, puer consciousness feels itself overcoming fate which sets and is limit.[8]

Rather than loving fate or being driven by it, ascending like Horus
to redeem the father, the puer escapes from fate in magical, ecstatic
flight. Puer aspirations are fed with new fuel: the potent combus-
tible of sexual and power drives whose source is in the instinctual
domain of the Great Goddess.[9] These exaggerations of the puer
impulse set him afire. He is the torch, the arrow, and the wing,
Aphrodite's son Eros. He seems able to realize in his sexual life and
his career every wish of his childhood's omnipotence fantasies. It's
all coming true. His being is a magic phallus, glowing and strong,
every act inspired, every word pregnant with deep, natural wisdom. The Great Goddess behind the scenes has handed him this
ecstatic wand. She governs both the animal desire and the horizon-
tal world of matter over which she offers promise of conquest.

Due to the emotionality of the great mother, the dynamus of the
son is unusually labile, unusually dependent upon emotion. Inspiration can no longer be differentiated from enthusiasm, the correct
and necessary ascension from ecstasy. The fire flares up and then
all but goes out, damp and smoky, clouding vision and afflicting
others with the noxious air of bad moods. The dependence of
spirit upon mood described in vertical language (heights and depths,
glory and despair) has its archetypal counterpart in the festivals
for Attis, Cybele's son, which were called *hilaria* and *tristia*.[10]

When the vertical direction toward transcendence is misdirected
through the great mother, the puer is no longer authentic. He takes
his role now from the relationship with the feminine. Ecstasy and
guilt are two parts of the pattern of sonship. Even more important
is heroism. Whether as hero-lover, or hero-hermit denying matter
but with an ear to nature's breast, or hero-conquerer who slays
some slimy dragon of public evil, or as Baldur, so perfect and so
unable to stanch the bleeding from his beautiful wounds, puer has
lost its freedom. Direct access to the spirit is no longer there; it requires drama, tragedy, heroics. Life becomes a performance acted
out through a role in the relationship with the eternal feminine
who stands behind every such son: martyr, messiah, devotee, hero,
lover. By playing these roles, we are part of the cult of the Great
Goddess.[11] Our identities are given by the enactment of these roles
and thus we become her sons, since our life depends on the roles
she gives. She thus can affect even the way that the puer seeks the
senex: exaggerating the discipleship of the student to his master,
the swagger of the battler with the old order, the exclusivity of the

messiah whose new truth refuses everything that has gone before. The mother-complex dulls *the precision of the spirit*; issues become quickly either/or, since the Great Goddess does not have much comprehension of the spirit. She only grasps it in relationship to her; that is, the mother-complex must make of spirit something *related*. It must have effects in the realm of matter: life, world, people. This sounds 'only human' and full of 'common sense,' again terms too often expressing the sentimentalism of the mother-complex. Even should a man recognize the mother in his actions and take flight from her relatedness into lofty abstraction and vast, impersonal fantasy, he is still the son filled with the animus of the Goddess, her pneuma, her breath and wind. And he serves her best by making such divisions between his light and her darkness, his spirit and her matter, between his world and hers.

This is the animus thinking of sonship, found as much in men as women. It is a thinking of coagulations and oppositions between them, rather than a thinking in distinctions between perspectives. For it is not that the mother is this or that and the puer this or that, as describable objects, things, but rather that mother and puer are ways of perceiving. More or less the same 'facts' can be found in puer and in the mother's son, so the real difference between them lies in the way in which we perceive these facts. But the mother does not want to be seen through. She throws up her veils of darkness, her opacity and emotionality, and presents crude, materialized divisions between God and Caesar, this world and the next, time and eternity, sacred and profane, introvert and extravert, and so on, ad infinitum, keeping her animus-son eternally occupied, preventing his need for an eternality of another sort. This eternality of the puer would see through all such opposites in terms of their fundamental likeness as a way of thought. The movement from son to puer, that is, the movement of restoration of the original puer vision, occurs when one sees through the challenge of opposites that the Great Goddess embroils us in so that one can refuse to do battle with her in the field of her entangling dilemmas. By this I do not mean that the puer vision is that of a Nietzschean superman, beyond good and evil. Rather I mean that the puer vision, because of its inherent connection with the senex, can live within this field, as the field of necessity, simply by seeing through to that ambiguity which is the identity of opposites. There is no need either to force choices as does the hero-son or to make a theology of conflict in the fashion of the priest-son. The puer vision is transcendent and beyond in the sense that it is not caught in her literal animus-game; therefore, puer consciousness does not have to be literally transcendent, leave the scene, cut out, blow.

V.

There is also the anti-hero, or hero-in-reverse, who is another puer substitute, another form of the great mother's son. He lives in her lap and off the lap of the land. Rather than all phallus, he is all castration—weak, gentle, yielding to life and its blows. He chooses to lose and his is the soft answer to wrath, which spirit he was unable to meet without the father. His way follows nature, the path of least resistance, eventually into the primeval swamp, bogged. Like water he flows downward, slips out of sight, and has effects underground, so like water that he evokes the divine child in the water-rushes. But this son is not separated from the water by cradle, basket, boat; he is the water. He gives the illusion of being on the right way, wending around obstacles, as the Tao is called water and child. But unlike Icarus he does not plunge into the water vertically, nor does he serve Olympian archetypal principles with wet enthusiasm as does Ganymede the cupbearer. He just goes along with what is going, a stream slipping through the great body of mother nature, ending ultimately in the amniotic estuary streaming into oceanic bliss. Whether hyperactive with heroics or ecstatics, or passive, the flow of energy results from the mother archetype. In the latter case of the anti-hero, there seems an attempt at resolving the puer-complex through the degradation of energy. The individual follows along, letting things happen, dropping out from the demands put upon the heroic ego. He makes few demands even on himself, wanting little and needing less and less. As tensions equalize he believes himself in rare balance, becoming cooler and less personal. His images and ideas become more archetypal, reflecting universal levels of the collective unconscious.

Because there appears to be a spiritual advance in visual, poetic, and metaphysical ideas, the term "regression" is refused as a misnomer. Regression means return to more childish or historically earlier behavior patterns, but in this instance one seems so obviously to be making spiritual advancement toward ever-widening values and general symbols, progressing through the perennial philosophy into truths of all religions—even if requiring sometimes financial support or hallucinogenic reinforcement. One can hardly be 'regressing' while quoting Hesse, Gurdjieff, Tagore, Eckhart, and Socrates! The philosophy, however, has a defensive note providing a wrap-around shield against heroics, will, and effort. For example, the anti-heroics of Ramakrishna: "The nearer you get to God, the less he gives you to do." These traits and the predictable pattern of the anti-hero—what he will do, read, say next—disclose that in his spiritual progress he is actually following the degradation of energy in its entropic direction, which is, in another language as Freud pointed out, Nirvana—or death. The entropy in a system is characterized by cooling and running down, by increase of statistical probability, equalization of tension, generalization (randomness), degradation from higher to lower descriptions of energy, and increasing disorder. All of this appears in individual behavior as well as in the behavior of any complex when it "gives up."

Although the theme of "giving up" belongs in another chapter of the book on puer consciousness and cannot be treated fully here, we may note a difference between the puer and the hero or anti-hero in this respect. The puer gives up because of an inadequate survival sense, that is, owing to a dynamus that does not know how to defend itself or keep itself in order in the senex sense. The hero/anti-hero gives up owing to the mother. The hero (and its opposite, the anti-hero) element in a complex would have the complex get rid of itself. Yet, as Jung points out, the complexes are the mother of psychic energy, and to conquer them, overcome them, or cure oneself of them is another way of trying to rid oneself of the mother.

The puer in the complex is self-destructive because it lacks psyche—containment, reflection, involvement. And it lacks, when separated from the senex, the ability to father itself, to put a roof over its head and a wall around its property. The self-destructiveness of the puer in any complex arises because the complex does not understand itself: it sees, it knows, it makes—but it does not see or know or make itself. There is an absence of psychic reflection of the spirit and an absence of spiritual realization within the psyche.

The hero is self-destructive because it would have done with the complex, and this may occur in various ways. It may appear as eros idealism, the inspiration of transforming the complexes into wholeness. It may appear as anti-heroic cooling of the complexes, depotentiating everything of tension (or its reverse, burning everything up in enthusiasm). It may appear as the cure of loving acceptance—which is also a death-wish, revealing how close eros and thanatos are to each other. For to be healed and made whole by love or to give up the tension by death are close indeed. Both refuse the complex as the fundamental necessity of psychic life, the only cure for which is death. Death alone puts an end to the complexes which are "normal phenomena of life"[12] and like the mother are the fundament of each individual's existence. We are complexed beings, and human nature is a composition of complexities. Without complexes there is no living reality, only a transcendent Nirvana of the Buddha whose last supposed words point to the complexity of the psyche as life's primary given: "Decay is inherent in all composite things—work your salvation with diligence."

Getting rid of and giving up this complexity through any formula for overcoming opposites, or dropping out, or curing misses psychic reality. Psychological therapy is less an overcoming and a getting rid than it is a decay, a decomposing of the way in which we are composed. This the alchemists called the *putrefactio*, the slow time-process of transformation through affliction, wastage, and moral horror. Both heroic getting-rid and passive giving-up attempt to speed decay and have done with it; they would avoid the work of psychic reality by escape into spiritual salvation. *But the cure is the decay.*

When the puer lives authentically to its structure, there is this smell of decadence, a fond attachment to one's mess, which is part of its resistance to analysis. In this sense the puer—seemingly so quick and flame-like—is slow to change, shows no development, seems forever stuck in the same old dirty habits. His putrefaction is in his intractable symptoms of colon and digestion, of eczema and acne, of piles, in his long, slow colds and sinuses, his chronic genital complaints, his money peculiarities, or in his low-life fascinations. These things analysis has wrongly attributed to the shadow repression owing to the mother-complex: he is bound to the mother in a compensatory materialistic way and cannot fight free. But against the background of decay, the slowness and the dirt in the puer can be seen as a way of following the path of putrefaction toward finding the senex. As such it is a digestive, fermentative process that should not be heroically hurried. Nor should it be forcefully 'rubbed in' as a treatment to integrate the shadow. The puer is not a dog; puer consciousness needs not house-breaking and heeling but a new attunement of his sensitivity to the odors of his own decay. His individuation is in the pathologizing process itself and not in his heroic efforts to over-come.

We can anyway not rid ourselves of complexes until they have given us up. Their decaying time is longer than the life of the in-dividual personality, since they continue in a kind of autonomous existence long after we have left the scene; they are part of the psychic inheritance of our children and their children, both natural and spiritual. The complexes are our dosage of sin, our karma, which if given up is really only passed on elsewhere. In the analysis of those men called "puer," one needs a nose for decay, for waste, for moldering ruin. By nursing the mess along we keep the puer alive and in touch with the prima materia; by whitewashing with bland acceptance (giving-up) or hurrying the process to get going (getting-rid), we put the authentic spirit into the old bottle marked "Mother."

VI.

In our consideration of puer and mother we should look, if only briefly, at Dionysos.[13] He has, of course, been perceived as a typical mother's son. The nurses, the milk, the emotionality, the dance, his unheroic behavior and weaponlessness, his softness and effeminacy, the women's favorite—all this has meant to our simple, so-called psychological minds nothing but one more strik-ing archetypal example of the mother-complex.[14]

But Dionysos may also be seen within the puer–senex structure. His name means Zeus-Son; his mythologems are in many aspects almost interchangeable with those of the Cretan Zeus, and in one of his birth performances he is delivered from the thigh of his father, male born of male. It is questionable whether we may call Dionysos puer in our modern psychological sense, even though *puer* was one of his Latin epithets. But since Dionysos was one of the young Gods and since his cult presented him, especially in later antiquity, in child form,[15] he shows traits relevant for our thoughts here, even if the quality of his masculinity differs from what our historical consciousness under its Greco-Roman and Judeo-Christian heroic dominants has decided is masculine. So we have written off "the Dionysian" to the mother; therewith we have missed the spiritual significance implied by Dionysos *puer*, and we have misappreciated the wine, the theatrical and its tragedy, the style of madness and phallicism, and other aspects of his nature and cult that bear on puer consciousness. Puer may find in Dionysos a background to traits and experiences that are not to be taken literally and acted out in dancing troops with tambourines but which offer another and softer means for the puer–senex, father–son, reunion. Dionysos presents the spiritual renewal in nature or the natural renewal of the spirit, encompassing in himself the cyclical and generative traits of mother nature with the culture, inspiration, and irrational excitement of puer consciousness.

Dionysos, they say, has several mothers. Demeter, Io, Dione, Persephone, Lethe, and Semele have been variously named. And the relationship between his mothers is *discontinuous*. Semele is killed by Zeus while still pregnant; Zeus is his second mother; he is mothered by nymphs in a cave, by Persephone, by his grandmother Rhea, who puts back together his dismembered pieces.

This discontinuity in the mother is not exclusive to Dionysos. Other Gods and heroes are 'motherless,' i.e., abandoned, suckled by animals, raised by foster mothers or nurses, the natural mother having disappeared or died. Psychoanalysis has made much of this theme of "the two mothers." It has become the good and bad breast; and Jung, too, devoted a large piece of his *Symbols of Transformation* to "The Dual Mother," by which is meant two sides of the same figure, a positive life-cherishing and a negative life-endangering aspect.

But I would look at the two (or more) mothers from another angle, not as different kinds or faces of one figure, but as an interruption in the relation between mother and child. I suggest that the rupture in natural continuity (Semele's not carrying the child to term) offers another way of regarding the relation between *mater* and *puer*. Owing to the intervention of Zeus's thunderbolt—or whatever other spiritual inroad into the natural continuity between mother and son, whether from Pharaoh (Moses) or from the oracle (Oedipus)—the son does not have to force a break with the mother. It has happened. It is given with his condition. He is no longer only her child. The only-natural has been broken because the spiritual has intervened, and so a separation of puer consciousness from mother occurs without the necessity of cutting or killing. Evidently, another archetype is activated to which the son also belongs, and this other archetype is as signal to his fate as is the mother from whom he is separated.

To make this point more clear let us turn to Leonardo da Vinci. The critical event in his early memory (as Freud and Neumann[16] have written) was indeed the bird that descended to him in the cradle. Leonardo lived with his grandmother and with two successive stepmothers; his natural mother married again and seems to have disappeared from Leonardo's life. Leonardo has a fantasy which he recounts as if it were an actual memory from infancy, that a *nibio* opened his mouth with its tail and struck him many times upon his lips. This bird was *not* a vulture, as Freud and then Neumann have declared. Neumann, despite noticing that a *nibio* is not a vulture and so correcting Freud's error, nonetheless sustains it by retaining the mistranslation as symbolically correct in order to analyze, along with Freud, Leonardo in terms of the mother-complex.[17]

No. The bird which came to Leonardo in his vision was a kite, a relative of the hawk and like it a variety of the genus *falconidae*. (Hawk is the wider term, kite one of its varieties.) We have here to do with a symbol that can best be amplified from Egypt to where Freud turned for his symbolic equation vulture = mother. But it is now the equation: hawk, kite, falcon = Horus = puer. The solar hawk descended upon the Kings at their coronation and was a spirit-soul, a *ka*, and the hawk in a series of other contexts (which I expose in another chapter of this work on the puer) is a puer emblem par excellence.

Because of the specific puer significance of this bird, the dual mother theme in Leonardo, on which Freud and Neumann base their interpretative case of his genius, may rather, and more correctly, be understood in terms of a discontinuity in the mother relation owing to the early intervention of the puer archetype in its apparition as a kite and which Leonardo kept as a valued memory. (I have not examined the biographical material enough to tell whether the intervention of the *nibio* image occurred precisely at a time between two of his many mothers. But I do not think the literal aspect of discontinuity is as important as are the two factors: the intervention of the puer and the discontinuity in mothers.)

Leonardo's interest in flying, his love of birds, as well as his supposed vegetarianism and homosexuality, may thus have a "hawk" in the background rather than a "vulture" and may be grasped as part of puer phenomenology rather than as a mother-complex. The various usages of the word "kite" in English emphasize the puer implications. A kite is a flying, triangular, light framed toy, a favorite of small boys, and a kite is "one who preys upon others." The term refers also to the highest sails of a ship which are set only in a light wind.

Moreover, the 'case' of Leonardo seems paradigmatic for both archetypal psychology in general and the psychology of genius in particular. By ignoring the true significance of an image (in this case the hawk–falcon–kite), one can attribute a crucial event of any life wrongly to an inappropriate archetypal constellation. Then genius is not viewed authentically in terms of the spirit and its early call but is rather attributed to peculiarities in the fate of the mother. Because the vulture-or-kite quarrel stands for the conflict in perspectives between mother and puer, we can see how important an investment early psychoanalysis had in the mother archetype and how there was a consequent mis-perception and repression of the puer which is only now beginning to be revalued.

VII.

A lesson we may draw from the Dionysos and the Leonardo examples is that what we see is determined by how we look, which is in turn determined by where we stand. When we stand within the consciousness influenced mainly by the great mother, all puer phenomena seem derivative of the mother complex, and even our consciousness itself becomes "her son," a resultant of the primordial matrix of the unconscious. Yet, there is no such thing as "the mother-complex." If we are strict and are not just led along by easy language, complexes do not belong to any specific archetype. The complexes—power, money, illness, sex, fear, ambition, jealousy, self-destruction, knowledge, etc.—which form the energetic cores and provide the fantasy stuff of our afflictions and transformations, do not belong to any single God.

First, there are no single Gods. In polytheism each God implies and involves others. *Theos* and *deus* (as well as the Celtic and Nordic roots of our God consciousness) arise in a polytheistic context where reference to God always meant a field of many Gods. A single God without others is unthinkable. Even our Judeo-Christian second commandment makes this statement, albeit in a negative fashion ("Thou shalt have no other Gods before me"). Second, the Gods interpenetrate, as the archetypes interfuse. The archetypes do not so much rule realms of being as they, like the Gods, rule all at once and together the same realm of being, this our world. But they provide distinction within this world, different ways of regarding things, different patterns for psychizing instinct, different modes of consciousness. So, third, complexes are not assigned either by definition or by nature to specific archetypal patterns. Any complex may at one time or another be under the aegis of this or that dominant, and any dominant may at any time take over this or that complex. For example, money may seem to belong to Saturn's greed, he who coined money, or to Mercury the trader, or to the hero's booty, or to Zeus who can appear as a shower of gold; or it may be the gold of Apollo, or belong within the Midas constellation; or money may even point a way into the psychic underworld, for Hades' other name was Pluto (wealth). So, too, for sexuality which takes on altogether different characteristics when Apollonic, Dionysian, Priapian, or in the service of Hera.[18]

Even the puer's orality—seemingly that one complex so certainly belonging to the mother archetype—may be envisioned otherwise. Psychology has surprisingly little to say about taste, food, hunger, eating, except 'orality.' Ever since the "oral stage" was laid out by Freud, everything to do with mouth, stomach, with food and cooking and drinking, with hungers of every sort goes back to Mom and her breasts (or bottle). But puer food behavior can show an asceticism, for instance, of a Pythagorean-Orphic sort. It can show a sensitivity in aesthetic flavors that belong (in the magical-astrological tradition of *Picatrix*) to Venus and not the Moon. Or, the puer hunger, which is usually not for nourishment at all, belongs more properly to Saturn and his greed, the wolf, Moloch, Bhoga, a rapacious eating of the world.

The shift of archetypal background to a complex is a common enough experience when a problematic and habitual knot is suddenly released and a wholly new perspective is disclosed. It is as if the complex has been redeemed by the grace, or the viewpoint, of a different God. We are equally familiar with the reverse: when a virtue suddenly is experienced through another archetype and becomes now "destructive" and a "shadow problem." Sometimes this shift from one archetype to another occurs as a breakdown. What previously supported one's ego-complex—say the nymphic anima, or the flaming, inspiring eros, or the conservative self-righteousness of moralistic Saturn—withdraws its domination. Then, a collapse and revolution take place until the complex can recognize its new Lord and find new archetypal sanction.

By giving over any complex to a single archetype, we condemn it to a single view, a diagnosis made too often in analysis. (This is your spiritual animus, your negative father, your neglected child, etc.) This frustrates the movement of the complex among the Gods, fixating it by definition and frustrating its Hermetic possibilities for transformation through movement of perspective. When we fix a complex to only one archetype, only one sort of insight can arise. It is crucially important to view moodiness, for example, not only as typically puer but also as typically anima, typically mother, and also as a power trick of the shadow, and even of the senex. As Eros does not belong only to Aphrodite because there are many kinds of loving, and as fighting can be governed by Ares, Athene, Nike, Apollo, Hercules, and Amazons, and as madness can be brought on and taken away by a variety of dominants, so may any complex be a tributary of the great mother and yet at the same time accord with the puer–senex.

By this I do not intend to deny complex, negative maternal phenomena. The 'negative mother' appears in the myths of destructive femininity (Hecate, Gorgo, Kali, Lua, and the other Great Goddesses who consume and lay waste). She is also evident in the barrenness of collective kindness, structures without milk, customs without tradition in a civilization that offers no support, nothing natural. The 'negative mother' is visible in the voices of the women with their children, the faces of ugly mouths and flat eyes, the resentment and hatred. It is a wonder anyone survives at all through the early years when mother-love comes with its double, mother-hate. Of course, we live in an age of Moms, for the culture is secular and the ordinary mortal must carry archetypal loads without help from the Gods. The mothers must support our survival without support themselves, having to become like Goddesses, everything too much, and they sacrifice us to their frustration as we in turn, becoming mothers and fathers, sacrifice our children to the same civilization.

The way to 'solve the mother-complex' would be not to cut from Mom but to cut the antagonism that makes me heroic and her negative. To 'solve the mother-complex' of the puer means to remove the puer phenomena from the mother, no longer viewing puer problems as mother-caused and mother-bound. (For in our civilization what cannot be blamed on the mother?) Rather than separate man and mother, we need to separate the archetypal necessity of their association and to consider puer phenomena in their own right. Then one can turn to each puer aspect and ask it where it belongs, in accordance with the procedure in ancient Greece when consulting an oracle. "To what god or hero must I pray or sacrifice to achieve such and such a purpose."[19] To what archetypal pattern do I relate my problem? Within which fantasy can I insight my complex? Once the problem has been placed upon a relevant altar, one can connect with it according to its own needs and connect to the God through it. (Had Freud and Neumann followed this method, they would not have placed Leonardo's genius on the altar of the mothers by mistaking the kite for a vulture and then retaining the mistake in order to fit theory.)

By taking for granted that puer phenomena belong to the great mother, analytical psychology has given the puer a mother-complex. Puer phenomena have received an inauthentic cast for which the epithet "neurotic" feels justified. By laying the complex on the altar of the great mother, rather than maintaining its connection with the *senex-et-puer* unity, we consume our own spiritual ground, giving over to the Goddess our eros, ideals, and inspirations, believing they are ultimately rooted in the maternal, either as my personal mother, or matter, or as a causally conditioned worldly field called society, economics, the family, etc. By making spirit her son, we make spirit itself neurotic. By taking the frailties and youthful follies necessary to all spiritual beginnings

merely as infantilisms of the mother-complex, we nip in the bud
the possibility of renewal in ourselves and our culture. This view
of things serves only to perpetuate the neurosis, preventing the reunion of senex and puer. Puer then seems opposite and enemy of
senex, and the age seems rightly characterized by what Freud suggested, a universal Oedipus complex, son against father because of
the mother.

In individuals, these distortions of the puer show themselves in
the personal mother-complex. In society, there are distortions of
spiritual goals and meanings, because an ambitiously heroic ego-
development has been the recipe for resolution of the puer syndrome. To assume that the puer is primarily the same as the son of
the great mother is to confirm the pathological distortions as an
authentic state of being. The distortion of puer into son is per-
petuated by the mother archetype which prefers the hero myth as
the model for ego-development since that model depicts the ego to
be primarily and necessarily embroiled with her. Our main Western psychological theories rest on a model which more or less declares the dynamics of the psyche to be derivatives of the family
and society, which are the preserve of the mother. Psychology itself
is her victim, not only in its therapeutics of ego development, but
more fundamentally: the spirit of psychology is lamed by materialism, literalism, and a genetic viewpoint toward its own subject
matter, the psyche. The spiritual nature and purposes of psychology never emerge because the puer never emerges from the mother.
Or it emerges still bound with a navel-cord, psychology as a heroic
mission of the priest-son whose urge is either to spread self
through the world or to become self in disdain of the world.

Psychology, as Jung insisted, always reflects our psychic condition.[20] A psychology that sees mother everywhere is a statement
about the psyche of the psychologist and not only a statement based
on empirical evidence. To advance the psyche through its collective
mother-complex, psychology itself must advance in its self-
reflection so that its subject, the soul, is no longer dominated by
naturalism and materialism, and the goals for that soul no longer
formulated via the mother archetype as "growth," "social adaptation," "human relatedness," "natural wholeness," etc.

Our ideas about the psyche affect the psyche. Ideas can be
poisonous or therapeutic. Psychological ideas are particularly important since they tell the psyche about itself, giving a mirror in

which to view its own events. Psychological concepts can work as liberating transformers, offering a new view of what had hitherto been condemned or misperceived. As Jung wrote: "Psychology inevitably merges with the psychic process itself"[21]—and of course as the psychic process moves it will continue to produce new aspects of psychology. In no other field is the state of the doer more involved with what is done than in psychology. Operator and material are indistinguishable; psychology is alchemy in a new dress. The more complicated and differentiated psychic life becomes, the more anachronistic to go on with simplest accounts in terms of bio-chemistry, sociology, psychodynamics, family genetics. Moreover, inadequate psychological accounts interfere with psychic differentiation, having a noxious effect on the soul. For this reason, among many others, psychology turns to mythology. Mythic accounts are the most open, most exploratory, most suggestively subtle yet precise, allowing the soul the widest imagination for its complexes.

Yet mythology for all its precision in detail leaves ambiguities about fundamentals, since the figures themselves, like the archetypes, are *dei ambigui*. We find the figures of hero, puer, and son not distinguished as clearly as our monocular minds would want. Myth offers possibilities for perceiving but not facts for building a case to prove that the puer is this and the son or hero is that. Proof is not the aim of myth; it does not set out to display an argument, to explain, or to demonstrate a single line of thought on any theme. Besides, the great mother is everywhere, because pervasiveness is at the essence of that dominant. So it is not independence from mother that separates puer out from son-hero but independence in our *conception* of the puer.

Perhaps the question—puer or son, authentic spirit or mother-derivative—can never be answered in the form of such sharp alternatives which too betray a kind of consciousness that asks questions in terms of swords and sunlight and would codify the psyche into the straight thinking of priestly dogma. Horus does not have to choose between father and mother; he is hero, puer, and son, all.

Hero, puer, and son are all the same in one basic respect: *youth*. Youth carries the significance of becoming, of self-correcting growth, of being beyond itself (ideals) since its reals are in *status nascendi*. So it is decisive how we envision this youth, whether embodied in a young person, as a dream figure, or as any young potential of the soul, since this youth is the emergence of spirit within the psyche. Just as there are young Gods and heroes, and young men of genius, who cannot all be understood in terms of the Great Goddess, so there are young men and young figures in our dreams who cannot all be interpreted through the mother-complex. Apollo, Hermes, and Dionysos have many typically puer characteristics that cannot be put down to mother, implying an authentic puer consciousness based on their authenticity as full and distinct Gods. Conversely, there are young men who have true mother-complexes in the sense of modern psychology, yet who do not show authentic puer characteristics. There is no fire, no spirit, no goal; the destructive and renegade tendencies are not present; fantasy is weak, and there is no exaggerated woundedness—distinguishing traits of the puer (which we take up in other chapters). So, the ideal therapist of the archetypal persuasion would watch carefully, not calling puer what is a mother-bind and not calling a mother-complex what is puer. And myth would help him note the differences.

The cosmos in which we place youth and through which we in-sight youth will influence its pattern of becoming. From the mother's perspective, male youth belongs with the female as a con-sort, part of her fertility and natural growth, her heroical culture drive, her realm of death. From the senex perspective, male youth is renewal both as hope and as threat, the same and the different in one figure, and a dynamus that calls for order, an innocence asking for knowledge, and a possibility to be realized through time and labor.

Although these two views of youth describe kinds of con-sciousness, we do not need to make a hierarchy of these kinds, demonstrating that matriarchy is prior to patriarchy or that son, hero, puer reflect levels of development. Levels of consciousness imply progress. They trigger the spiritual heroics of self-improvement from mother and matter to enlightenment. (Often the entire climb and the great enlightenment can still be on her ground and a gift of her optical orality, her reward for being good and loving her.) It is not a matter of which is right in terms of which comes first. We are not concerned with the "origins and history of consciousness" or the origins of son, hero, puer, or of Gods. The search for origins has to lead back to the mother anyway who must always come "first," since genetic analysis, analysis in terms of origins, is an obeisance to her and is determined by her kind of consciousness. It is enough to realize that insight can shift perspective from one archetypal background to another and that phenomena now seeming to be of the son can move elsewhere and offer another kind of psychological movement.

VIII.

By laying to rest the notion that the puer is only the son of the great mother, we may also abandon former notions of ego-development. Delivery through battle against an overwhelming mother is no longer the only way.[22] The hero of the will—who has been disappearing from drama and fiction, and political history too—is not always a viable role for ego, nor must battle be the way. The dragon demands battle and the hero myth tells us how to proceed. But suppose we were to step out altogether from the great mother, from Jocasta and Oedipus and the exhausting, blinding heroics that so often kill the feminine opposite—not just 'out there' in the enemy but within the heroic psyche itself.

If Emerson considered the hero to be he who was immovably centered (which can be reversed to mean he who is so fixed on the center that he has lost his mobility), we might define the hero as he who has maimed femininity. In compensation to this, analytical psychology has long concentrated on the anima as therapy for the ego (or persona) identification. But the basic notions of the anima, and the therapeutic sentimentalisms about her, are in turn the result of the same psychology's efforts to strengthen the ego. The anima would not have to carry feeling, femininity, soul, imagination, introversion, subtlety, and what have you if the ego were not so bound to the hero myth, so fixed in its central focus on 'reality,' 'problems,' and 'moral choice.'

Suppose we were no longer to conceive of the ego's relation to its development and to the spirit on the heroic model, achieving through fighting, keeping in shape, trusting in the right arm, overcoming all darkness with the enlightenment of the ego over the id. Is this the only way to consciousness and culture?

Freud defined the intention of psychoanalysis: ". . . to strengthen the ego, to make it more independent of the super-ego, to widen its field of perception and enlarge its organization, so that it can appropriate fresh portions of the id. Where id was, there ego shall be. It is a work of culture."[23] Oedipus, hero and king, determines not only the content of psychoanalysis but also its impetus, its heroism. Analysis, psychological development, becoming conscious are new models of cultural heroism so that the culture hero is the thoroughly analyzed man, sublimated, integrated, whole, conscious. And analysis, as a way of achieving this goal, becomes a suffering pilgrimage or trial by ordeal of the hero. If Freud was right that Oedipus is the stuff of neurosis, then the corollary follows that Oedipus-heroics are the dynamism of neurosis. Heroism is thus a kind of neurosis and the heroic ego is neurotic ego. Creative spirit and fertile matter are there embraced and embattled to the destruction of both. Ego-development that is patterned on the hero will have as part of this pattern the shadow of the hero —estrangement from the feminine and compulsive masculinity —foreshadowing the sterile and bitter senex as outcome of the heroic course.

The wandering loneliness of such figures as Jason, Bellerophon, Oedipus (and perhaps Orestes who lived on to seventy) after their great deeds were done, and their failures, may be seen in two different ways. On the one hand, this wandering loneliness is temporal, belonging to the heroic course which issues into the used-up old king. (The hero—was he a puer?—of F. Scott Fitzgerald's *Tender Is the Night* slowly falls away, aimless like Bellerophon, wandering to ever smaller towns through the great plains.) But, on the other hand, we may regard synchronically this behavior trait as a senex aspect of the puer from the beginning, his steady companion.

The hero and the puer seem to have to go it alone (unlike Dionysos, who sometimes is the lonely stranger but who is usually together with a crowd). Yes, this characteristic shows something renegade, psychopathic, schizoid; however, if it is a senex attribute within the puer figure, the attempt to socialize a young man who is following a puer pattern violates the style of his individuation and the integration of the senex component. Leave it alone, says the style itself. The socializing impetus is again that of the mother, whereas the spirit does indeed blow in gusts, free, where it will, and often where no one else can go along. For the mother this is hard to take because she is 'by nature' everywhere and wants no phase, no part off on its own, unconnected, out of touch. As a myth can be read two ways—strung out into successive events or condensed where all parts are present at any one time—so we may look at a life in the same way. Assertive masculinity results in aimlessness, or assertive masculinity results from aimlessness. Owing to the proximity of puer and senex, we cannot tell which comes first.

Assertive masculinity is suspicious. Somewhere we know that it must be reactive to feminine attachment. Mythical levels of the psyche support the suspicion, for there it is recollected that hero and female opponent are inseparable. Although they meet in battle, the hero shouting, they could as well be in bed and groaning, because battle with the mother is a manner of incest. Whether as lover or as enemy, his role is determined by his opposite, his polarity with the mother. When mother determines the role, then regardless how it is played its essence is always the same: son. And, as Jung says of assertive heroism: "Unfortunately, however, this heroic deed has no lasting effects. Again and again the hero must renew the struggle, and always under the symbol of deliverance from the mother. . . . The mother is thus the daemon who challenges the hero to his deeds and lays in his path the poisonous serpent that will strike him."[24] As long as psychotherapy is conceived in terms of ego development, the development will never be strong enough and the task will never be done. Rather than being therapists of psyche, we are therapists (servants and devotees) of mother.

Even the *imitatio Christi*—and especially as it is exhibited in the contemporary program of Christianity in social action—supports the heroic ego and keeps it embroiled in the hassle with the archetypal mother. The "Church in Action" belongs to the myth of the culture hero, a Herculean absorption of Jesus,[25] where Jesus fades into the older archetypal patterns of Gilgamesh, Shamash, and Hercules, losing the special relation of Father and Son which Jesus' words themselves so emphasize. Yet, Jesus does bring a sword in the heroic fashion, and this blade from the beginning of the Christian era until today is plunged century after century into the body of the dragon, now meaning this, now meaning that, but always consciousness is defined through this slaughter. If in traditional Christian heroics the knife slays the evil, in Greek mythic thought the knife *is* the evil.[26] Have we gone far enough when we reflect upon our Western history of incredible bloodshed only in terms of aggression and the aggressive instinct in animals? This takes evil right out of the psyche and puts it safely into some objective field. Let us once look closer at the knife (which animals don't have) and interiorize, psychologize aggression in terms of our very *definition of consciousness:* the logos sword of discrimination in the hands of the heroic ego in his mission to clean up the mother-benighted world. What we have taken for consciousness, this too has been determined by the mother. To be conscious has meant and continues to mean: to kill.

Discrimination is the essential, the sword only a secondary instrument. Consciousness requires discrimination, for, as Jung said, there is no consciousness without perception of differences. But this perception can use the delicacy of fingers, sensitivity of ear, eye, and taste, a feeling for values and tones and images. There can be puer aesthetic distinctions without swords. The puer has this talent for craft in his background—Joseph the carpenter, Daedalus the inventor (cf. *CW* 5, §515); these fathers put the knife to another use.

Hercules is a primordial figure of assertive masculinity and is the killer-culture-hero par excellence. His cult was the most widely observed in Greek antiquity, yet his name means simply Glory of Hera.[27] Although this Goddess acts as his enemy before his birth and from his cradle where she sent serpents to kill him, it is this Great Goddess who spurs his deeds as culture hero. In the madness of Hercules described by Euripides, the hero claims he was driven beyond the borders of sanity into heroic extremes by Hera, who plagued his life throughout. Yet, he is explicitly her servant, even coming to her rescue when she had been accosted by Silenus,[28] and he receives as his bride in final reward Hebe, who is none other than Hera herself in her younger, sweeter, seductive form.

Hercules is merely one of the heroes driven by this Great Goddess to perform his deeds for her civilization. Hera sends the Sphinx to Oedipus; she (Juno) is the specific persecutor of Aeneas and is the background to Jason's exploits. Hera, the tales say, mothered the monster Typhon and nourished the Hydra and Nemean lion. She had a part in the persecutions and slaying of Dionysos. Hera is the "Enemy's consort."[29] Her own children are

Ares[30] of the battle-rage and Hephaistos[31] the ironworker, the volcano.

We are so used to assuming that the son of the great mother appears as a beautiful ineffectual who has laid his testicles on her altar and nourishes her soil with his blood, and we are so used to believing that the hero pattern leads away from her, that we have lost sight of the role of the Great Goddess in what is closest to us: our ego-formation. The adapted ego of reality is in her "yoke,"[32] a meaning of Hera, just as the words *hero* and *Hera* are taken by many scholars to be cognate.[33] When outer life, or inner life, is conceived as a contest for light, an arena of struggles, success versus failure, coping versus collapse, work versus sleep, pleasure and love, then we are a child of Hera.[34] And the ego that results is the mother-complex in a jockstrap.

My point here is to reverse the usual order: puer is weak and mother-bound; hero is strong and mother-free. If the hero is really the son and strength what the mother wants, then we might look at the puer's weaknesses differently.

The son disguises himself as the hyperactive culture hero of civilization, all of whose conquests, glories, triumphs, and spoils ultimately serve the mother of material civilization. The hero of antiquity was so fond of his trophies. Heroic consciousness must have something to show; the ego must have its concrete proof, for such is its definition of reality. Battle has always been for booty and not only for the fun of fighting and pride of winning. But the loot and spoils soon decorate a city, become the furnishings of domestic life, and the hero begins to accumulate possessions. (A votary object to Hera in Paestum was a little terracotta *domus,* house.) The domestication of the marauding, careless adventurer finally takes place through marriage, mimesis not of his archetype but of hers, the *hieros gamos* with Zeus, and, in the case of Hercules and Hebe, a place in the upper world at her side. (Hercules was married to, or the consort of, Hera "from the beginning" before Zeus, so that Hebe is the *dénouement* that brings the tale full circle.[35]) Hero and puer here differ considerably, since the exploits of the former show a preponderance of civilizing virtues, viz., Hercules, Jason, and Theseus. The puer's task is more an odyssey of the spirit, a wandering that never comes home to any hearth or city. (For exploration of the wandering and longing theme in puer psychology, see the chapter "Pothos" in my *Loose Ends.*[36])

These considerations of the hero/mother relation must take into account one more essential element in the hero: death. Pointing to any element in heroic psychology as 'essential' is always subject to counter-arguments. After all, the hero has been a principal focus for historians of Greek religion and for psychologists, whose writings on this theme reach heroic proportions, as if the theme drives its student into spectacular efforts of mastery. Of the major themes that characterize the hero analyzed and abstracted by Brelich, Farnell, Fontenrose, Kerényi, Nock, Campbell, Harding, Neumann, and Roheim[37] (to extend the list would drive us, too, further into heroics), let us single out *the cult of the burial tumulus* as a central focus of the hero myth. Of course the hero's spectacular mantic and healing powers, his virtue and strength, his cultural deeds, his role as model in initiation and as founder of cult, city, clan, and family should not be overlooked, but most writers agree that the hero cult is bound to a distinct locus and the locus indicated by a burial mound.

When reference is made to a hero in antiquity it is an evocation of something dead; there are no present heroes, no heroes now, living in the present tense. To be a hero (or the hero-in-reverse as anti-hero) one must be 'dead.' The hero is dead because he is an imaginal power, a fantasy. The hero is present not in actuality but as a psychic projection through his cult, in his local tumulus where he is buried, and only 'after' the events and through legends of them. The hero himself has been translated to the Isles of the Blest, removed, distant, out of it. The hero is a revenant, providing a fantasy for what the complex can do with itself. The hero gives us the model for that peculiar process upon which our civilization rests: dissociation. We worship the drive of the complex and refuse its inertia. The inertia we call unconscious, regressive, dragon, mother; the drive we call consciousness. We all, whose 'family' and 'city' are founded upon heroic consciousness and whose initiation is modeled upon the hero, are haunted by this revenant spirit that takes the basic element of psychic life, the complex, from one side only, the negentropic upward direction, calling the dynamic movement which it releases 'ego.' In this manner the complex civilizes itself through achievements, casting off its inertia into unconsciousness. The heroic presents an ascending spirit, active in its questing and transcendent to life (dead) and in the Isles of the Blest.[38] These characteristics are also (as we set out in other chapters) puer themes. Therefore, the puer is readily caught up in heroics. But there is a difference, and this difference may be conceived in regard to death, the element we have considered central to the idea of the hero.

The son, the hero, and the puer may all die the same death. But I would hazard a sugestion about differences: the son's 'death' is for the mother (Attis, say); the hero's 'death' is because of the mother (Hercules and Hera, Baldur and Frigg, Achilles and Thetis[39]), or the mother helps the hero to his translation to heroic stature by being his carrier (to the Isles of the Blest) or by keeping him sacred after death, i.e., keeping death more sacred than life (cf. the Gardens of Adonis, the groves sacred to Hippolytus, Orpheus buried by the Muses, his Aunts); the puer's death is independent of the mother. These distinctions are again one of attitude, perspective, not of mythical 'fact,' and bespeak the place that death holds within the psyche for son, hero, and puer. Where death means sacrifice (the son) or victory (hero)—"death, where is thy sting"—the mother is playing her significant role. Death connected with the senex, its survival, its depression, its penetrating insight, presents another image and emotion.

IX.

Son and great mother metamorphose into hero and serpent—or do they? Jung says that the hero and the dragon he overcomes are brothers or even one; the man who has power over the daemonic is himself touched by the daemonic.[40] Harrison wrote that the snake as *daimon* is the double of the hero; the early hero had snake form, and even the higher Gods (Ares, Apollo, Hermes, Zeus) have their serpent aspect as did Demeter and Athene.[41] If hero and serpent are one, then the battle turns the hero against his own nature. But what precisely does he turn against, and how does the animal double of his own structure, this daimon or dragon or serpent, become 'mother'? Psychology's approach to this motif is usually in terms of development. 'Development' has been the master-key to all the locked riddles in modern psychology, just as fertility once opened what we did not understand in mythology and archeology. The supposed development of consciousness occurs from a darker level to a lighter one, from only matter to also spirit, from only nature to also culture. This "development of consciousness" supposedly occurs historically in civilizations, phylogenetically in the species and race, and ontogenetically in each individual from maternal attachment to paternal self-reliance. The hero against serpent is thus *the paradigm* for the kernel structure in our personal and collective consciousness.

Were we to be interviewed by an aboriginal anthropologist from Australia for our "dream," our "Gods," and our "cosmology," this would be the story we would tell. We would tell of the struggle each day brings to Ego who must rise and do battle with Depression and Seduction and Entanglement, so as to keep the world safe from Chaos, Evil, and Regression, which coil round it like an oppressive Swallowing Serpent. This gives account to our inquirer of our peculiar irrationalities: why we sweep the streets, why we pay taxes, why we go to school and to war—all with compulsive ritualistic energy so as to keep the Serpent at bay. This is our true cosmology; for Ego, who changes rivers in their course and shoots to the moon, acts not out of hunger or Gods or tribal persecutions, as the inquiring aboriginal might imagine in his savage mind, so inert and lazy, bound to the maternal uroboros, with his "weak ego." No, our civilization's excessive activism is all to keep back the night of the Serpent, requiring a single monotheistic singlemindedness, a cyclop's dynamism of all the Gods which She and Ego have partaken in together at a Western banquet lasting three thousand years and perhaps now coming to its indigestible conclusion as Ego weakens in what we call "neurosis" and the swallowed Gods stir again in the imaginal dark of his shadow and of her belly. Ego and Unconscious, Hero and Serpent, Son and Mother, their battle, their bed and their banquet—this is the sustaining myth we must tell to account for our strange ways: why we are always at war, why we have eaten up the world, why we have so little imaginative power, and why we have only one God and He so far away.

Snake and dragon are *not* one and the same. The snake is a piece of nature and well represents instinctual being, especially the hard-to-grasp movements of introverting libido. But the dragon, as we pointed out above, does not exist in external nature. It is a fantasy instinct, or the instinct of fantasy, which the hero slays, thereby becoming the singleminded ego of will-power. If the snake is the *daimon* of the instinctual psyche, the dragon, who shoots fire from his tongue and eyes, blazes with color, and controls the waters, who lives below our daily world but could as well with his wings inhabit the sky, is the *daimon* of our imaginal psyche. The masculine sword of reason in the masculine hand of will kills both snake and dragon, both instinct and imagination, in daily combat as the ego enacts our central myth.

Undoubtedly, the dragon has moon associations; and the snake has feminine connotations in mythological and in psychological material and can be found in our culture in association with the Great Goddess. But the snake can as well be found with heroes, kings, and Gods. It is strongly sexual, phallic even, yet transcends gender. It appears in the religion of primordial man. (Adam too has his snake.) Like nature, instinct, libido, or the *mercurius* of alchemy—for each of which the serpent stands—it is a primordial form of life, or life in its primordiality, *Ur*-life. *The serpent is primordiality itself,* which can transform into anything, so that we experience it in sexuality, project it backward into ancestors as their ghost, envision it in earth or below it, hear its wisdom, fear its death. It is a power, a numinosity, a primordiality of religion. Its meanings renew with its skin and peel off as we try to grasp hold. (The dragon's many-heads say we cannot meet it with one idea alone.) The slippery flow of meanings makes it possible for Great Goddess and *daimon* to merge, to lose their distinction, so that by means of the serpent (Hera sending the snakes to baby Hercules) the mother gets at the puer and brings his fall into heroism. She tempts him into the fight for deliverance from her. By falling for the challenge he is delivered of his own *daimon*. Like Beowulf he dies when he kills the dragon. The Dragon-Fight is his undoing.

In the mixture of the three components—man, mother, snake—the snake loses its life, the man loses his snake, but the mother has her hero. This leaves him without wisdom, without chthonic depths, vital imagination, or phallic consciousness, a one-sided solar-hero for a civilization ruled by the mother or by the senex whose snakes have gone into the sewers. By losing chthonic consciousness, which means his psychoid *daimon* root that trails into the ancestors in Hades, he loses his root in death, becoming the real victim of the "Battle for Deliverance,"[42] and ready for Hebe. Because the heroic way to spirit goes against the snake, it is secretly a self-destruction.

By turning against the snake, heroic consciousness also tends to lose the other animals of the mother world, especially the cow of nature. With this goes the warmth, the muzzle and the eyes, the rumination and the slowness, the pastures for the soul, Hera as Hathor, the holiness of life and its rhythm. In the struggle for independence and self-reliance, he can no longer return to the stable without fearing decomposition. (Hercules cleans stables.) So of course heroic consciousness cannot get through, as fairytales say, without the helpful animal. A consciousness that had not defined itself by refusing the animal in the first place would not be in this predicament of lost animal help, its sureness and knowledge of survival.

Furthermore, heroic consciousness constellates its fundamental opposite as feminine and as enemy. The great figures on whose patterns we build our ego strength—Oedipus and Hercules, Achilles, Hippolytus, and Orpheus—in different ways opposed the feminine and fell victim to it.[43] Could we not turn another way? Could we become conscious without that struggle? Ego development has so long been conceived through the heroics of tough aggression, paranoid misogyny, selfishness, and distance of feeling so typical of the mother's son that we have neglected other paths opened by the puer.

Must the feminine continue to be the primary enemy to be magnified into a magna mater whom one succumbs to, worships, or battles, but with whom one never simply pairs as equal though different? Whenever we are sons of this Great Feminine, the feminine is experienced as "great." Woman is idealized. She is endowed with the divine power to save or destroy. We look for the wonderful woman to be our salvation, which then constellates the other side, betrayal and destruction. Every idealization of the feminine is only a propitiation of her other components: the Amazons, the Furies, the Graeae, the Sirens, the Harpies, Circe, Phaedra, Medea, Baubo, Persephone, Hecate, Gorgo, Medusa. The expectation to be saved by a woman goes hand in hand with the fear of being destroyed by her.

Here we come upon one more difference between puer and heroic son. The magnification of the mother-complex is a sure sign that we are choosing the heroic role whose purpose is less spirit and less psyche than it is the traditional ego, its strengthening and its development. The epic dramas in which the hero is cast with impossible tasks, miraculous weapons, overwhelming enemies, and where mother is a dragon, witch, or Goddess can well make a man forget the ordinary mother in the case. But in many tales the mother is merely human, or a lowly nymph, reminding consciousness of its commonness. By keeping to this personal, ordinary, human mother, her specific pathological lacks and her unique graces, we can keep at our backs as support the sense of human ordinariness given by the limits of our actual personal mother-complex, what she passes to us and how we descend from her, for which we have gratitude. She is our history, and it is from her simple lap that we fell (*casus*) as a case. By keeping her in proportion, we can then reserve the *magnificatio* for the puer archetype itself, its narcissism and high-flying ambition to create. The hero's *hybris* (inflation) arises from his hidden identity with the mother; the puer's *superbia* (arrogance) reflects his cocky, narcissistic conviction that he is about his father's business, a child of the spirit, bearing its message. (But of this, his necessary ascensionism, we cannot speak here, for it too belongs to a separate chapter.)

Released from these mystiques of the son–great mother, the feminine could show other individualities, as in the *Odyssey*. There the feminine plays many roles: Goddess (Athene), Mistress (Calypso), Devourer (Scylla and Charybdis), Enchantress (Circe), Mother–Daughter (Arete–Nausicaa), Personal Mother (Anticleia), Rescuer (Ino), Seductress (Sirens), Nurse (Eurykleia), and Wife (Penelope).[44] With each, man finds individual ways of coming to terms, loving, and being furthered. There, the feminine does not threaten the eventual rapprochement of father and son. (But Ulysses, like the King figure in alchemy, is himself *senex-et-puer*.) The feminine in the *Odyssey* works throughout for the reunion of the divided house of Ithaca, giving us a model for the way in which feminine patterns can weave together puer and senex, rather than divide them further through the penchant of the great mother for heroics which magnify her into a man's main concern, literalizing his psychic reality, clouding his puer vision, and distracting him away from his puer necessities.

X.

If I could sum up into one main thought the many ideas we have touched upon, it would be this. Jung makes a clear distinction between the role of the mother archetype as regressive and devouring, on the one hand, and as the creative matrix, on the other. He places this duality within the fantasy of another duality—the first and second halves of life. For young consciousness "entry into the mother" is a fatal incest; for old consciousness it is the way of renewal and even that which he calls the way of individuation.[45] We do not need to keep this important idea of Jung's within the frame of its presentation. First and second half, young and old, are another way of putting the puer–senex duality, which are structures of consciousness valid always and not only as they are divided from each other into first and second halves of life. Because our culture appears now to be in a period when its heroic ego has peaked and where the senex dominant, and so the puer complement, is now of extreme relevance, collective consciousness itself is in what Jung would call "the second half." For anyone in this culture at this time the battle with the mother and the heroic stance of the "first half" cannot but be archetypally wrong, regardless of one's age. This stance is anachronistic in the true sense of being out of tune with time, and every victory over the mother is a defeat for the fundamental task of the present culture: becoming aware of the senex in all its archetypal significance and relating puer phenomena to it.

1.   Jung's main remarks directly on the puer aeternus in relation with the mother-complex are in CW 5, §393: "The lovely apparition of the puer aeternus is, alas, a form of illusion. In reality he is a parasite on the mother, a creature of her imagination, who only lives when rooted in the maternal body." Cf. CW 5, §§392, 394, 526 (but also passim in that volume on the mother's son and the hero) and CW 16, §336 ("provisional life"). In CW 9, i, "Psychological Aspects of the Mother Archetype," "The Psychology of the Child Archetype," and "On the Psychology of the Trickster Figure" are important for puer psychology in relation with and distinction from the mother. In CW 13, "The Spirit Mercurius" is useful for some puer phenomenology independent of the mother-complex. For classical cases of the mother-complex in the son, see, for instance, CW 7, §§167 ff. and also J. Jacobi, "Symbols in an Individual Analysis," in Man and His Symbols, ed. C. G. Jung (London: Aldus, 1964), pp. 272 ff. This last case might look quite different were it to have been viewed through the eyes of the puer–senex constellation.
           Following Jung's early (pre-alchemical) view of the puer would be M.-L. von Franz: "With the concept of the eternal youth, puer aeternus, we in psychology describe a definite form of neurosis in men, which is distinguished by a fixation [Steckenbleiben] in the age of adolescence as a result of an all too strong

mother-bind. The main characteristics are therefore those corresponding with
C. G. Jung's elaborations in his essay on the mother archetype . . ." in her "Ueber
religiöse Hintegründe des Puer-Aeternus-Problems," in *The Archetype*, ed. A.
Guggenbühl-Craig (Basel: Karger, 1964), p. 141 (trans. mine); and J. L. Henderson, *Thresholds of Initiation* (Middletown, Conn.: Wesleyan University Press,
1967), p. 24: "we may conjecture that when things go wrong with the archetype
of the *puer aeternus*, it is because the mother is too demanding or too rejecting,
thus frustrating the youth in his normal orientation to the feminine principle as
anima-function, or because the youth for some other reason falls into a passive-
dependent attitude upon the mother or her substitute." In the same vein: E.
Neumann and M. E. Harding, whose works are cited below in the relevant
places, and also G. F. Heyer, "Die Grosse Mutter im Seelenleben des heutigen
Menschen," *Eranos Jahrbuch 6—1938* (Zürich: Rhein, 1939), pp. 454, 474. For
intimations of a new view of the puer, this time in connection with Artemis
(rather than the mother): R. Malamud, "The Amazon Problem," in *Facing the
Gods* (Dallas: Spring Publications, 1980), pp. 47–66.

2.   Not all young male figures show the same pattern. For instance: Hercules is threatened by Hera and even complains of being driven mad by her, while
Icarus is altogether with the father; Ganymede and Hyacinthus are loved by male
figures, Zeus and Apollo. The interest of the mothers in Achilles, Theseus, and
Perseus is more protective than erotic—so, too, in the Nordic-Baldur, and in
Moses, Jacob, and Jesus. In these latter examples, where protection and pushing
the son forward are the mother's concern, the entanglement through incestuous
libido is not the paramount theme. Each mythologem tells another story. The *differences* are more important for an individual destiny than are the generalizations
about the "mother-complex."

There are as well differences among the heroes. Various types have been
sorted out: messianic hero, culture hero, suffering martyr, trickster, etc. Just as
the word *hero* of mythology has become the word *ego* of psychology, so there is a
variety of heroic styles as there is a variety of ego styles. What is characteristic of
both hero and ego is the central importance of action. Action may be expressed
by deeds, by importance of honor and reputation, by a remarkable journey or, in
reverse, by desolate, impotent suffering. For action the specific psychological attitude of literalizing is necessary. Both hero and ego—no matter the variety of
styles and differences between, say, the Venus-hero and the Mars-hero and the
Apollo-hero—require a literalization of the challenge. The maiden must be won,
the dragon fought, the culture produced, the death accomplished. Literalism, in
my view, is a more fundamental trait of hero psychology than the compulsion to
act.

3.   Cf. my discussion of this theme in both *The Myth of Analysis* (Evanston:
Northwestern University Press, 1972), pp. 169–90, and in *Re-Visioning Psychology* (New York: Harper & Row, 1975).

4.   CW 16, §181.

5.   Concerning the father (and the senex) as meaning and order, see my
"On Senex Consciousness" and the paper of A. Vitale both elsewhere in the present volume.

6. "These are three essential aspects of the mother: her cherishing and nourishing goodness, her orgiastic emotionality, and her Stygian depths," and as Jung goes on to say, *not* "discriminating knowledge" (*CW* 9, i, §158 and elsewhere in the present volume).

7. *CW* 5, §199.

8. R. B. Onians, *The Origins of European Thought,* 2d. ed. (Cambridge: Cambridge University Press, 1954), pp. 349–95.

9. Cf. J. Fontenrose, *Python: A Study of Delphic Myth* (Berkeley: University of California Press, 1959), p. 582, for references to the Venusberg–Siren theme, relevant to the mother–anima contamination.

10. "The Roman ceremonies which were held in Attis' honor during the month of March were divided into two principal parts: the *tristia,* the commemoration of Attis' passion and death, and the *hilaria,* the festivities of his followers, who believed that the god comes to life again after a long winter sleep" (M. J. Vermaseren, *The Legend of Attis in Greek and Roman Art* [Leiden, 1966], p. 39). Attis is another of the appearing and disappearing Gods whose cyclical return has been interpreted as the vegetative rhythm and the *tristia* and *hilaria* ultimately as fertility rituals. By substituting "libido" for "fertility," we can transpose the entire pattern from the external and natural to the internal and psychological level. Then the *tristia* and *hilaria* refer to the rhythm of the libido, the discontinuities (comings and goings) of the puer impulse, at whose appearance we rejoice and feel Spring, and in whose absence there is the sadness of Winter which Attis too represented (i.e., his senex side). These seasons and this fertility are not just 'out there' in nature but 'inside' experienced as the natural cycle of psychic energy.

11. Curious how the mother archetype has encroached upon areas that once belonged to other archetypes. The earth in ancient Egyptian mythology was Geb, a God (not a Goddess). The sea, taken so stereotypically in the analytical interpretation of dreams as a 'symbol for' (hence, 'sign of') the collective unconscious as matrix and thus as the maternal element, was once the province of Father Okeanos, who was a source of all things (Homer), and the rivers of life were fathering river Gods, e.g., Achelous, Poseidon (Helikon). Cf. K. Kerényi, "Man and Mask" in *Spiritual Disciplines,* Papers from the Eranos Yearbooks 4 (London: Routledge, 1961), p. 158.

In Jung's English-language *Collected Works,* the only archetype that consistently receives capital letters is the Great Mother, an honoring not offered to the wise old man, anima, animus, or even self; the "gods" and "goddesses" are also written small.

12. *CW* 8, §§211, 213.

13. The best modern treatment of Dionysos in English is that of W. F. Otto, *Dionysus: Myth and Cult,* trans. R. Palmer (Bloomington: Indiana University Press, 1965; reprinted, Dallas: Spring Publications, 1981). I have given further literature on Dionysos in my *The Myth of Analysis,* pp. 258–81 and have reviewed how Jung regards this figure in my "Dionysos in Jung's Writings," in *Facing the Gods,* pp. 151–64.

14. E. Neumann, whose main line of thinking (feeling?) is within the mother archetype, of course places Dionysos in her train. He speaks of Leonardo's painting of Bacchus as a portrayal of the puer aeternus: "The relaxed and indolent way in which the hermaphroditic god sits resting in the countryside is wholly in keeping with the ancient conception of Dionysus. . . . Leonardo, unconsciously no doubt, portrayed a central figure of the matriarchal mystery world, closely related to the vulture goddess. For Dionysus is the mystery god of feminine existence." He continues this for several paragraphs; his point is that Dionysos is another "divine luminous son of the Great Mother" (E. Neumann, "Leonardo and the Mother Archetype," in his *Art and the Creative Unconscious,* trans. R. Manheim, Bollingen Series [New York: Pantheon, 1959], p. 70). I would not disabuse the reader from Neumann's view: any archetype may be viewed from within any perspective so that Dionysian events may well be seen as matriarchal. I would only disabuse the reader from Neumann's argument, as if it were based on evidence. The vulture has nothing to do either with Dionysos or with the puer; Egypt is only one of many 'alien' and 'border' areas from which Dionysos and his cult were said to spring; Dionysos did not come "late to Greece" (Neumann) but appears even in the early Cretan culture. Mythical statements about archetypes are anyway to be read mythically, psychologically, and not historically, literally.

There is a significant difference between Jung and Neumann in regard to the puer nature of Dionysos. Although Jung does once place Dionysos (Iacchus/Zagreus) as a puer aeternus within the Eleusinian mystery cult, and thus within the mother archetype (*CW* 5, §§526–27), he noted already in 1911 (*CW* 5, §184): "The double figure of the adult and infant Dionysus . . . ," speaking of him in the context of the "giant and dwarf," "big and little," "father and son." Thus Jung saw what Neumann did not: Dionysos is himself a *senex-et-puer* and can as well be regarded from this perspective as from within that of the mother.

15. Cf. M. P. Nilsson, "The Dionysiac Mysteries of the Hellenistic and Roman Age," *Skrift. Utgv. Svenska Instit. Athen* 8/5 (1957): 111.

16. S. Freud, "Leonardo da Vinci and a Memory of His Childhood," in *The Standard Edition of the Complete Psychological Works of Sigmund Freud,* ed. James Strachey, 24 vols. (London: Hogarth Press, 1953–1974), vol. 11; E. Neumann, "Leonardo and the Mother Archetype."

17. Neumann, "Leonardo," p. 14: "Against the background of archetypal relations, the bird of Leonardo's childhood fantasy, considered in its creative-uroboric unity of breast-mother and phallus-father, is symbolically a 'vulture' even if Leonardo called it a '*nibio*'. . . . For this reason we are perfectly justified in retaining the term 'vulture', which Freud chose 'by mistake', for it was through this very 'blunder' that his keen intuition penetrated to the core of the matter. . ." (i.e., "the symbolic equation *vulture = mother*" [p. 7]).

This vulture was 'seen' by Oskar Pfister in Leonardo's painting of St. Anne with Virgin and Christ Child as a negative form in the blue cloth that drapes and links the figures. Jung too 'saw' a vulture in that painting. In a letter to Freud of 17 June 1919, Jung writes that he has seen a vulture (*Geier* in German) in a different place from the one seen by Pfister. Jung's vulture has its "beak precisely in the pubic region."

Strachey, who edited Freud's works for the *Standard Edition*, said the hidden vulture idea must be abandoned in the light of the kite-hawk-falcon (*nibio*) which was Leonardo's actual bird. But Neumann responds to this by saying that, in Pfister, Freud, and in Leonardo too, "the symbolic image of the Great Mother proved stronger than the actual image of the 'kite'" ("Leonardo," pp. 64–66). The power of the archetypal image of the Great Mother certainly dominated the psychoanalytic interpretation in all these commentators, but this does not establish that it also dominated Leonardo in the same way.

For a succinct devastation of Freud's Leonardo thesis, based on the vulture–kite confusion, see D. E. Stannard, *Shrinking History: On Freud and the Failure of Psychohistory* (New York: Oxford University Press, 1980), pp. 5–21.

18. For a more thorough sketch of the mobility of the complex among different archetypal dominants and their perspectives, see my *The Myth of Analysis,* pp. 40–49, where I present the notion (and complex) of creativity as it can be experienced by seven different archetypal structures.

19. H. W. Parke, *Greek Oracles* (London, 1967), p. 87.

20. *CW* 8, §223.

21. Ibid., §429.

22. Jung's classic work *Symbols of Transformation* (*CW* 5) provides a full description of the development of consciousness in terms of the hero's struggle with the mother. More or less in the same line are the works of E. Neumann, *The Origins and History of Consciousness,* Bollingen Series (New York: Pantheon, 1954), esp. pp. 44–52, and M. E. Harding, *Psychic Energy: Its Source and Goal,* Bollingen Series (New York: Pantheon, 1947). It is against this background of classic Jungian literature that my critique of the heroic way should be read.

23. Freud, "New Introductory Lectures," in *The Standard Edition,* vol. 22, p. 80.

24. *CW* 5, §540.

25. On the Hercules–Christ identifications, see E. R. Goodenough, *Jewish Symbols in the Greco–Roman Period,* Bollingen Series (New York: Pantheon, 1964), 10: 122–23 with notes, and M. Simon, *Hercule et le Christianism* (Paris, 1955); also, G. K. Galinsky, *The Herakles Theme* (London, 1972).

26. K. Kerényi, "Evil in Greek Mythology can be symbolized by the knife. . . ." "A man desires to kill if he is 'evil', and that *is* the nature of the 'evil'" ("The Problem of Evil in Mythology," in *Evil* [Evanston: Northwestern University Press, 1967], pp. 15 f.).

27. Cf. P. Slater's *The Glory of Hera* (Boston: Beacon, 1971). The book reviews the major Greek mythical figures, especially heroes, and sees them all from within the sociology of the mother-complex, represented by Hera. The Gods and heroes he treats are ultimately projections of different styles of the mother-complex. His view is not archetypal; that is, he has not learned from Jung that ". . . we are obliged to reverse our rationalistic causal sequence, and instead of deriving these figures from our psychic conditions, must derive our psychic conditions from these figures" (*CW* 13, §299).

28. K. Kerényi, *The Heroes of the Greeks* (London, 1959), p. 193.

29. Fontenrose, *Python*, pp. 256–60.

30. For insights on the psychological importance of Ares, see R. Grinnell, "Reflections on the Archetype of Consciousness," *Spring 1970*: 25–28, and E. C. Whitmont, "On Aggression," pp. 52 ff. in the same volume; also R. Malamud, "The Amazon Problem," pp. 50–52, 54. See also my essay "Wars, Arms, Rams, Mars: On the Love of War," in *Facing Apocalypse* (Dallas: Spring Publications, 1987), pp. 117–36.

31. For the psychological importance of Hephaistos, see M. Stein, "Hephaistos: A Pattern of Introversion," *Facing the Gods*, pp. 67–86.

32. W. K. C. Guthrie, *The Greeks and Their Gods* (London: Methuen, 1968), p. 70. The Hera of Argos was called the "Goddess of the yoke."

33. Fontenrose, *Python*, p. 119, n. 53. Further on the name of Hercules, see M. P. Nilsson, *The Mycenean Origin of Greek Mythology* (Cambridge, 1932), pp. 189 ff. Nilsson, however, misses the psychological point that the opposites are one when he writes that the name of Herakles is clearly composed of Hera and *kles* but finds it "forced and improbable" that Hercules should be called 'the fame of Hera' "while this goddess dealt the severest blow to him and imposed pain, grief, and labor upon him."

34. We may read the following description of the hero in the light of psychology's ideals of 'ego-strength': "the Homeric hero loved battle, and fighting was his life. . . . A hero's activity . . . is concentrated on the most testing kind of action, war. . . ." "The hero must use his superior qualities at all times to excel and win applause. . . . He makes honour his paramount code, and glory the driving force and aim of his existence. . . . his ideals are courage, endurance, strength and beauty. . . . he relies upon his own ability to make the fullest use of his powers." "The heroic outlook shook off primitive superstitions and taboos by showing that man can do amazing things by his own effort and by his own nature, indeed that he can almost rise *above* his own nature. . . ." M. Grant, *Myths of the Greeks and Romans* (New York: Mentor Books, 1962), pp. 45–47. This description covers heroic consciousness as such and not only its extraverted manifestations. The same attitudes and the same battle can take place in the confines of a consulting room, as the heroic attitude wrestles introvertedly with 'the unconscious' in order to rise above its own nature.

35. J. E. Harrison, *Themis* (Cambridge: Cambridge University Press, 1927), p. 491; Guthrie, *The Greeks*, p. 66n.

36. J. Hillman, *Loose Ends* (Dallas: Spring Publications, 1975), pp. 49–62.

37. A. Brelich, *Gli eroi greci* (Rome, 1958); L. R. Farnell, *Greek Hero Cults and Ideas of Immortality* (Oxford, 1921); J. Fontenrose, *Python*; K. Kerényi, *The Heroes of the Greeks*; A. D. Nock, "The Cult of Heroes," *Harvard Theological Review* 37 (1944); J. Campbell, *The Hero with a Thousand Faces* (New York, 1949); M. E. Harding, "The Inner Conflict: The Dragon and the Hero," in *Psychic Energy*; E. Neumann, *The Origins and History of Consciousness*; G. Roheim, "The Dragon and the Hero," *American Imago* 1, 2, 3 (1940). This list is by no means intended to be complete, especially as it does not extend into the area of heroic literature (epic) or the hero in various sorts of fiction, nor does it

refer to the hero figure in nonclassical accounts, e.g., fairytale and folklore and in exotic cultures, etc. For a comparative study of the hero in poetry and the heroic style, see C. M. Bowra's massive opus, *Heroic Poetry*, 2d. ed. (London: Mac-Millan, 1961).

38. Frequently, the hero is translated to the Isles of the Blest without 'dying.' He simply 'leaves the scene,' because a God favors him, and is removed into isolation (Cf. E. Rohde, *Psyche*, 8th ed. [London: Routledge, 1925], pp. 64–76). Often it is the mother who raises the hero to immortality—Phaethon by Aphrodite, Telegonos by Circe, Achilles by Thetis, Memnon by Eos, but Hercules from his flaming funeral pyre was borne aloft by Zeus. The Isles of the Blest are ruled over by Kronos (the senex), so that even in this mythologem there recurs the motif of the reunion with the senex, the mother being in these cases the detour (through heroism) and then the necessary helper.

39. The overt cause of Achilles' death is Apollo (or Paris), but the spot hit is the heel, that place where Thetis held Achilles while dipping him into invulnerability. His ultimate cause of death was where she had touched and held him to keep him safe.

40. CW 5, §§575, 580, 593, 671; cf. Harding, *Psychic Energy*, pp. 259 ff. Harding makes the hero–dragon issue excessively moral, as if she were in a Christian version of that myth herself, saying of the kinship between dragon and dragon slayer: "The renegade in man is closely related in its nature to the slothful aspect of the dragon, while the forward-going, heroic element in him is more nearly related to the energy of the dragon. Thus the human being who has conquered the dragon and assimilated its power through tasting its blood or eating its heart becomes a superman." If dragon be translated into "the unconscious," what high hopes, what Nietzschean hopes, analysis bodes the striving ego. If dragon be translated into "imagination" or "vitality" or "Mercurius," what devastation!

41. On the snake forms of the Gods and heroes, see Harrison, *Themis,* section "Daimon and Hero"; E. Kuster, *Die Schlange in der Griechischen Kunst und Religion* (Giessen, 1913); Fontenrose, *Python,* passim. Artemidorus (*Oneirocriticus* 1, 13) said that the "snake is the symbol of all gods to whom it is sacred, viz. Zeus, Sabazius, Helios, Demeter, Core, Hecate, Asclepius, and the Heroes." On Apollo and snake, K. Kerényi, "Apollonian Epiphanies," in his *Apollo: The Wind, the Spirit, and the God—Four Studies,* trans. Jon Solomon (Dallas: Spring Publications, 1983), pp. 21–45.

42. CW 5, part two, chap. 6.

43. Cf. next note below for details.

44. Cf. W. B. Stanford, chap. 4: "Personal Relationships," in his *The Ulysses Theme* (Oxford: Blackwell, 1963). In contrast with ULYSSES, let us review the relation to feminine figures in certain other Greek heroes. OEDIPUS belonged to the race Spartoi, "Dragon people," supposedly a matriarchy without paternal principle. He did not recognize his own father because "The child does not know his own begetter, and this is what makes patricide possible" (J. J. Bachofen, *Myth, Religion, and Mother Right,* trans. R. Manheim, Bollingen Series [Princeton: Princeton University Press, 1967], pp. 180–81). As OEDIPUS is conceived in the line of the Dragons, so is he inconceivable without that complementary

mother / dragon, first as Sphinx (sent by Hera, or her fantasy), then as Jocasta. HERCULES' relation with women is summed up by Bachofen (p. 176): "It is characteristic that Hercules alone of all the heroes remained on board the Argo and reproached his friends for lying with the Amazons. . . . In all his myths he is the irreconcilable foe of matriarchy, the indefatigable battler of Amazons, the misogynist, in whose sacrifice no woman takes part, by whose name no woman swears, and who finally meets his death from a woman's poisoned garment." ACHILLES, of the Greek heroes at Troy, was the only one who was a son of a Goddess (Kerényi, *Heroes*, p. 347) and was finally overcome by an arrow of Paris, the favorite of Aphrodite and the paramour of Helen. Although a most unheroic and unmilitaristic figure, Paris of "the soft weak ways" (R. Bespaloff, *On the Iliad*, Bollingen Series [New York: Pantheon, 1947], p. 64) is the one who overcomes ACHILLES. Paris is the Achilles' heel of the hero. HIPPOLYTUS was slain through the revenge of Aphrodite whom he had spurned. ORPHEUS, as Vergil and Ovid describe him, shunned entirely the company of women after he had lost Eurydice—or did his misogyny result in her loss to the serpent's bite? (W. K. C. Guthrie, *Orpheus and Greek Religion* [London: Methuen, 1952], p. 31). He let no women in his cult; and thus "in the established tradition it is the women of Thrace who make him their victim" (ibid., p. 32). Aeschylus, who is the earliest source for the legend of his death, presents the Maenads of Dionysus as his slayers. But, as Guthrie points out (ibid., p. 33), other legends tell it differently: the women themselves excluded by Orphic misogyny took their revenge. Furthermore, earlier evidence of vase paintings shows him not torn to pieces (maenad-style), but speared and hacked and stoned by women in a melée of feminine wrath rather than in a Dionysian ritual. However we view it, the point remains: feminine figures were his enemy and did him in. Achilles' son NEOPTOLEMOS ("renewer of war"), also called PYRRHOS ("red-head") (M. Delcourt, *Pyrrhos et Pyrrha: Recherches sur les valeurs du feu dans les légendes hélleniques*, Bibl. Faculté Philos. et Lettres, Univ. de. Liége [Paris, 1965], chap. 2), is the one who murders Priam of Troy and the boy infant who would have been the carrier of its line (Euripides, *Trojan Women*). "Vase paintings often combine the death of the old king and that of his grandson at the hands of Neoptolemo" (M. L. Scherrer, *The Legends of Troy* [London: Phaidon, 1964], p. 123). This renewer of Achilles' spirit is the murderer of a senex–puer pair, and he follows the heroic pattern by meeting death at the hands of women: either at the instigation of the Pythian priestess or in the form of a Pyrrhus, King of Epirus, killed by a woman who hurls a tile at him from a rooftop. What comes first: killed by a woman, his woman-killer nature, or his killing the senex–puer pair? Contrast Ulysses!

45. *CW* 5, § 459.

On the Moon and Matriarchal Consciousness
Erich Neumann

IN THE HISTORY of the beginnings of consciousness, we can discern successive phases of development during which the ego frees itself from containment in the unconscious, the original uroboric situation, and finally, at the end of the process, having become the center of modern Western consciousness, confronts the unconscious as a separated system in the psyche. During this development, leading to a liberation from the ascendancy of the unconscious, the symbolism of consciousness is masculine and that of the unconscious, insofar as it stands in opposition to the emancipation of the ego, is feminine, as we learn from mythology and the symbolism of the collective unconscious.

The phase in which ego-consciousness is still childlike, that is, dependent in its relation to the unconscious, is represented in myth by the archetype of the Great Mother. The constellation of this psychic situation, as well as of its forms of expression and projection, we have termed "matriarchy," and, in contradistinction to this, we will speak of the tendency of the ego to free itself from the unconscious and to dominate it, as the "patriarchal accent" in the development of consciousness.

Therefore, matriarchy and patriarchy are psychic stages which are characterized by different developments of the conscious and the unconscious and, especially, by different attitudes of the one toward the other. Matriarchy not only signifies the dominance of the Great Mother archetype but also, in a general way, a total psychic situation in which the unconscious (and the feminine) is dominant and consciousness (and the masculine) has not yet reached self-reliance and independence. ("Masculine" and "feminine" are here symbolic magnitudes, not to be identified with the "man" or the "woman" as carriers of specific sexual characteristics.) In this sense, a psychological stage, a religion, a neurosis, and also a stage in the development of consciousness can be called "matriarchal"; and "patriarchal" does not mean the sociological rule of men but the dominance of a masculine consciousness which succeeds in separating the systems of consciousness and unconsciousness and which is relatively firmly established in a position opposite to, and independent of, the unconscious. For this reason, modern woman must also go through all those developments which lead to the formation of the patriarchal consciousness which is now typical of, and taken for granted in, the Western conscious situation, being dominant in patriarchal culture.

However, along with this "patriarchal consciousness" exists a "matriarchal consciousness" whose effectiveness is hidden but significant. "Matriarchal consciousness" belongs to the matriarchal layer of the psyche that shaped civilization in the early period of human history. It characterizes the spiritual nature of woman—apart from the cultural contribution of woman to patriarchal consciousness—but it also plays an important role in the life of man. Wherever consciousness is not liberated in a patriarchal way from the unconscious, "matriarchal consciousness" dominates: that is, in the early days of humanity and, ontogenetically, in the corresponding phases of childhood—likewise, in the man in whom occurs an accentuated activity on the part of the anima, the feminine side of his psychology, in psychological crises, as well as in creative processes.

Before seeking to reach a deeper psychological understanding of matriarchal consciousness, let us indulge in an "etymological intermezzo on the moon," which will tell us something about the structure of the moon archetype. We will find that the psychological aspect of the archetype may provide an inner, central point of relationship between roots that have hitherto been considered as having no linguistic connection.

Etymology has attempted to separate two roots: on the one hand, the moon-root which, with *men* (moon) and *mênsis* (month), belongs to the root *mā* and the Sanscrit root *mâs* and, on the other, the Sanscrit root *manas*, with *menos* (Greek), *mens* (Latin), etc., which represents the spirit par excellence.[1]

From the spirit-root stems a wide ramification of significant spiritual meanings: *menos*, spirit, heart, soul, courage, ardency; *menoinan*, to consider, meditate, wish; *memona*, to have in mind, to intend; *mainomai*, to think, but also to be lost in thoughts and to rave, with which belong *mania*, madness, possession, and also *manteia*, prophecy. Other branches of the same spirit-stem are *menis, menos,* anger; *menuō*, indicate, reveal; *menō*, remain, linger; *manthanō*, to learn; *memini*, to remember; and *mentiri*, to lie. All these spirit-roots stem from the one original Sanscrit root *mati-h*, which means thought, intention.

On no grounds whatever, this root has been set in opposition to the moon-root: *men*, moon; *mensis*, month; *mâs*, which is connected with *ma*, to measure. From it stems not only *matra-m*, measure, but also *mentis*, cleverness, wisdom; *metiesthai*, to meditate, to have in mind, to dream; and, moreover, to our surprise we ascertain that this moon-root, purportedly opposed to the spirit-root, is likewise derived from the Sanscrit root *mati-h*, meaning measure, knowing.[2]

Hence, the single archetypal root underlying these meanings is the moon-spirit, which expresses itself in all of the diversified branchings, thus revealing to us its nature and its primal meaning. What emanates from the moon-spirit is an emotional movement closely related to the activities of the unconscious. In active eruption it is a fiery spirit—it is courage, anger, possession, and rage; its self-revelation leads to prophecy, cogitation, and lying, but also to poetry. Along with this fiery productivity, however, goes another, more "measured" attitude which meditates, dreams, waits and wishes, hesitates and lingers, which is related to memory and learning, and whose outcome is moderation, wisdom, and meaning.

In discussing this subject elsewhere I mentioned, as a primary activity of the unconscious, the *Einfall*, that is, the hunch or thought that 'pops' into the head.[3] The appearance of spiritual contents which thrust themselves into consciousness with sufficient convincing force to fascinate and control it probably represents the first form of the emergence of the spirit in man. While, with an expanded consciousness and a stronger ego, this emerging factor is introjected and thought of as an inner psychic manifestation, in the beginning it appears to approach the psyche from outside as a sacred revelation and a numinous message from the "powers" or Gods. The ego, experiencing these contents as arriving from without, even when it calls them intuitions or inspirations, meets the spontaneous spiritual phenomenon with the attitude characteristic of the ego of matriarchal consciousness. For it is still as true as ever that the revelations of the moon-spirit are more easily received when night animates the unconscious and brings introversion than in the bright light of day.

Naturally, matriarchal consciousness is not confined to women; it exists also in men insofar as their consciousness is an anima-consciousness. This is particularly true of creative people; yet the consciousness of everyone depends upon the activity of the unconscious for inspiration and hunches, as well as for the functioning of instincts, and the "provision of libido" for consciousness. All these things are ruled by the moon and therefore require a harmony with the moon, an adjustment to it—that is, a moon-cult.

Of prime significance in the moon-cult is the role of the moon as measurer of time. But moon-time is not the abstract, quantitative time of scientific, patriarchal consciousness. It is qualitative time; it changes and, in changing, assumes different qualities. Moon-time has periods and rhythms, it waxes and wanes, is favorable or unfavorable. As the time that rules the cosmos, it also rules the earth, and all things that live, and the feminine.

The waxing moon is more than a measurer of time. It is a symbol, like the waning moon, the full moon, and the dark moon, for an inner and outer quality of life and humanity. We can most clearly represent to ourselves the archetypal character of the moon's periods by the changing force of their radiations. For they are centers of the waves of vibration, the streams of power, which, from within and without, pulse through the world and permeate psycho-biological life. Moon-time conditions human living, too. New moon and full moon were the earliest sacred times; the dark of the moon, as the victory of the dark night dragon, was the first typical time of darkness and evil. Moreover, seeding and harvest, growth and ripeness, the success and the failure of every enterprise and action were also dependent on the constellation of cosmic moon-time.

It is, of course, in the feminine that the nature and periodicity of the moon are particularly manifested, and therefore the masculine mind continues to identify the feminine with the moon. Not only is the feminine physically bound to the moon by the monthly change (though no longer dependent on the outer moon period), but also the whole of feminine mentality is determined by the moon, and its form of spirituality is impressed upon it by the moon archetype, as the epitome of matriarchal consciousness.

The periodicity of the moon, with its nocturnal background, is the symbol of a spirit that waxes and wanes, conforming to the dark processes of the unconscious. Moon-consciousness, as matriarchal consciousness might be called, is never divorced from the unconscious, for it is a phase, a spiritual phase, of the unconscious itself. The ego of matriarchal consciousness possesses no free, independent activity of its own; it waits passively, attuned to the spirit-impulse carried toward it by the unconscious.

A time is favorable or unfavorable according to whether the spiritual activity determined by the unconscious turns toward the ego and reveals itself or turns away, darkens, and disappears. At this stage of matriarchal consciousness, the ego's task is to wait and watch for the favorable or unfavorable time, to put itself in harmony with the changing moon, to bring about a consonance, a unison with the rhythm of the moon's emanations.

In other words, matriarchal consciousness is dependent upon mood, upon harmony with the unconscious. This moon-dependency can be viewed as instability or caprice, yet it provides a backdrop which acts like a sounding board, endowing matriarchal consciousness with a special and positive character. Its response to the rhythm, the times and tides of waxing and waning, of crescendo and decrescendo, gives it something of the quality of music. Therefore, music and dance, because of their accented rhythm, play an important role in creating and activating matriarchal consciousness and in establishing a consonance between the ego and femininity and its ruler, the moon-spirit.[4]

A musical character of an intoxicating, orgiastic nature appertains to the deepest involvements and greatest heights of feminine being. Here, as in music, an emotion driving toward disintegration and a simultaneous, irrational experience of harmony combine together, according to an inner, invisible law. The source of seduction and transport ranges from the *fascinans*[5] of a singing voice or the Pied Piper's flute to the ecstatic music of the Dionysian mysteries, the dissolving power of music in orgiastic ritual, and the effect of music on modern woman.[6]

The connection between time, the unconscious, and the moon-spirit belongs, even more profoundly than has so far been shown, to the essential nature of matriarchal consciousness; and it is only by an adequate grasp of the spirit-character of the moon-archetype that we can understand the meaning of matriarchal consciousness and of feminine spirit.

The way in which an idea, an inspiration, or an intoxication arising from the unconscious seizes a personality as if by a sudden, violent assault—driving it to ecstasy, insanity, poetry, or prophecy —represents one part of the spirit's working. The corresponding trait of matriarchal consciousness is its dependence for every intuition and inspiration upon what emerges from the unconscious, mysteriously and almost beyond influence, when, where, and how it will. From this point of view, all shamanism, including prophecy, is a passive sufferance; its activity is more that of conceiving than of a willed act; and the essential contribution of the ego consists in a readiness to accept the emerging unconscious content and to come into harmony with it. Since, however, this independence of consciousness is characteristic of the autonomous emergence of all unconscious contents, the moon very frequently appears as the symbol of the unconscious in general.

The relation between time and the moon in matriarchal consciousness, the moon's lordship of time, becomes clear to us only when we pursue the time significance of the moon beyond the cosmic-mythological realm into its effect on the psychology of the individual.

The development of patriarchal consciousness culminates in a relative liberation and independence from the unconscious which leaves the ego in command of a differentiated system of consciousness with a certain amount of disposable libido, libido that can be applied at will. We must understand the importance of this patriarchal form of consciousness, even while rejecting the self-deception which makes it interpret itself as an absolutely free system. Masculine patriarchal consciousness, as shown by the development of the species "man," is a highly practical and effective organ of adaptation and accomplishment. Among its advantages are its constant readiness to react and the extraordinary swiftness of its reactions and adaptations for, although instinctual reactions guided by the sense organs are prompt indeed, the speed that the consciousness of modern man has achieved by specialization far outstrips them. This speeding up of conscious reactions is brought about by the same processes that led to the detachment of patriarchal consciousness from the unconscious.[7] As a final development, we see processes of abstraction, which assist in the free disposal and application of ideas and, in the differentiated thinking type, lead to the manipulation of abstractions, like numbers in mathematics and concepts in logic. In the psychological sense, such abstractions are in the highest degree without emotional content.

While patriarchal consciousness annihilates time and outstrips nature's slow processes of transformation and evolution by its purposive use of experiment and calculation, matriarchal consciousness remains caught in the spell of the changing moon. Like the moon, its illumination and its luminosity are bound to the flow of time and to periodicity. It must wait for time to ripen, while with time, like sown seed, comprehension ripens too.

In ritual and cult, waiting and awaiting are identical with encirclement, with circumambulation. In the wonderful story told by the Brothers Grimm about the nixie in the mill pond, as well as in many other fairytales, the woman must wait until the moon is full again.[8] Till then she must continue circling the lake in silence, or she must spin her spool full. Only when the time is "fulfilled" does understanding come as an illumination. Similarly, in woman's primal mysteries—in boiling, baking, fermenting, and roasting —the ripening and getting done, the transformation, is always connected with a period of waiting. The ego of matriarchal consciousness is accustomed to keeping still until the time is favorable, until the process is complete, until the fruit of the moon-tree has ripened into a full moon—that is, until comprehension has been born out of the unconscious. For the moon is not only lord of growth but also, as moon-tree and life-tree, always itself a growth, "the fruit that begets itself."

It is in the act of understanding that the peculiar and specific difference between the processes of matriarchal and patriarchal consciousness first becomes apparent. For matriarchal consciousness, understanding is not an act of the intellect, functioning as an organ for swift registration, development, and organization; rather, it has the meaning of a "conception."[9] Whatever is to be understood must first enter matriarchal consciousness in the full, sexual, symbolic meaning of a fructification.

But this feminine symbolism does not stop here, for that which has entered must come forth. The phrase "to come forth" marvelously expresses the double aspect of matriarchal consciousness, which experiences the light of consciousness like seed that has sprouted. But when something enters and then even comes forth again, this something involves the whole psyche, which is now permeated through and through with the full-grown perception that it must realize, must make real, with its full self. This means that the conceiving and understanding have brought about a personality change. The new content has seized and stirred the whole being, whereas in patriarchal consciousness it would too often only have been filed in one intellectual pigeon-hole or another. Just as a patriarchal consciousness finds it difficult to realize fully and not merely to meet with "superb" understanding, so a matriarchal consciousness finds it difficult to understand without first realizing. And here, to realize means to "bear," to bring to birth; it means submitting to a mutual relation and interaction like that of the mother and the embryo in pregnancy.

Matriarchal, qualitative time is always a unique and single occurrence, like a pregnancy, in contrast to the quantitative time of patriarchal consciousness. To patriarchal ego-consciousness, every section of time is equal; but matriarchal consciousness has learned, from the timing of the moon, to know the individuality of cosmic time, if not yet that of the ego. The uniqueness and indestructibility of time are constellated for the eye of one schooled to perceive the growth of living things, able to experience and realize the pregnancy of a moment, its readiness for birth. A fairytale relates that once in a hundred years, on a certain day, at a definite hour, a treasure rises from the deep and will belong to him who finds it at this right moment of its growth.[10] Only a matriarchal consciousness, adjusted to the processes of the unconscious, can recognize the individual time element; a patriarchal consciousness, to which this is one of innumerable, similar moments, will necessarily miss it. In this respect, the matriarchal consciousness is more concrete and closer to actual life, while the patriarchal is more abstract and further from reality.

Therefore, the language of symbolism would, as a rule, situate matriarchal consciousness not in the head but in the heart. Here, understanding means also an act of inclusive feeling, and very often this act—as, for instance, in creative work—has to be accompanied by the most intense affect-participation if anything is to shine forth and illuminate. The abstract thought of patriarchal consciousness is cold in comparison, for the objectivity demanded of it presupposes an aloofness possible only to cold blood and a cool head.

Moon-consciousness has been generally associated with the heart by all peoples for whom the head has not yet become the center of a patriarchal consciousness detached from the unconscious. In Egypt the heart was believed to be the original source of thought and of the creative spirit. In India, where it was cosmically associated with the moon, the heart was held to be the seat of the *manas*—another word belonging to the root *men*, signifying a psychical organ of the spirit—and so became the place of manifestation for the highest divinity. This heart-center of matriarchal consciousness, with its relation to moon-time, is still the valid orienting factor in all processes of growth and transformation. Its dominance is also typical of the processes of the creative spirit, in the course of which contents are slowly constellated in the unconscious, more or less independent of conscious participation, until they flow up into a consciousness which is neither systematized nor insulated, but open and ready to expand.

That the seat of matriarchal consciousness is in the heart and not the head means—to point out only one implication of the symbolism—that the ego of patriarchal consciousness, our familiar head-ego, often knows nothing of what goes on in the deeper center of consciousness in the heart.

For it is essential to bear in mind that the processes of matriarchal consciousness have their relation to an ego and can therefore not be described as unconscious. To be sure, this ego is of a different kind than the one familiar to us in patriarchal consciousness, but it nevertheless plays an active part in the process of matriarchal consciousness. Its presence constitutes the difference between human functioning at the matriarchal stage and a totally unconscious existence.

The common identification of our ego with patriarchal head-consciousness and the corresponding unrelatedness to matriarchal consciousness often lead to our not knowing what is really happening to us. In such cases we find out later that we have been deeply impressed by things, situations, and people, of which our head-ego has taken no cognizance whatever. Then, the other way round, a seemingly dull lack of reaction may appear in someone —often a woman—whose head cannot react promptly but whose heart-consciousness has conceived. The fact that, like lightning, something has 'struck' and been realized will become visible later in the fruitfulness of a personality change. Here the saying of Heraclitus holds true: "Nature loves to hide itself."[11]

The moment of conception is veiled and mysterious, often submitted to by the ego of matriarchal consciousness without any awareness on the part of the head-ego. But a deeper introspection, taking dreams, images, and fantasies into account, will show that in the matriarchal consciousness the moment and the event have been registered and have by no means passed without a consciousness participating.

There is much meaning in the veiling of these moments of conception which are often so vitally important. Growth needs stillness and invisibility, not loudness and light. It is no accident that the symbols of patriarchal consciousness are daylight and the sun. The validity of this law, for biological as for psychological increase, is confirmed by Nietzsche, that great connoisseur of the creative soul, when he says: "In the state of pregnancy we hide ourselves."[12]

It is not under the burning rays of the sun but in the cool, reflected light of the moon, when the darkness of unconsciousness is at the full, that the creative process fulfills itself; the night, not the day, is the time of procreation. It wants darkness and quiet, secrecy, muteness, and hiddenness. Therefore, the moon is lord of life and growth in opposition to the lethal, devouring sun. The moist night time is the time of sleep but also of healing and recovery. For this reason, the moon-God Sin is a physician, and it is said in a cuneiform inscription of his healing plant that "after the sun goes down and with a veiled head, it [the plant] must be encircled with a magic ring of flour, and cut before the sun rises."[13] Here we see, associated with the magic circle and with flour, the mystery symbol of "veiling" which belongs to the moon and the secretness of the night. The realms of healing and healer, healing plant and recuperative growth, meet in this configuration.[14] It is the regenerating power of the unconscious that in nocturnal darkness or by the light of the moon performs its task, a *mysterium* in a *mysterium*, working from out of itself, out of nature, with no aid from the head-ego. This is why healing pills and herbs are ascribed to the moon and their secrets guarded by women or, better, by womanliness, which belongs to the moon.

Here the symbolism of vegetative growth is to be interpreted in the wide sense which conceives every symbol to be a synthesis of inner as well as outer reality. To the nocturnal realm of the healing moon belong the regenerating power of sleep which heals the body and its wounds, the darkness where the recovery takes place, and also those events in the soul which in obscurity, by processes only the heart can know, allow men to 'outgrow' their insolvable crises.

It is not, as has been thought, because the moon often looks green in the east that green has been supposed to be the color of the moon;[15] it is because of the moon's inherent kinship with vegetation, of which it is said: "When Sin's word descends to the earth, the green comes forth."[16] This green of Osiris, of Chidher, of Shiva's sprout, and of the green alchemical stone is not only the color of physical development but also of the development of the spirit and the soul. The moon as ruler of matriarchal consciousness is connected with a specific knowledge and a particular form of comprehension. This is consciousness that has come to birth, spirit as something born, light as the offspring of night.

Comprehension, as fruit, belongs to the essence of matriarchal consciousness. As Nietzsche put it: "Everything about woman is a riddle, and everything about woman has one solution. It is called pregnancy." Again and again the Tree of Life is a moon-tree and its fruit the delicious fruit of the full moon. The draft, or "pill of immortality," sublime knowledge, illumination, ecstasy—all these are the radiant fruit of the tree of transforming growth. Also, in India, the moon is King Soma, the intoxicating juice, of which it is said: "As King Soma, the self of nourishment, I worship him."[17]

We have seen that the moon is lord of fertility and of fertility magic. This magic associated with matriarchal consciousness is always used for the increase or insurance of growth, in contrast to the directed magic of the will, the magic act which, like a hunting spell, for instance, is a tool of active, male, patriarchal consciousness. Processes of growth are processes of transformation and subject to the self. Matriarchal consciousness mirrors these processes and in its specific way accompanies and supports them. On the other hand, form-giving processes, in which the initiative and activity lie with the ego, belong to the domain of the masculine, patriarchal spirit.

To 'carry' a knowledge and allow it to ripen mean, at the same time, to accept it; and acceptance, which here includes the idea of assimilation, is a typically feminine form of activity, not to be confused with passive submission or drifting. The comparative passivity of matriarchal consciousness is not due to any incapacity for action but rather to an awareness of subjection to a process in which it can 'do' nothing but can only 'let happen.' In all decisive life situations, the feminine, in a far greater degree than the nothing-but masculine, is subjected to the numinous elements in nature or, still better, has these brought home to it. Therefore, its relation to nature and to God is more familiar and intimate, and its tie to an anonymous transpersonal allegiance forms earlier and goes deeper than its personal tie to a man.

Although matriarchal consciousness exists in all human beings and plays an important role in men, especially if they are creative, women are still the real representatives of this consciousness, even now when they have a patriarchal consciousness at their disposal too, and the opposition between the two attitudes has become a source of deep conflict. For woman has held the attitude of receptivity and acceptance, which is basic to matriarchal consciousness, since the beginning of time. She takes this attitude for granted. It is not only during the menstrual period that, to live wisely, she must place her harmony with the moon above the desires and plans of the masculine side of her ego-consciousness. Pregnancy and birth bring total psycho-biological changes also, demanding and presupposing adaptations and adjustments lasting for years on end. In regard to the unknown nature of the child, its character, its sex (a matter of decisive importance in many cultures, both matriarchal and patriarchal), its health, its fate—in all these things, woman is delivered over to the mercy and power of God and condemned, as an ego, to helpless non-activity and non-intervention.

Similarly, at a later stage, she is subjected in an entirely different way by men to the overwhelming force of a love-relation. For this reason, the male faith in the ego and in consciousness is alien to women; indeed, it seems to them slightly absurd and childish. From this stems the profound skepticism and the kind of indifference with which they tend to react toward patriarchal consciousness and the masculine mental world, especially when, as frequently happens, they confuse the two worlds of spirit and consciousness. Masculinity is attached to the ego and to consciousness; it has deliberately broken the relation to nature and to destiny in which matriarchal consciousness is so deeply rooted. The patriarchal emphasis on the ego, on will and freedom, contradicts the feminine experience of the "potencies and powers" of the unconscious and of fate, of the way that existence depends on the non-ego and the "thou."

The subdued activity of the ego at the matriarchal stage accords with its preference—as contrasted to that of the head-ego—for the attitude of an observing consciousness. It is more concerned with awareness and attentiveness than with directed thought or judgment. Observant, matriarchal consciousness must not be confused with the sensation function of masculine ego-consciousness or with its aloofness, which leads to scientific objectivity. Matriarchal consciousness is directed by attendant feelings and intuitions that are based on half-conscious processes and assist the emotionally participating ego in its task of orientation.

Matriarchal consciousness reflects unconscious processes, sums them up, and guides itself by them; that is, it behaves more or less passively, without willed ego-intentions. It functions as a kind of total realization in which the whole psyche participates and in which the ego has the task of turning the libido toward a particular psychic event and intensifying its effect, rather than using the experience as a basis for abstract conclusions and an expansion of consciousness. The typical activity of this observing consciousness is contemplation. In contemplation, the energies are directed toward an emotionally colored content, event, or center, with which the ego establishes a relation and by which it allows itself to be filled and permeated; from this it never withdraws or abstracts, as in an extremely patriarchal consciousness.

The observant, emotionally determined nature of the moon-spirit is designated in the German language by words belonging to the root *Sinn*, signifying: to muse, to have in mind, to ponder, to consider, and to be contemplative; also contemplation, bent of mind, as well as senses and sensual; and last, not least, the *Eigen-Sinn* (self-will, stubbornness) which the male usually ascribes to the female. Matriarchal consciousness circumambulates and broods; it lacks the purposiveness of directed thought, of logical conclusion and judgment. Its characteristic action is a movement around a circle, a contemplation (*Betrachtung*, once interpreted by Jung as *trächtigmachen*, making pregnant). It has not the direct aim of masculine consciousness nor the knife-sharp edge of its analysis. Matriarchal consciousness is more interested in the meaningful than in facts and dates and is oriented teleologically to organic growth rather than to mechanical or logical causation.

Since the process of cognition in such a moon-consciousness is a pregnancy and its product a birth, a process in which the whole personality participates, its 'knowledge' cannot be imparted, accounted for, or proved. It is an inner possession, realized and assimilated by the personality but not easily discussed, for the inner experience behind it is scarcely capable of adequate verbal expression and can hardly be transmitted to anyone who has not undergone the same experience.

For this reason, a plain and simple masculine consciousness finds the knowledge of matriarchal consciousness unverifiable, willful, and, par excellence, mystic. This, in fact, is in a positive sense the heart of the matter. It is the same kind of knowledge which is revealed in the true mysteries and in mysticism; it consists not of imparted truths but of experienced transformations and so necessarily has validity only for people who have passed through a similar experience. For them, Goethe's advice still holds:

> Sagt es niemand, nur den Weisen,
> Weil die Menge gleich verhohnet.
>
> (Tell it to none, but to the wise
> For the crowd is quick in scoffing.)

This is to say that the realizations of matriarchal consciousness are conditioned by the personality which has them. They are not abstract and de-emotionalized, for matriarchal consciousness conserves the tie with the unconscious realms from which its knowledge springs. Its insights are therefore often in direct opposition to those of masculine consciousness, which ideally consist of isolated and abstract conscious contents, free of emotionalism and possessing a universal validity unaffected by personal factors.

A fundamental trend of Western development has been to expand the domain of patriarchal consciousness and draw to it everything that could possibly be added. Yet matriarchal consciousness is by no means an outdated mode of functioning or an area of undeveloped contents which only lethargy has kept from evolving to the patriarchal level. What the moon-side perceives is in large part, at least to the contemporary psyche, beyond the grasp of scientific understanding. It relates to those general experiences of life which have always been the subject matter of mysteries and religions and which belong to the domain of wisdom, not to that of science.

The moon-spirit bestows culture too but not in the sense that stargazing and astrology have led to mathematics and astronomy; rather, the celestial prototype of its cultural influence is the "fruit which begets itself," the conqueror of death and bestower of rebirth. As lord of ghosts and the departed, it summons the natural and spiritual powers of the unconscious to arise from the watery depths, when their time is come, and so bestows upon mankind not only growth and sustenance but also prophecy, poetry, wisdom, and immortality.

Matriarchal consciousness experiences the dark and mysterious process of growing comprehension as something in which the self functions as a totality. The self here dominates as the (male) moon, but above and beyond its moon-aspect it rules as the Great Mother, as the wholeness of the nocturnal. Because of its relation to growth, matriarchal consciousness presupposes this unbroken connection with the root-bed of all growing things, with the nocturnal mother—a connection broken on principle and with heroic determination by the masculine ego; yet for matriarchal consciousness, the influence of the Great Mother and that of the masculine moon often seem to come together in the moon symbol. The relationship, amounting to participation between the matriarchal ego and the moon, like that of the Great Mother herself, goes further than partnership with a moon-lover: it reaches identity. The likeness of the hermaphroditic nature of the Great Mother is shown not only by the reception of the moon-spirit, the lord and lover from without, as may be supposed at once rightly and wrongly, but also by the carrying within itself of its own masculine side, as a divinity, a son-lover, and at once a father and a child.

The ego of matriarchal consciousness experiences the fructifying power of the moon as the fructifying side of the unconscious, as a portion of the power of the uroboric Great Mother.[18] And through this experience of unbroken union with the wholeness appearing before it in the Great Mother image, it can see its own likeness. The wholeness of the Great Mother, like its own, encircles what it conceives and recognizes the engenderer as something born of itself, as the son and fruit of its own growth.

So the moon has not only a male manifestation as the center of the spiritual world of matriarchal consciousness; it has also a feminine manifestation as the highest form of the feminine spirit-self, as Sophia, as wisdom. It is a wisdom relating to the indissoluble and paradoxical unity of life and death, of nature and spirit, to the laws of time and fate, of growth, of death and death's overcoming. This figure of feminine wisdom accords with no abstract, unrelated code of law by which dead stars or atoms circulate in empty space; it is a wisdom that is bound and stays bound to the earth, to organic growth, and to ancestral experience. It is the wisdom of the unconscious, of the instincts, of life, and of relationship.

Hence, matriarchal consciousness is the wisdom of the earth, of peasants and, naturally, of women. The teachings of China, particularly of the *I Ching* and of Lao-tzu, are an expression of this matriarchal consciousness, which loves the hidden and the dark and which has time. It renounces quick results, prompt reactions, and visible effects. More turned to the night than to the day, it dreams and watches more than it wakes and acts. It has less love for brightness and clarity than seems desirable to patriarchal consciousness, which, turning its back to the moon-side, only too gladly ignores its own dependence upon the dark aspect of the unconscious. Matriarchal wisdom is paradoxical. It never separates and juxtaposes opposites with the clear discrimination of patriarchal consciousness; rather, it relates them to one another by an "as well as" or an "also."

From this point of view—not to be misinterpreted—matriarchal consciousness is relativistic, for it is less oriented to the absolute unambiguity of truth than to a wisdom which remains imbedded in a cosmo-psychological system of ever-changing forces. This relativistic attitude often may even appear like enmity toward the 'absolute,' if a difference in kind and a tendency toward relationship can be termed enmity.

The dependence of matriarchal consciousness upon its partner the moon-spirit, its consonance with the moon-spirit's changing phases, contains an element of Eros, a dependence on the thou of the partner as moon-lover, which distinguishes matriarchal from patriarchal consciousness as a consciousness of relationship. Patriarchal consciousness is free to act and think when, how, and what it wants. In its detached, abstract way, it is self-sufficient or ego-sufficient, supreme within the circle of its conscious contents. But matriarchal consciousness is not self-sufficient; it is bound to the moon and to the unconscious and, aware of its dependence, adjusts itself accordingly.

For this reason the wisdom of the moon-Sophia lacks that abstract, non-individual, universal, and absolute character which the patriarchal male asserts to be the highest spirituality, revering it as the celestial spirit-sphere of sun and daylight and setting it above the moon-world. From this point of view, the moon-spirit of matriarchal consciousness is 'only' moon-spirit, 'only' soul, and the eternal feminine. But by forfeiting the character of remote divinity, matriarchal consciousness retains the milder and less blinding light of the human spirit. Woman's wisdom is non-speculative; it is close to nature and life, bound to fate and to living reality. Its illusionless view of actuality may shock an idealistic, masculine mentality; yet it is related to this actuality as nourisher, helper, comforter, and lover and leads it beyond death to ever-renewed transformation and rebirth.

The moon-wisdom of waiting, accepting, ripening admits everything into its totality, transforming it as well as its own being. It is always concerned with wholeness, with shaping and realizing, with the creative. One must never forget that the creative is by its inherent nature related to matriarchal consciousness. It is not the conscious but the unconscious which is creative, and every creative achievement, like a pregnancy, presupposes an attitude of patience and relatedness such as we have found characteristic of matriarchal consciousness.

However, while all creative cultural achievement—at least in its highest form—represents a synthesis of receptive matriarchal and formative patriarchal consciousness, woman's predominant dependence upon matriarchal consciousness and its form of wisdom entails, with all its blessings, some inherent dangers. It is certainly consonant with the moon-spirit and the process of growth that silence and realization should come before formulation and understanding; but woman's tendency to realization, one of the creative elements of matriarchal consciousness, often gets entangled in mere naturalness.

In that early phase of its development, the "self-establishment" phase, when the feminine can without danger still remain caught in the Great Mother, matriarchal consciousness is quite unaware of being dominated by the unconscious.[19] But even when the matriarchal ego becomes conscious of its separate existence, it still adheres to the basic condition of its former existence, which is never to be split. Even when the feminine, as will be shown, has to progress from the task of self-establishment to that of self-surrender, it still wants to be totally involved. It is never satisfied with the fulfillment of a partial psychic structure such as a conscious differentiation of the ego; the feminine wishes the whole of itself included. That, on the spiritual or psychological plane, means realization.

But here woman's nature often plays a trick. Instead of realizing, she concretizes and, by a natural projection, transposes the creative process of pregnancy onto the external plane. That is to say, woman takes the symbols of this phase of matriarchal consciousness literally; she loves, becomes pregnant, bears, nourishes, cherishes, and so on, and lives her femininity outwardly but not in the inner world. This tendency may explain the smallness of her spiritual achievements as compared to men, her lack of creative productivity. It seems to a woman (rightly or wrongly?) that to be the source of life in pregnancy and birth is creative enough. Matriarchal consciousness is written into a woman's body, and through her body she lives in outer actuality all which for a man must become a psychological happening, if it is to be realized.[20] In this sense, man, with his developed patriarchal consciousness, is a step ahead, since nature permits him to experience the matriarchal phase of consciousness only as a spiritual advancement and not in concrete form.

As a result, when mankind is forced to come to patriarchal consciousness and to break with the unconscious, matriarchal consciousness—like matriarchy and, along with it, the moon— becomes something negative to be surmounted. Any development, at any stage, that strives toward patriarchal consciousness, toward the sun, looks on the moon-spirit as the spirit of regression, as the terrible mother, as a witch. Whether this negative moon is experienced as masculine or feminine, it is in either case a symbol of the devouring unconscious. Especially as the dark moon, it becomes the blood-sucker, the child-murderer, the eater of human flesh; it symbolizes the danger of inundation by the unconscious, of moodiness, lunacy, and madness.[21] The English "to moon," to be melancholy, to waste time, shows that to be "withdrawn" can mean to be "drawn to the moon" with its dangerous pull toward the unconscious.

Here, as everywhere, comes the question as to what value a psychic phase has at any special stage of development. Moon-consciousness or matriarchal consciousness is creative and productive at the beginning and end. Moon-light is the first light to illumine the dark world of the unconscious, whence consciousness is born and to which it remains bound; and all things that are childlike, growing, creative, and feminine remain faithful to their relation to the moon-spirit.

But as development goes on, that which was a progression out from the unconscious comes to be a holding fast to the unconsciousness. At this point, the new and superior sun-world comes into opposition with the world of the moon, as patriarchy does with matriarchy, when they are considered as two psychological phases. Only in later periods of development, when patriarchy has fulfilled itself or gone to absurd lengths, losing its connection with Mother Earth, does individuation bring about a reversal. Then, patriarchal sun-consciousness reunites with the earlier, more fundamental phase, and matriarchal consciousness, with its central symbol the moon, arises from the deep, imbued with the regenerating power of its primal waters, to celebrate the ancient *hieros gamos* of moon and sun on a new and higher plane, the plane of the human psyche.

For the masculine as for the feminine, wholeness is attainable only when, in a union of opposites, day and night, upper and lower, patriarchal consciousness and matriarchal come to their own kind of productivity and mutually supplement and fructify one another.

The Jewish *Midrash* relates that at the beginning of creation the sun and moon were of equal size, but the moon, because it committed a sin, was made smaller, and the sun became the ruling star of the universe. However, God's promise to the moon foretells the re-establishment of the original situation:

At that time thou wilt again be large as the sun;
And the moon's light will be like the sun's light.[22]

1. Cf. the following etymological dictionaries: J. Grimm and W. Grimm, *Deutsches Wörterbuch;* E. Littré, *Dictionnaire de la langue francaise;* E. Boisacq, *Dictionnaire etymologique de la langue grecque* (1916).

2. E. Boisacq, *Dictionnaire de la langue grecque.*

3. See Part I of this article in the *Eranos Jahrbuch 18* (here untranslated).

4. It is not an accident that the sphere of the muses, that is, of the feminine powers who preside over music, rhythm, dance, soothsaying, and everything artistically creative, is associated through the numbers three and nine with the moon. (Cf. K. Kerényi, "Die orphische Kosmogonie und der Ursprung der Orphik," in *Eranos Jahrbuch 17* [Rascher Verlag, 1949]). Similarly, it is the figures of Musaios, of his son Eumolpos, and of Orpheus (see Bachofen, *Mutterrecht,* 3d ed., 2: 849, 856 ff.) which become so especially important for the traditions of matriarchal consciousness in the Orphic and Eleusinian mysteries. A further example is that in China the origin of the theater was ascribed to the moon. An emperor who visited the moon, as the legend relates, was so enchanted by the singing and dancing fairies that on his return to earth he instructed some youths to make a terrestrial copy of their songs and postures and so created the beginning of the Chinese theater (J. Bredon, *Das Mondjahr* [1937], p. 420).

5. See R. Otto, *The Idea of the Holy,* trans. J. W. Harvey, rev. ed. (London: Oxford University Press, 1929), especially translator's note, p. xv or chap. 6, "The Element of Fascination."

6. Music is not only the specific art of the temporal but also of moon-symbolism as a whole; the concept of qualitative time, of rhythm, of phases, etc., determines its fundamental structure—and by no means only in primitive music.

7. E. Neumann, *The Origins and History of Consciousness,* Bollingen Series 42 (New York: Pantheon Books, 1954; Princeton: Princeton University Press).

8. *Grimm's Fairy Tales* (New York: Pantheon Books, 1944), p. 736.

9. Here, and in the following, thinking is taken only as the clearest example of a differentiated function, whose dominance is characteristic of patriarchal consciousness. See C. G. Jung, *Psychological Types,* trans. H. G. Baynes (New York: Harcourt Brace & Co., 1926; revised edition, vol. 6 of *The Collected Works* [Princeton: Princeton University Press, 1971]), p. 611; and the author's *Origins and History of Consciousness.*

10. Characteristically, it is often said that the treasure "blooms."

11. Diels, Fragment 123, *Heraklit.*

12. F. Nietzsche, *Gesammelte Werke,* vol. 11, p. 305.

13. A. Jeremias, *Handbuch der altorientalischen Geisteskultur* (Berlin: W. de Gruyter, 1929), p. 240.

14. C. Kerényi, *Asklepios: Archetypal Image of the Physician's Existence,*

trans. R. Manheim, Bollingen Series 65.3 (New York: Pantheon Books, 1959); and C. A. Meier, *Antike Inkubation und moderne Psychotherapie,* Studien aus der C. G. Jung Institut (Zürich: Rascher Verlag, 1948).

15.   The symbol of silver which belongs to the moon and, among other things connected with it, the "silver age" of Hesiod will not be included in this discussion.

16.   A. Jeremias, *Handbuch,* p. 248.

17.   P. Deussen, *Sechzig Upanishaden* (Leipzig: F. A. Brockhaus, 1897), p. 53.

18.   The uroboros, because of its essential duality, includes, among other things, male and female, maternal and paternal. While the female-maternal uroboros rules over the psychological phase of matriarchy, the male uroboros, in which the actively procreative and mobile side of the uroboros is manifested, leads over into patriarchy.

19.   See Part I of this paper (n. 3, above).

20.   Not entirely without justification, and certainly not without humor, one woman's psychoanalytic theory—a kind of answer to the penis-envy imputed to the feminine by man—was that the cultural achievement of man is only a compensation for his incapacity to give birth and so stems, in a way, from his "uterus-envy."

21.   R. Briffault, *The Mothers* (New York: The Macmillan Co., 1927).

22.   M. J. bin Gorion, *Die Sagen der Juden* (Frankfurt a. M.: Rutter & Loening, 1913–1927).

The Psychological Aspects of the Mother Archetype
C. G. Jung

I. On the Concept of the Archetype

THE CONCEPT OF "The Great Mother" originates in the field of comparative religion and comprises a great many modifications of the mother goddess image. Psychology is not directly concerned with it, because the image of the Great Mother in this form is to be met with rarely in psychotherapy and only under very special conditions. It is, however, obviously a derivative of the mother archetype. If, therefore, we venture to investigate the Great Mother image in the light of psychology, the mother archetype, as the more inclusive concept of the two, must be taken as the basis of our discussion. First I will briefly review fundamental assumptions about the concept of an archetype.

In former times, despite dissenting opinion and the pervasive influence of Aristotle, it was not found too difficult to understand Plato's conception of the Idea as supra-ordinate and pre-existent to all phenomena. The term *archetype,* far from being modern, was already in use before the time of St. Augustine and was synonymous with the term *Idea* in the Platonic usage. When the *Corpus Hermeticum,* which probably dates from the third century, describes God as *to archetypon phōs,* it expresses the idea that he is the prototype of all light, i.e., pre-existent and supra-ordinate to the phenomenon "light." If I were a philosopher, I should continue, true to my temperament, in this Platonic strain and say, "Somewhere, in 'some celestial place,' there is a prototype or

primordial image of the mother which is pre-existent and supra-
ordinate to every phenomenon in which the maternal evinces
itself." But since I am not a philosopher, but an empirical investigator, I cannot allow myself to presuppose that my peculiar
temperament, that is, my individual attitude toward intellectual
problems, is of necessity universally valid. Apparently, this is an
assumption in which only the philosopher may indulge, who
always takes it for granted that his own disposition and attitude
are universal and who will not recognize the fact—if he can avoid
it—that his individual temperament or his individual problem conditions his philosophy.

As an empirical investigator, I must state that there is a temperament which regards ideas as real entities and not merely as *nomina*.
By chance, one might also say, the contrary view has obtained for
the past two hundred years; it has become unpopular or even
unintelligible to assume that ideas could be anything but mere
nomina. Any man who, true to his temperament, continued to
think as Plato thought was doomed to pay for his anachronism by
seeing the "celestial," i.e., metaphysical, entity of the Idea
relegated to the unverifiable realm of faith and superstition or
charitably turned over to the poet. Once again, in the secular strife
of the universals, the nominalistic point of view had overcome the
realistic, and the Idea evaporated into a mere *flatus vocis*. This
change was accompanied—and, indeed, to a considerable degree
caused—by the marked rise of empiricism, whose advantages were
only too obvious. Since that time, the Idea is no longer something
a priori but is secondary and derived. The new nominalism, too,
forthwith claimed universal validity in spite of the fact that it also
is based on a definite and limited premise due to a special temperament. This premise is as follows: we accept as valid that which
comes from without and can therefore be verified. The ideal case is
verification by experiment.

The antithesis is that we accept as valid that which comes from
within and cannot be verified. The hopelessness of this latter
standpoint is obvious. Greek nature philosophy with its interest in
matter, together with Aristotelian reasoning, has achieved a
belated but overwhelming victory over Plato.

In every victory, however, the germ of future defeat lies hidden.
In our own day, symptoms are rapidly increasing which fore-
shadow a change of attitude. Significantly enough, it is Kant's

doctrine of categories more than anything else which, on the one hand, destroys every attempt to revive metaphysics in the old sense of the word but, on the other, paves the way for a rebirth of the Platonic spirit. If it be true that there can be no metaphysics transcending human reason, it is no less true that there can be no empirical knowledge that is not already given and limited by the a priori structure of the cognitive faculty. During the one-and-a-half centuries that have elapsed since the appearance of the *Critique of Pure Reason,* the conviction has gradually gained ground that thinking, understanding, and reasoning cannot be regarded as independent processes subject only to the eternal laws of logic; on the contrary, they are psychical functions which form part of a personality and are subordinate to it. We no longer ask, "Has this or that been seen, heard, handled, weighed, counted, thought, and found to be logical?" We rather ask, "*Who* saw, heard, or thought?"

Beginning with the "personal equation" in the observation and measurement of minimal processes, this critical attitude has gone on to the creation of an empirical psychology such as no time before our own has known. Today we are convinced that in all fields of knowledge psychological premises exist which exert a decisive influence upon the selection of the material, the method of investigation, the nature of the conclusions, and the formulation of hypotheses and theories. We have even come to believe that Kant's personality was a decisive conditioning factor of his *Critique of Pure Reason.* Not only our philosophers, but also our own predilections in philosophy, and even what we are fond of calling our "best" truths, are affected, if not dangerously undermined, by this recognition of a personal premise. All creative freedom, we cry out, is taken away from us! What! Can it be possible that a man only thinks or says or does what he himself *is?*

Provided that we do not again exaggerate and thus fall prey to unrestrained "psychologizing," it seems to me that the critical standpoint here defined is inescapable. This critical standpoint constitutes the essence, source, and method of modern psychology: there is an a priori factor in all human activities—namely, the inborn and therefore pre-conscious and unconscious individual structure of the psyche. The pre-conscious psyche—for example, that of a newborn infant—is by no means an empty vessel into which, granted favorable conditions, practically anything can be poured. It is, on the contrary, a tremendously complicated, sharply and individually defined potentiality which only appears indeterminate to us because we cannot see it directly. But the moment the first visible manifestations of psychical life begin to appear, only the blind could fail to recognize their individual character, that is, the unique personality which they bespeak. It is scarcely possible to assume that all these details only come into being at the moment in which they appear. When it is a case of morbid predispositions which were already present in the parents, we infer hereditary transmission through the germ plasm; we do not dream of regarding epilepsy in the child of an epileptic mother as a miraculous mutation. Again, we explain by heredity the gifts and talents which can be traced through whole generations. In the same way we explain the reappearance of complicated instinctive actions on the part of animals which have never set eyes on their parents and therefore could not possibly have been 'taught' by them.

We have to start today from the hypothesis that, as far as predisposition is concerned, there is no essential difference between man and all other creatures. Like every animal, he possesses a preformed psyche which is true to his species and which, moreover, upon closer examination reveals distinct features traceable to family antecedents. There is not the slightest reason for us to assume that there are certain human activities or functions that could be exempted from this rule. We are unable to form any idea of what those dispositions or aptitudes look like which make instinctive actions in animals possible. And it is just as impossible for us to know the makeup of the pre-conscious psychical dispositions by virtue of which a child can react in a human manner. We can only assume that they result from patterns of functioning, which I have also described as "images." This term *image* is intended to express not only the form of the activity taking place but also the typical situation in which the activity is released.[1] These images are primordial images insofar as they are peculiar to whole species and, if they ever "originated," their origin must have coincided at least with the beginning of the species. They are the "humanness" of the human being, the factors which make his activities specifically "human." These specific properties are hereditary and are already present in the germ plasm. The idea that they are not inherited, but come into being in every child anew, would be just as preposterous as the primitive belief that the sun rising in the morning is a different sun from that which had set the evening before.

Since the psyche is preformed, this must also be true of the individual psychical functions, of which one of the most important is creative imagination. In the products of the imagination the primordial images are made visible, and it is here that the concept of the archetype may be specifically applied. I am far from claiming the merit of having been the first to point out this fact. The honor belongs to Plato. The first in the field of ethnological psychology to draw attention to the occurrence of certain universal archetypal ideas was Adolf Bastian. Mention is further due to two later investigators, Hubert and Mauss, followers of Dürkheim, who speak of "categories" of the imagination.[2] And it was no less an authority than Hermann Usener who first recognized unconscious preformation in the form of "unconscious thinking."[3] If I have any share in these discoveries at all, it consists in my having shown that archetypes are by no means disseminated only by tradition, by language, and by migration, but that they can arise again spontaneously, at any time, at any place, and without any outside influence.[4]

The significance of this statement should not be underestimated. For it means that there exist in every psyche unconscious, but nevertheless active, forms; they are living dispositions, Ideas in the Platonic sense, which preform and continually influence our thoughts and feelings and actions.[5]

Again and again I encounter the mistaken notion that an archetype is determined in regard to its content or, in other words, that it is a kind of unconscious idea (if that expression is even admissible). It is therefore necessary to point out once more that the archetypes are not determined as regards their content, but only so far as their form is concerned—and even this only to a limited degree. A primordial image is determined in regard to its content only when it has become part of consciousness and is therefore filled with the material of conscious experience. Its form, on the other hand, can be compared, as I have explained elsewhere, to the axial system of a crystal, which to a certain degree preforms a crystal in the mother liquid, without having any material existence of its own. The axial system manifests itself only in the specific way in which the ions and molecules align themselves. The archetype in itself is empty and purely formal, nothing but a *facultas praeformandi,* a given a priori possibility of representation. The representations themselves are not inherited, only the forms, and in that respect they correspond in every way to the instincts which are also determined in form only. There is another aspect on which the comparison to a crystal throws light. The axial system determines only the stereometric structure, but not the concrete appearance of the individual crystal. The latter may be either large or small and may vary endlessly by reason of the different size of its planes or by the formation of twins. The only thing which remains constant is the axial system or, rather, the invariable geometrical relations underlying it. The same is true of the archetype. In principle it can be named and has an invariable nucleus of meaning which determines its manifestations—but always only in principle, never as regards its concrete representation. For instance, the specific form in which the mother image appears in any given instance cannot be deduced from the mother archetype, but depends on an endless number of other factors.

II. The Mother Archetype

Like any other archetype, the mother archetype appears under an almost infinite variety of aspects. I mention here only some of the more characteristic. First in importance are the personal mother and grandmother; then, any woman with whom a relationship exists—for example, a nurse or governess; or perhaps a remote ancestress may become a mother archetype. Then there are what might be termed mothers in a figurative sense. To this category belong the goddess and, especially, the Mother of God, the Virgin, and Sophia. Mythology offers many variations of the mother archetype, as for instance the mother who reappears as the maiden in the myth of Demeter and Kore; or the mother who is also the beloved, as in the Cybele–Attis myth. Other symbols of the mother, but in a figurative sense, appear in things representing the goal of our yearning for redemption, such as Paradise, the Kingdom of God, the Heavenly Jerusalem, and many things arousing devotion—as, for instance, church, university, city or country, Heaven, Earth, the woods, the sea or any still waters. Matter, even, and the underworld can be mother symbols. The archetype is often associated with things and places standing for fertility and fruitfulness: the cornucopia, a plowed field, a garden. It can be attached to a rock, a cave, a tree, a spring, a deep well, or to various vessels such as the baptismal font or to vessel-shaped objects such as the rose or the lotus. Because of the implication of protection, the magic circle or mandala can be a form of the mother archetype. Hollow objects such as ovens and cooking vessels are associated with the mother archetype and, of course, the uterus and anything with a similar shape. Added to this list there are many animals associated with the mother archetype, chief among them being the helpful animals such as the cow.

All these symbols may have a positive, favorable meaning or a negative, evil meaning. An ambivalent aspect is seen in the goddess of fate (Moira, Gracae, Norns). Evil symbols are the witch, the dragon (or any devouring and entwining animal, such as a large fish or a serpent); the grave; the sarcophagus; deep water; death; nightmares and bogies (cf. Empusa, Lilith, etc.). This enumeration is not, of course, complete; it presents only the most essential features of the mother archetype.

The qualities associated with it are maternal solicitude and sympathy; the magic authority of the female principle; the wisdom and spiritual exaltation that transcend reason; also, all that is benign, all that cherishes and sustains, furthers growth and fertility. The place of magic transformation and rebirth, together with the underworld and its inhabitants, is presided over by the mother. On the negative side, the mother archetype may connote what devours, seduces, and poisons; it is terrifying and inescapable like fate.[6] I have expressed the ambivalence of these attributes in the phrase "the loving and the terrible mother." No doubt the historical example of the dual nature of the mother most familiar to us is the Virgin Mary, who is not only the Lord's mother but also, according to the medieval allegories, his cross. In India, "the loving and the terrible mother" is the ruthlessly paradoxical Kali. The Sankhya philosophy has elaborated the mother archetype into the concept of *prakrti* (potential matter) and attributed to it the three *gunas* or fundamental attributes: *sattvam, rajas, tamas* (kindness, passion, and darkness).[7] These are three essential aspects of the mother: namely, her cherishing and nourishing kindness, her orgiastic emotionality, and her Stygian depths.[8]

Although the figure of the mother as it appears in folklore also

comes to the fore more or less obviously in the empirical psychology of the Western world, the image changes markedly when it
appears in the individual psyche. In treating patients one is at first
impressed, and indeed arrested, by the apparent significance of the
personal mother. This figure of the personal mother looms so large
in all the psychologies dealing with individuals that, as is generally
known, it has been difficult to get beyond it even in theory to other
important etiological factors. My own view differs from that of
other medico-psychological theories principally in the fact that I
attribute to the personal mother only a limited etiological significance. That is to say, all those influences exerted on the children as
described in medical literature do not come from the mother, but
rather from the archetype which is projected upon the mother. The
etiological or traumatic effects produced by the mother should be
differentiated into two groups: (1) those really corresponding to
traits of character or attitudes actually manifested by the mother,
and (2) those referring to traits which the mother only seems to
possess, whereas the reality is composed of more or less fantastic
projections on the part of the child. Freud himself had already seen
that the real etiology of neuroses is not to be found in traumatic effects, as he had at first suspected, but rather in a peculiar and abnormal development of the infantile imagination. This, however,
does not deny the possibility that this abnormal development may
be traced back to disturbing influences on the part of the mother. I
myself make it a rule to look for the cause of infantile neuroses first
in the mother, for I know from experience that a child is much
more likely to develop normally than neurotically and that, in the
great majority of cases, definite causes of disturbances are to be
found in the parents, especially in the mother.

But as far as the products of a disordered imagination are concerned, the mother is responsible for them only in part, since they
often contain clear and unmistakable allusions which could not
possibly have reference to human beings. This is true especially
where definitely mythological themes are concerned, as is frequently the case in infantile phobias where the mother may appear
as a wild beast, a witch, a specter, an ogre, a hermaphrodite, and
so on. It must be borne in mind, however, that such fantasies are
not always of unmistakably mythological origin, and even if they
are they may not always be rooted in the hereditary archetype but
may have been occasioned by fairytales or accidental remarks.

Therefore, a thorough investigation is indicated in each particular case. For practical reasons, such investigations cannot be undertaken as readily with children as with adults. The latter almost invariably transfer such fantasies to the physician during the treatment—or, to put it more exactly, the fantasies automatically transfer themselves.

When that happens, nothing is gained by brushing them aside as ridiculous, for archetypes are among the inalienable assets of every psyche; they form that "treasure in the field of obscure ideas" of which Kant spoke and of which we have ample evidence in the countless treasure motifs of mythology. An archetype as such is in no sense something troublesome and prejudicial; it becomes so only when in the wrong place. In themselves, archetypal images are among the highest values of the human soul; they have peopled the heavens of all races from time immemorial. To discard them as valueless would mean a distinct loss. What would Faust be without the transfigured beauty of the divine Mother, Our Lady of Grace! Our task is not, therefore, to deny the archetype, but to dissolve the projections in order to restore their content to him who has involuntarily lost them in projecting them outside of himself.

III. The Mother-Complex

The mother archetype forms the foundation of the so-called mother-complex. It is an open question whether a mother-complex can develop without the mother having taken part in its formation as a demonstrable causal factor. My own experience leads me to believe that the mother always plays an active part in the origin of the disturbance, especially in infantile neuroses or in neuroses whose etiology undoubtedly dates back to early childhood.[9] In any case, the child's instincts are disturbed, and this leads to a constellation of archetypes which, in their turn, produce fantasies intervening between the child and the mother as an alien element and frequently arousing fear. Thus, if the children of an over-anxious mother regularly dream about her as a wild beast or a witch, these experiences point to a split in the psyche of the child such as predisposes it to a neurosis.

1. *The Mother-Complex of the Son*

The effects of the mother-complex are different according to whether a son or a daughter is concerned. Typical effects in the case of a son are homosexuality and Don Juanism, and sometimes also impotence.[10] In homosexuality the son's entire heterosexuality is attached to the mother in an unconscious form; in Don Juanism he unconsciously looks for the mother in every woman. The effects of a mother-complex on the son may be seen in many myths, typical of which is the Cybele–Attis story. These effects may be grouped roughly under the heading of castration or its opposite, hypersexuality. Because of the difference in sex, a son's mother-complex does not appear in a clear-cut form. Thus in every mother-complex in a man, side by side with the mother archetype a significant part is played by the image of the man's sexual counterpart, that is, the anima. Moreover, the mother is the first woman with whom the future man comes in contact; and, crudely or delicately, consciously or unconsciously, she cannot help touching in some way upon the son's masculinity. The son, too, in his turn becomes increasingly aware of his mother's femininity or responds to it instinctively, at least unconsciously. In the case of the son, therefore, the simple relationships of identity or of discriminating simple relationships of identity or of discriminating resistance are continually crossed by the factors of erotic attraction or repulsion, which complicate matters very considerably. I do not mean to say, however, that the mother-complex of a son ought for this reason to be regarded as more serious than that of a daughter. The investigation of these complex mental phenomena is still at its very beginning, in the pioneer stage. Comparisons will not become feasible until we have at our disposal methods of measurement of one sort or another; and so far, there is no sign of these.

It is only in the daughter that the mother-complex is a clear and uncomplicated case. Here we have to deal, on the one hand, with an overdevelopment of the feminine instincts indirectly due to the mother or, on the other, with a weakening of these same instincts to the point of complete extinction. In the first instance, the preponderance of the world of the instincts makes the daughter unconscious of her own personality; in the latter, the instincts are projected upon the mother. For the present we must content ourselves with the statement that in the daughter the mother-complex either furthers or inhibits the feminine instinct to an excessive degree, whereas, in the son, it injures the masculine instinct through an unnatural sexualization.

Since a "mother-complex" is a concept belonging to psychopathology, it is always associated with the idea of injury and illness. But if we take the concept of a complex out of this narrow psychopathological frame and give it a purely psychological connotation, we can see at once that it has beneficial effects as well. Thus a man with a mother-complex may show instead of homosexuality, or in addition to it, many really valuable traits. He may show a subtly differentiated eros (cf. Plato's *Symposium*), and he may have a great capacity for friendship; indeed he may even rescue friendship between the sexes from the realm of the impossible. He may have esthetic taste which is fostered rather than hindered by a certain degree of femininity. Then he may be gifted as a teacher because of his sympathetic insight. He is apt to value tradition and be conservative in the best sense. Again, a man with a mother-complex often has a strong religious feeling and is able to translate the *Ecclesia Spiritualis* into reality. Finally, he may be endowed with a spiritual receptivity which makes possible profound psychological experience.

In the same way, what from the negative point of view is Don Juanism can assume the following positive aspects: bold and self-assertive manliness; ambitious striving after the highest goals; violent opposition to all stupidity, narrow-mindedness, and laziness; an almost ascetic willingness to make sacrifices for what is regarded as right; perseverance, inflexibility, and stubbornness of will; a curiosity that does not shrink even from the riddles of the universe; and finally, a revolutionary spirit which strives to put a new face upon the world.

All these possibilities are reflected in the mythological motifs enumerated above as different aspects of the mother archetype. I have already dealt with the mother-complex of the son, including the anima complication in a series of previous publications, and since my subject here is the figure of the mother, in the following discussion I shall relegate masculine psychology to the background.

2. The Mother-Complex in the Daughter[11]

(a) *Exaggeration of the maternal element.* It has already been
stated that in the daughter the mother-complex leads either to a
hypertrophy of the feminine side or to its corresponding atrophy.
The exaggeration of the feminine side means an intensification of
all female instincts and, above all, of the maternal instinct; a
negative aspect of this intensification is seen in the woman whose
only goal is childbirth. To such a woman the husband is obviously
of secondary import; he is first and foremost the instrument of
procreation, and she merely regards him as an object to be looked
after, along with children, poor relations, cats, dogs, and household furniture. Even her own personality is a matter of secondary
importance; she often remains entirely unconscious of it, for her
life is led in others and through others, in more or less complete
identification with all the objects of her care. First she gives birth
to the children, and from then on she clings to them, for without
them she has no existence whatsoever. Like Demeter, she compels
the gods by her stubborn persistence to grant her the right of
possession over her daughter. The eros develops exclusively as a
maternal relationship while remaining unconscious on the personal side. An unconscious eros, however, always expresses itself
as will to power.[12] Therefore, despite what might seem maternal
self-sacrifice, women of this type are, as a matter of fact, unable to
make any real sacrifice. Driven by ruthless will to power and a
fanatical insistence on their own maternal rights, they often succeed in repressing not only their own personality but also the personal lives of their children. The less conscious such a mother is of
her own personality, the greater and the more violent is her unconscious will to power. For many such women, Baubo rather
than Demeter would be the fitting symbol. The mind is not
cultivated for its own sake but usually remains in its original condition—that is, altogether primitive, ruthless, and unrelated to the
environment, but at the same time true, sometimes even profound,
like Nature herself.[13] But such a woman does not know this and is
therefore unable to appreciate the wittiness of her own mind or to
marvel philosophically at its profundity; like as not she will immediately forget what she said.

(b) *Exaggeration of the eros.* It does not follow by any means
that the complex caused in the daughter by such a mother nec-

essarily leads in turn to an exaggeration of the maternal instinct. Quite the contrary, this instinct may be wiped out in the daughter. As a substitute, an exaggerated eros results, which almost invariably leads to an unconscious incestuous relationship with the father.[14] Jealousy of the mother and the desire to outdo her become the leading motives for subsequent enterprises, often of a destructive nature. For a woman of this type loves romantic and sensational relationships for their own sake. She takes an interest in married men, less, it should be said, for their own well-being than because of the fact that they are married and therefore give her an opportunity to destroy a marriage, that being the main purpose of her maneuvers. If the goal is attained, her interest evaporates for lack of any maternal instinct, and then it will be someone else's turn.[15] This type is characterized by a remarkable unconsciousness. Such women really seem to be utterly blind to what they are doing, which is anything but advantageous either for themselves or for the others concerned. I need hardly point out that men with a passive eros find in this type an excellent opportunity for the projection of the anima.

(c) *Identity with the mother.* If a mother-complex in a woman does not produce overdevelopment of the eros, it leads to identification with the mother and a laming of the daughter's own feminine initiative. There is a complete projection of her personality on the mother, due to the fact that she is unconscious both of her maternal and of her erotic instincts. Everything in this girl which reminds her of motherhood, responsibility, personal attachment and erotic demands arouses feelings of inferiority and compels her to run away—to her mother, naturally, who lives all that seems unattainable to her daughter in the most perfect way. As a sort of superpersonality (admired involuntarily by the daughter), the mother lives in advance all that the girl might have lived herself. The latter is content to cling to the mother in selfless devotion, while at the same time unconsciously striving against her own will to achieve tyranny over her mother, at first, it is true, under the mask of complete loyalty and devotion. She leads a shadow-existence, often visibly sucked dry by the mother, and prolongs the latter's life by what one might call continual blood transfusions.

Such pallid maidens are by no means proof against marriage. On the contrary, despite their vagueness and their inner apathy, or perhaps for these very reasons, they command a high value in the marriage market. First, they are so empty that a man is free to assume that they contain everything he can think of. In addition, they are so unconscious that the unconscious stretches out countless invisible feelers, veritable octopus arms that suck up all masculine projections; and this pleases men enormously. This great degree of feminine indeterminateness is the longed-for counterpart of a masculine definiteness and clarity of vision that can only be achieved satisfactorily if the man can unload all that is ambiguous, vague, and obscure upon the projection he has made on some charming example of feminine innocence.[16] Because of the woman's characteristic lack of interest and because of the feelings of inferiority which make her continually pose as injured innocence, the man finds himself cast in an inspiring role; he has the privilege of putting up with the familiar feminine deficiencies with real superiority, and yet with forbearance, like a true knight. (Fortunately, he remains ignorant of the fact that the deficiencies are largely part and parcel of his own projections.) This girl's obvious helplessness is a special attraction. She is so completely an appendage of her mother that she can only flutter in a frightened way when a man approaches. She is so helpless, so greatly in need of help, and so utterly innocent that even the gentlest swain becomes a daring abductor and brutally robs a mother of her daughter! Such a marvelous opportunity to show off as a devil of a fellow does not occur every day, and therefore it offers a strong incentive. It was in this way that Pluto abducted Persephone from the inconsolable Demeter. But by a decree of the gods, he had to surrender his wife every year to his mother-in-law for the summer season. (The attentive reader will note that such legends do not arise by chance!)

(d) *Resistance to the mother.* These three extreme types are connected by many intermediate stages; I shall content myself here with the mention of only one important example. In the particular intermediate type I have in mind, the problem is less an exaggeration or an inhibition of the feminine instincts than a resistance to the maternal supremacy to the absolute exclusion of all else. The leading motto of this type is "Anything whatever, so long as it is not like Mother!" We have to deal here, on one hand, with a fascination exerted by the mother which, however, never becomes identification and, on the other, with a certain intensification of the eros which exhausts itself in a futile jealous resistance to the mother. The daughter is in no doubt about what she does *not* want but is usually completely at sea as to what she would choose her fate to be. All her instincts are concentrated upon the mother in the negative form of defense against her, and therefore they are of no use to her in building her own life. Should she get married after all, either her marriage is designed solely to rid her of her mother, or a devilish fate will present her with a husband who shares the principal traits of her mother's character! All instinctive processes and needs meet with unexpected difficulties; either there are sexual inhibitions, or children are not wanted, or maternal duties seem unbearable, or the demands of marital life are responded to with impatience and irritation.

This is quite natural, because none of this has anything to do with the essential realities of life when the stubborn resistance to the power of the mother in every form has come to be life's highest aim. In such cases one can often see the attributes of the mother archetype demonstrated in every detail. For example, the mother as representative of the family (or clan) causes either violent resistances or complete indifference to anything that comes under the head of family, community, society, convention, and the like. Inasmuch as the uterus is *the* maternal symbol, resistance to the mother often manifests itself in these women by menstrual disturbances, failure of conception, abhorrence of pregnancy, hemorrhages and undue vomiting during pregnancy, miscarriages, and so on. We have noted above that matter can be one of the symbols of the mother archetype. Hence a negative projection of the mother in this type may cause impatience with objects, clumsy handling of tools and crockery, and also bad taste in clothes.

Or resistance to the mother in this type can sometimes engender a spontaneous intellectual development for the purpose of creating a sphere in which the mother has no place. This development springs from the daughter's own needs and is not for the sake of a man whom she would like to impress or dazzle by a semblance of intellectual comradeship. Its real purpose is to break the mother's power by intellectual criticism and superior knowledge in order to be able to enumerate to her all her stupidities, mistakes in logic, and gaps in education. This intellectual development often goes hand in hand with a certain manifestation of masculine traits in general.

IV. The Positive Aspects of the Mother-Complex

1. The Mother

The positive aspect of the first type of complex that we have discussed—that is, the exaggeration of the maternal instinct— brings to mind that well-known image of the mother which has been glorified in all ages and all tongues. It is that mother-love we know as one of the most moving and unforgettable memories of our lives, the mysterious root of all growth and change; it is the love which stands for homecoming and for quiet contemplation; it is the primordial silence from which everything takes its beginning and in which everything ends. Intimately known and yet strange like Nature, lovingly tender and yet cruel like fate, the joyous and untiring giver of life—the *mater dolorosa* and the mute, implacable portal that closes upon the dead. Mother is mother-love, is *my* experience and *my* secret. Why risk saying too much, then, that is inadequate and beside the point about that human being who was our mother, the carrier—we might almost say, accidentally—of that great experience which includes herself and myself and all mankind, and indeed the whole of created nature, the experience of life whose children we are?

The attempt to say these things has always been made and probably always will be; but a person of understanding cannot in all fairness load that enormous burden of significance, responsibility, and duty, of heaven and hell, on the shoulders of the one frail and fallible human being—so deserving of love, indulgence, understanding, and forgiveness—who was our mother. He knows that the mother carries for us that image of the *mater natura* and *mater spiritualis* inborn in us, the image of the totality of life of which we are a small and helpless part. Nor should he hesitate for one moment to release the human mother from this appalling burden, for his own sake as well as hers. For it is the weight of that meaningfulness which ties us to the mother and chains her to her child, to the great physical and mental harm of both alike. A mother-complex is not dissolved by one-sidedly reducing the mother to human proportions. In such an attempt there is the danger of entirely dissolving the living experience known through "mother," and that means destroying a supreme value and throwing away the golden key which a kind fairy had laid in our cradle. That is why man has always instinctively added the divine pair to the two parents—the "god"-father and "god"-mother of the new-born child—so that a sinful rationalism should never cause the child so far to forget himself as to invest his own parents with divinity.

The archetype is really far less a scientific problem than a burn-ing question of mental hygiene. Even if all proofs of the existence of archetypes were lacking and if all the wiseacres in the world suc-ceeded in convincing us that there could not possibly be such things as archetypes, we should have to invent them forthwith in order to keep our highest and most important values from disap-pearing into the unconscious. For when they fall into the un-conscious, the whole elemental force of creative experience is lost to us. In its place appears the fixation on the mother image, and when this image has been sufficiently rationalized we are tied fast to the human *ratio* and doomed from then on to believe exclusively in what is rational—that is, in the League of Nations, the purchasing-power theory, planned economy, autarchy, the New Deal, and the State as the sole source of salvation, although we well know that the latter has no existence except as an idée fixe of pathological proportions.

Let us invent as many utopias as we like, but in the meantime let us find some place in our lives for those images of what is greatest and profoundest in human experience. For unless we succeed in doing so, the tremendous sum of energy stored in these images, which is also the source of the fascination back of the infantile parental complex, drops into the unconscious. The unconscious thus becomes charged with a force which acts as an irresistible *vis a tergo* to whatever view or idea or tendency our intellect may choose to dangle enticingly before our *concupiscentia*. In this way man is delivered over to his conscious side, and Reason becomes arbiter of right and wrong, of good and evil. Nothing could be far-ther from my intention than to belittle the divine gift of reason, man's highest faculty. But in the role of an absolute tyrant it has no meaning—no more than light would have in a world where its counterpart, darkness, was lacking. Man would do well to heed the wise counsel of the mother and obey the inexorable law of nature which sets limits to the existence of every being. He ought never to forget the fact that the world exists only because opposing forces are in equilibrium. So the rational is counterbalanced by the non-rational, and what is planned is governed by what is given.

This excursion into the realm of generalities was unavoidable, because the mother is the first world of the child and the last world of the adult. We are all wrapped as her children in the mantle of this great Isis. But now let us return to the different types of the feminine mother-complex. It may seem strange that I am devoting so much more time to the mother-complex in woman than to its counterpart in man. But the reason has already been mentioned: in a man, the mother-complex is never "pure." It is always mixed with the anima archetype, and the consequence is that the statements of men about the mother are always emotionally prejudiced in the sense of showing "animosity." Thus, as a man when speaking of the mother, I must constantly submit myself to self-criticism, and that is why I prefer to present the mother-complex in its feminine phenomenology. For it is only in woman herself that we have the possibility of investigating the effects of the mother-complex without admixture of animosity.

2. The Exaggerated Eros

I drew a very unfavorable picture of this type as we encountered it in the field of psychopathology. But this type, too, uninviting as it appears, has a positive aspect which society could ill do without. Indeed, behind what is possibly the worst effect of the attitude portrayed, the unscrupulous destruction of marriages, we may see an extremely significant and purposeful arrangement of nature. This type frequently develops in reaction to a mother who is wholly a thrall of nature, purely instinctive and therefore all-devouring. This mother type is an anachronism, a throwback to a primitive state of matriarchy in which the man leads a tedious existence as a somewhat futile procreator and serf of the soil. The exaggeration of the eros in the daughter is directed toward the man who is to be rescued from the preponderance of the female-maternal in his life. A woman of this type instinctively intervenes when a marriage begins to be hopelessly dull and shallow. She will disturb that comfortable ease so dangerous to the personality of a man but frequently regarded by him as marital faithfulness. This ease and comfort lead to his becoming unconscious of his own personality and end in those supposedly ideal marriages where he is nothing but Dad and she nothing but Mother, and they even address each other thus. This is a hazardous road which can easily lead to degrading marriage to the level of a mere breeding pen. I know the deeper reasons justifying the Encyclical on Christian Marriage. But a man who has reached a certain level of consciousness ought to subject that encyclical to the most unsparing criticism. And then—mindful of the biblical saying "Woe to him by whom the offence cometh"—he had perhaps better keep this criticism to himself.

A woman of the type under discussion directs the burning ray of her eros upon a man whose life is overshadowed by the maternal, and by doing so she arouses moral conflict. Yet without the latter there can be no consciousness of personality. "But why in all the world," you may ask, "should it be necessary for man to achieve, à tort et à travers, a higher level of consciousness?" This is truly the crucial question, and I do not find the answer easy. My answer is in fact a confession of faith: I believe that someone finally had to realize that this wonderful world of mountains and oceans, suns and moons, galaxies and nebulae exists. From a low hill, in the Athi plains of East Africa, I once watched the vast herds of wild animals grazing in a soundless stillness, as they had done from time immemorial, touched only by the breath of a primeval world. I felt then as if I were the first man, the first creature, to know that all this is! That entire world surrounding me was still in its primeval state; it did not know that it was. And then, in that one moment in which I came to know, the world came into being; without that moment it would never have been. All nature seeks this goal and finds it fulfilled in man, but only in the most highly developed and most fully conscious man. Every advance, even the smallest, on this path of consciousness adds that much to the world, to the visible and tangible God.

There is no consciousness without discrimination between opposites. This is the paternal principle, the logos, which eternally struggles to extricate itself from the primal warmth and primal darkness of the maternal womb, in a word, from unconsciousness. Divine curiosity yearns to be born and does not shrink from conflict, suffering, or sin; for as we read in Saint Paul, "The spirit searcheth all things, yea, the deep things of God." To the logos, unconsciousness is the primal sin, evil itself. Therefore, its creative act of liberation is matricide. And the spirit that dared all heights and all depths must, as Synesius says, also suffer the divine punishment, enchainment on the rocks of the Caucasus. For nothing can exist without its opposite; the two were one in the beginning and will be one again in the end. Consciousness can only exist by virtue of continual subordination to the unconscious, just as everything living must pass through many deaths.

The stirring up of conflict is a Luciferian virtue in the true sense of the word. Conflict engenders fire, the fire of affects and emotions, and like every other, this fire, too, has two aspects, that of combustion and that of creating light. On the one hand, emotion is the alchemical fire whose warmth brings everything into existence and whose heat burns all superfluities to ashes (*omnes superfluitates comburit*). But on the other hand, emotion is the moment when steel meets flint and a spark leaps forth; for emotion is the chief source of consciousness. There is no change from darkness to light or from inertia to movement without emotion.

The woman whose fate it is to be a disturbing element is not solely destructive, except in pathological cases. Normally, she who is the disturber is herself caught in the disturbance; she who works the change is thereby changed herself; and the glare of the fire she ignites both illuminates and enlightens all the victims of the entanglement. What seemed a senseless disturbance becomes a process of purification: "So that all that is vain / Might dwindle and wane."[17] If a woman of this type remains unconscious of the meaning of her function or, in other words, if she does not know that she is ". . . part of the power that would / At all times bring forth evil, and always works the good,"[18] then she will herself perish by the sword she brings. Consciousness, however, transforms her into a deliverer and a redeemer.

3. *The Nothing-But-Daughter*

The woman of the third type who is identified with the mother to the detriment of her own instincts need not necessarily be a hopeless nonentity. On the contrary, within the wide margin provided by normality, there is every chance of the empty vessel being filled by an intensive anima projection. The fate of such a woman, it is true, depends on that eventuality; she can never find herself at all, not even approximately, without a man's help; she has to be literally abducted or stolen from her mother. Moreover, she then has to play the role mapped out for her, for a long time, until she actually comes to loathe it. In this way, she may perhaps discover who she really is. Such women may become devoted wives of husbands whose whole existence turns on their identification with a profession or a great talent, but who, for the rest, are unconscious. Since they are nothing but masks themselves, the wife, too, must be able to play the accompanying part with a certain degree of naturalness. But it may happen that such women have valuable gifts which had remained undeveloped only because they were unconscious of their own personality. Such cases may project the gift or talent upon the husband who lacks it himself, and then we can see a totally insignificant man who seemed to have no chance whatsoever suddenly soar as if on a magic carpet to the highest summits of achievement. *Cherchez la femme,* and you have the secret of such success.

Finally, it must be added that emptiness is a great feminine secret. It is that which is absolutely alien to man, the unplumbed depths, the *Yin* principle. The pitiable wretchedness of this nonentity (I am speaking as a man) is—I feel tempted to say, unfortunately—the mighty mystery of the incomprehensibility of woman. Such a woman is fate itself. A man may say what he likes about it, be for it or against it, or both at once. In the end he falls, absurdly happy, into this pit, or, if not, he has missed and bungled his only chance of making a man of himself. In the first case one cannot disprove his foolish good luck to the man; in the latter, one cannot make his misfortune seem plausible. "The mothers, the mothers—how strange it sounds!"[19] With this sigh, which seals man's capitulation as he approaches the realm of the mothers, let us turn to the fourth type.

4. The Negative Mother-Complex

As a pathological phenomenon this type is an unpleasant, exacting, and anything but satisfactory companion to her husband, since she rebels in every fiber of her being against everything that springs from natural soil. However, there is no reason why her increasing experience of life should not teach her something, so that as a first step she gives up fighting the mother in the personal or restricted sense. At her best she will be hostile to all that is dark, unclear, and ambiguous, while cultivating and emphasizing all that is certain and clear and reasonable. Excelling her more feminine sister in her objectivity and coolness of judgment, she may become the friend, sister, and competent adviser of her husband. She can do this by virtue of her own masculine aspirations which make it possible for her to have a human understanding of the individuality of her husband quite transcending the realm of the erotic. The woman with this type of mother-complex probably has the best chance of all to make her marriage an outstanding success during the second half of life. But this is true only if she succeeds in overcoming the hell of the "nothing-but-female," the chaos of the maternal womb, which is her greatest danger because of the negative complex. For as we all know, a complex can only be really overcome when it has been drained to the last depths by life. In other words, if we are to develop further we have to draw to us and drink down to the very dregs what, because of complexes, we have held at a distance.

This type started out in the world with an averted face, like Lot's wife looking back on Sodom and Gomorrah. And all the while, the world and life pass her by like a dream—an annoying source of illusions, disappointments, and irritations, all of which are due solely to the fact that she cannot bring herself to look straight ahead for once. Thus, because of her lack of consciousness in her attitude toward reality, her life actually becomes what she fought hardest against, nothing but maternal. But if she should later turn her face, she will see the world for the first time, so to speak, in the light of maturity and see it embellished with the colors and all the cherished marvels of youth. Such vision means knowledge and discovery of truth, which is the indispensable prerequisite of consciousness. A part of life was lost, but the meaning of life was salvaged for her.

The woman who fights against the father still has the possibility of an instinctive female existence open to her because she rejects only what is alien to her. When she fights against the mother she can, at the risk of injury to her instincts, attain to greater consciousness because, in repudiating the mother, she repudiates all that is obscure, instinctive, ambiguous, and unconscious in her own nature.

Because of her clarity, objectivity, and masculinity, a woman of this type is frequently to be found in important positions in which her tardily discovered maternal quality, guided by a cool intelligence, exerts a most beneficial influence. Not only in external matters does this combination of womanliness and masculine understanding demonstrate itself but also in the realm of intimate relationships. As the spiritual guide and adviser of a man, such a woman, unknown to the world, may play a highly influential part. Owing to her qualities, she is more understandable to a masculine observer than are women representing other forms of the mother-complex, and for this reason she is often favored by men with the projection of positive mother-complexes. The "all-too-female" terrifies men who have a certain type of mother-complex characterized by great sensitivity. But this woman does not terrify a man because she builds bridges to the masculine mind over which he can safely guide his feelings to the opposite shore. Her articulate understanding inspires the man with confidence, a factor not to be underrated and much more often absent from the relationship between a man and a woman than one might think. The man's eros leads not only upward but also downward into that uncanny, dark world of a Hecate or a Kali that is a horror to any intellectual man. The understanding possessed by this type of woman will be a guiding star to him in the mazes of a complicated existence.

V. Conclusion

From what has been said, it should be clear that, in the last analysis, all the data of mythology, as well as the observed effects of the mother-complex when stripped of their confusing detail, point to the unconscious as their place of origin. Why should man have ever understood day and night, summer and winter, as an analogy of the division of the cosmos into a light world of day and a dark world of supernatural beings, if he had not found the prototype within himself, in the polarity of the conscious and the unconscious?[20] Our perception of objects is conditioned only partly by the objective behavior of the things themselves, whereas a much greater part is often played by intrapsychical facts which are not related to the external things except by way of projection. This is quite simply due to the fact that the primitive has not yet experienced that ascesis of the mind known to us as the critique of knowledge. To him the world is a more or less fluid phenomenon within his own fantasy, and subject and object interpenetrate without discrimination on his part. "All without is within, too!" one may very well say with Goethe. But this "within" that modern rationalism is so eager to derive from the "without" has a structure of its own which antedates all conscious experience and which is an a priori even of unconscious experience. For it is difficult to conceive how "experience" in the widest sense or, for that matter, anything psychical could originate exclusively in the outside world. The psyche belongs to the inmost mystery of life and has its own peculiar structure and form like every other organic thing. Whether this psychical structure and its elements, the archetypes, came into being at a particular time is a metaphysical problem and therefore unanswerable. The structure is the pre-existent datum; that is, it is what in each instance is already there, a precondition. That is the mother.

This is why the mother archetype has all the paradoxical features I enumerated at the beginning. Primarily it is the personal mother herself, because at first the child lives in complete participation with her. In the fullest sense the mother is the psychical precondition of the child. With the awakening of ego-consciousness the participation gradually weakens, and consciousness begins to enter into opposition to the unconscious, its own precondition. This leads to discrimination between the ego and the mother, whose personal individuality gradually becomes distinct. All the fabulous and mysterious connotations attaching to her image begin to fall away and are transferred to the next closest being, for instance, the grandmother. As the mother of the mother, she is greater than the latter; she is in truth the "grand mother." Not infrequently, she assumes the attributes of wisdom as well as those of a witch. For the farther the archetype recedes from consciousness, the clearer the latter becomes, and the greater the certainty with which the archetype can be recognized as such. The transition from the mother to the grandmother means that the archetype is elevated to a higher rank. This is clearly demonstrated, for example, in a notion held by the Batakas. The funeral sacrifice in honor of a dead father is modest, consisting of ordinary food. But if the son has a son of his own, then the father has become a grandfather and has thereby attained to higher dignity in the Beyond, and very important offerings are made to him.[21]

From then on, as the archetype phases out of consciousness, the distance between the conscious and the unconscious grows greater, and the grandmother is elevated further and is transformed into the Great Mother; and then it often happens that the opposites contained in the image split apart. We get a good fairy and a wicked fairy, or a benevolent goddess and one who is malevolent and dangerous. In primitive cultures, owing to the lack of development of consciousness, the conscious functions, too, are insufficiently differentiated, and this permits all sorts of paradoxes to come about; but these do not disturb a primitive mind.

The legends of the gods are as full of contradictions as are the moral characters of their personalities. Efforts at unification appear early in history, such as the reforms by Amenophis IV, and philosophical interpretations of the gods are also undertaken, as for example in India. In the West, feeling values gained the upper hand and led to criticism of the moral primitiveness of the gods. It would seem as if the predominance of feeling which came about in occidental man had forced him to make that decision between good and evil which divided the godhead into opposing aspects. In India, as opposed to the West, the predominantly intuitive and intellectual attitude did not allow feeling any voice in the decision, and the gods—Kali is a case in point—could retain their original paradoxical morality undisturbed.[22]

So we have the antithesis of Kali and the Madonna. The latter has entirely forfeited the shadow that still followed her from afar in the allegories of the Middle Ages. The shadow has been relegated to the Hell familiar to popular imagination, where it now leads an insignificant existence as the devil's grandmother.[23] Thanks to the development of the feeling values, the splendor of the godhead as a power of light has been enhanced beyond measure, but the dark attributes have been swallowed by man himself and made by him into original sin and the fundamental wickedness of the heart. Even the devil has been done away with to a great extent—i.e., introjected—so that in medieval times already the European could confess "*omne bonum a Deo, omne malum a homine.*"

In recent times this development has been reversed in an infernal manner, and the wolf in sheep's clothing goes about everywhere and whispers in our ear that evil is really nothing but a misunderstanding of the good. It is believed that the world of darkness has thus been done away with once and for all, and no one realizes that man has thus poisoned his own mind. Indeed by doing this man transforms himself into the devil, for the latter is one aspect of that archetype whose irresistible power makes even the skeptic exclaim, "Oh God!" upon every suitable and unsuitable occasion. If one can possibly avoid it, one ought never to identify oneself with an archetype, because, as psychopathology shows, the consequences are terrifying. Western man has already sunk to such a low level spiritually that he even has to deny the power of the godhead itself so that after swallowing evil he may take possession of the good as well. If we read Nietzsche's *Zarathustra* with close attention and with psychological understanding, we see that he has delineated with consistency and with the passion of a truly religious man the psychology of that "superman" whose god is dead, that man who is shattered because he imprisoned the divine paradox within the narrow framework of mortal man. Goethe, the sage, has well said: "What shuddering awe then seizes the superman!" and has won for himself a supercilious smile of superiority from the Philistines. He has even been accused of "Catholic tendencies," an interpretation that really marks the summit of stupidity. His glorification of the Mother whose greatness embraces the Queen of Heaven as well as Maria Aegyptiaca is the height of wisdom and profoundly significant to anyone willing to reflect upon it.

I have tried in the foregoing to give a survey of those phenomena which are to be attributed to the predominance of the mother image in the psyche. Though I have not called attention to the features characterizing the Great Mother as she appears in mythology, they have undoubtedly been recognized as such, even if somewhat obscured. Whenever we ask those of our patients who are dominated by the mother image to express in words or by a picture what confronts them as "mother," be it positive or negative, we are presented with symbolical figures which are to be regarded as direct analogies to the mythological mother image.

These analogies take us into a field whose clarification calls for a great deal of additional work. At any rate, I personally do not feel able to make any final statements about these matters. If, nevertheless, I venture to offer a few suggestions, they are to be regarded as altogether provisional and tentative.

Above all, I would like to call your attention to the fact that the mother image is of an altogether different character in a man's psychology from what it is in a woman's. To a woman, the mother typifies her own conscious life conditioned by her sex. To a man, however, the figure of the mother typifies an alien something which he has yet to experience; it is surrounded by images from the latent unconscious. For this reason, if for no other, the mother image of a man is essentially different from that of a woman. Accordingly, the mother from the outset has a decidedly symbolical character for a man, which probably accounts for his tendency to idealize her. Idealization is a hidden apotropaism; one idealizes when there is a fear to be exorcised. In this instance, what is feared is the unconscious and its magic influence.

Whereas to a man the mother is ipso facto symbolical, to a woman she becomes a symbol only in the course of her psychological development. Experience shows the striking fact that the Urania type of mother image predominates the masculine psychology, whereas in a woman the chthonic type, or Earth-Mother, is the most frequent. During the phase in which the archetype manifests itself, a more or less complete identification with the type takes place. A woman is able to identify herself directly with the Earth-Mother; a man, on the other hand, cannot do so except in case of a psychosis. As mythology shows, one of the peculiarities of the Great Mother is that she frequently appears paired with her male counterpart. The man therefore identifies himself with the son-lover, the wise man on whom the grace of Sophia, the Mother, has descended. The companion of the chthonic mother, on the other hand, represents the reverse relationship: he is an ithyphallic Hermes or a lingam. In India this symbol is of the highest spiritual significance, and Hermes is one of the most contradictory figures of Hellenistic syncretism, in which the most important spiritual developments of the occidental world originated. Hermes is also the god of revelation; and in the unofficial early-medieval philosophy of nature which took the place of the religion of the Paraclete after its suppression by the Church, he is nothing less than the world-creating *Nous* itself. This mystery has probably found its most appropriate expression in the esoteric words of the *Tabula Smaragdina: "omne superius sicut inferius."*

It is a psychological fact that when we touch upon these identifications we enter the field of the syzygies, the paired opposites, where the one is never separated from the other, its antithesis. It is that sphere of personal experience which leads directly to the experience of individuation, the attainment of the Self. A very great number of symbols of this process could be adduced from the medieval literature of the occident and even more from the store-houses of Eastern lore, but in this matter words and ideas count for little. Indeed, they are dangerous bypaths; but ignorance is small protection. In this still very obscure field of psychological ex-perience, where we are in direct contact with the archetype, its spiritual force is also most evident. This realm is so entirely one of immediate experience that it cannot be captured by any formula but can only be indicated to one who already knows. He will need no commentary to understand the tension between the opposites expressed by Apuleius in his magnificent *Regina Coeli* prayer when he associated *nocturnis ululatibus horrenda Proserpina* with *coelestis Venus*. He will even feel an irresistible need to add to the "eternal-feminine" which "draws us aloft" that other sinister figure which draws us down—not merely *amor et visio Dei,* but rather *amor et timor Dei.*

1. Cf. C. G. Jung, "Instinct and the Unconscious," *CW* 8, §277.

2. Cf. "Concerning the Archetypes, with Special Reference to the Anima Concept," Jung, *CW* 9, i, §137, n. 25.

3. H. Usener, *Das Weihnachtsfest*, 2d ed. (1911), p. 3.

4. Cf. "Concerning the Archetypes."

5. Lévy-Bruhl shows this conception to be a phenomenon of primitive myth-ology. He also uses the expression *"archétype"* (*La Mythologie Primitive* [Paris, 1935]).

6. All these attributes of the mother archetype are fully described in Jung, *CW* 5.

7. This is the etymological sense of the names of the three *gunas.* See A. Weckerling, *Anandaraya-makhi: Das Glück des Lebens* (1937), pp. 21 ff. and R. Garbe, *Die Sankhya Philosophie* (1917), pp. 272 ff.

8. The special feature of the philosophical myth, which shows Prakrti danc-ing before Purusha in order to remind him of "discriminating knowledge," does not belong to the mother archetype but to the anima archetype, which in male psychology invariably first appears mingled with the image of his mother.

9. I do not share the conviction that this is the case in all neuroses, or what are generally known as such.

10. In this latter respect, however, the father-complex also plays an impor-tant part.

11. In the present section I propose to present a series of different "types" of the mother-complex; in formulating them, I am drawing on my own therapeutic experiences. "Types" are not individual cases, as any educated person ought to know without being told. Nor is a "type" a freely invented schema into which all

individual cases have to be forced. "Types" are intellectual constructs, images representing an average of numerous experiences, with which no single individual case can ever be identified. The trouble is that so many people whose experience has remained confined to books or psychological laboratories can form no idea of the cumulative experience of a practicing physician.

12. This statement is based on the experience that, wherever love is absent, the vacancy is occupied by power.

13. In my English seminars I have called this the "natural mind."

14. In such a case the difficulty lies with the daughter. In other cases the father is responsible; through projection of the anima he induces an incestuous fixation in the daughter.

15. This marks the difference between this type of complex and the father-complex in the daughter, which is related to it, and in which, quite in the opposite way, the "father" is mothered and coddled.

16. This type of woman exerts a curiously soothing influence on the husband, but only until he discovers who it is that he has married and with whom he shares his nuptial bed—namely, his mother-in-law.

17. Goethe, *Faust*, Part 2, Act 5.

18. Ibid., Part 1, Act 1.

19. Ibid., Part 2, Act 1.

20. See Jung, *The Integration of the Personality* (New York, 1939), p. 54: "All the mythologized occurrences of nature, such as summer and winter, the phases of the moon, the rainy seasons, and so forth, are anything but allegories of these same objective experiences, nor are they to be understood as 'explanations' of sunrise, sunset, and the rest of the natural phenomena. They are, rather, symbolic expressions for the inner psychic drama that becomes accessible to human consciousness by way of projection—that is, mirrored in the events of nature. This projection is so thorough-going that it has taken several thousand years of culture to separate it in some measure from the outer object." (Trans.)

21. Warnecke, *Die Religion der Batak* (1909).

22. Where moral questions are concerned, the intuitive type can boast a remarkably robust digestion.

23. A familiar figure in German folklore. (Trans.)

A Family of Books

Broodmales
Nor Hall, Warren R. Dawson
In the folk customs of couvade—"brooding" or "hatching"—a man takes on the events of a woman's body—pregnancy, labor, nursing—so that her experience becomes his. Introducing Dawson's 1929 "Custom of Couvade," Hall supplies biographical data about social anthropologists at the turn of the century and then looks inward at the physical ground of the customs they labeled bizarre. Dawson's ethnological classic collects material from accounts of explorers and informants from the 1700s to the 1900s. Index. (173 pp.)

The Cult of Childhood
George Boas
Could our fascination with our early years and the issues of child abuse and abortion—and even developmental psychology—be recapitulations of what Boas calls "cultural primitivism," that theory which holds earlier states are better, purer because more innocent? Innocence, rather than the primary characteristic of children, may be a fond fantasy about them. By examining the *idea* of childhood from Plato to Norman O. Brown, Boas exposes the buried assumptions that continue to influence nearly everything we do and say about children. Index. (120 pp.)

Inscapes of the Child's World
Jungian Counseling in Schools and Clinics
John Allan
The fruit of over twenty years of clinical work with children—"normal" ones as well as those abused, neglected, and terminally ill. The book describes different ways to use art: drawing, guided imagery, and active imagination. Rooted in Jung's theory of the regenerative ability of psyche, Allan's approach is pragmatic and sensitive. The drawings, paintings, and writings by children open a profound dimension of their suffering and strength. (235 pp.)

Rosegarden and Labyrinth
Seonaid M. Robertson
With care and precision and aided by years of experience, Seonaid Robertson explores the relationship between art and psyche. Focusing on the drawings of children and adolescents, she views these first products of the imagination against the background of artistic and cultural history. Illustrations, index. (xxix, 216 pp.)

SPRING PUBLICATIONS, INC. • P.O. BOX 222069 • DALLAS, TX 75222